INFLATION, FISCAL POLICY AND CENTRAL BANKS

INFLATION, FISCAL POLICY AND CENTRAL BANKS

LEO N. BARTOLOTTI
EDITOR

Nova Science Publishers, Inc.
New York

For permission to use material from this book please contact us:
Telephone 631-231-7269; Fax 631-231-8175
Web Site: http://www.novapublishers.com

NOTICE TO THE READER

LIBRARY OF CONGRESS CATALOGING-IN-PUBLICATION DATA
Available upon request

ISBN 1-60021-122-4

Published by Nova Science Publishers, Inc. ✤ *New York*

CONTENTS

PREFACE

This new book brings together new research on three areas of ongoing interest in the area of international finance: 1. Inflation; 2. Fiscal Policy and 3. Central Policy. Several of the papers deal with the G-8 countries.

Chapter 1 studies the effects of fiscal policies on external and budget deficits. From a tractable small open-economy, overlapping-generation model, the effects are measured by the responses of the external deficit to an increase in the budget deficit due to a tax-cut. The responses are positively affected by the birth rate and the degree of persistence of the budget deficit. Empirical results for the G7 countries over the post-1975 period reveal that the values of birth rate are small for all, but one, countries; but the responses of external and budget deficits are substantial and persistent for most countries. In particular, the fiscal policy has the most important effects on the external deficits for Canada, Japan, and the United States; somewhat smaller impacts for France, Germany, and the United Kingdom; and negligible effects for Italy.

Chapter 2 aims at assessing the long-run determinants and the short-run dynamics of inflation in each country belonging to the European Monetary Union (EMU). Our work complements the recent literature on this topic for the Euro Area as a whole. Detecting such determinants can be crucial in designing structural reforms acting as aside instruments of monetary policy in maintaining price stability. The empirical methodology consists of a re-interpretation of the structural cointegrating VAR approach, which allows for a structural long-run analysis of inflation determinants along with an accurate assessment of its short-run dynamics. The main conclusion emerging from the estimates is that not only the determinants of inflation differ in the countries belonging to the Euro Area, but also that cost-push factors have a considerable role in explaining inflation in most of the countries examined. As a policy implication, a tight monetary policy pursued in those countries whose inflation is mainly driven by costs would result in a contraction of economic activity without exerting relevant effects on price dynamics.

The design of a central bank's monetary policy operational framework is likely to aaffect short-term interest rates and credit institutions' bidding behaviour. Within the euro area, from mid-1999 until 2003, the Eurosystem witnessed several episodes of instable bidding behaviour from credit institutions in periods of imminent expectations of interest rate changes -the so called "overbidding" and "underbidding" phenomena. Chapter 3 gives a brief overview on the Eurosystem's operational framework for monetary policy and its performance since its inception six years ago. Despite some unstability in bidding behaviour, the operational framework has overall proved very robust and has catered for an efficient transmission of the monetary policy stance. In this paper, a particular attention is given to the changes to the Eurosystem's monetary policy operational framework that were introduced in March 2004, with a view to provide an assessment of the experience under the new framework until December 2004.

Chapter 4 analyzes how the inflation bias to discretionary monetary policy is affected when we extend the basic principal-agent framework to allow for the existence of two principals, namely, the government and an interest group which design Wash inflation contracts. We begin by considering an scenario where the interest group has an output objective that exceeds the government's. We show that, in this case, a deflation bias arises. Then, we analyze a setting where the interest group's dislike of deviations of inflation from its objective is higher than the government's. In this context, we conclude that a deflation bias also occurs but it is smaller than the one arising in the first scenario.

The importance of inflation persistence has received considerable attention over the last two decades. This interest, especially in the recent years, is mainly due to the fact that the size of inflation persistence directly affects the conduct of monetary policy. Chapter 5 estimates inflation persistence in Euro-area employing quarterly data for the period 1971 to 2002. Four empirical procedures, the recursive OLS, the rolling OLS, the Kalman filter and the second-generation random coefficient procedures (RC), are employed to estimate inflation persistence using a univariate autoregressive (AR) modeling. The RC estimation procedure allows the profiles of the inflation persistence to be traced over time and relaxes several restrictions imposed in applied work. The empirical results from all the estimation procedures indicate that inflation persistence might have changed over this period. This empirical finding is very important since inflation persistence has immediate consequences for conducting monetary policy. Changes in the degree of inflation persistence overtime indicates different time horizons at which monetary policy successfully can preserve price stability, facilitate economic growth and achieve efficient use of resources.

Chapter 6 updates the research in Karras (2000) estimating the productivity of government and private employment for a panel of 22 OECD economies over the 1961-2001 period, effectively adding the decade of the 1990s to the time frame of the earlier study. The paper finds that (i) the output elasticity of private employment is six to seven times higher than government employment's; (ii) the difference between the marginal products of private and government employment is not statistically significant, so that government employment can be characterized as neither overprovided nor underprovided; and (iii) in most of the countries examined, government workers continue to be overpaid in the sense that the government/private wage ratio exceeds the corresponding ratio of marginal products.

Lobbying is costly and differs between groups as a function of the groups needs and possibility to obtain resources from government. In Chapter 7 we start by reviewing the different reasons for the existence for lobbying over fiscal policy. We consider how the needs of each of the groups affect its lobbying activities and therefore, how these lobbying activities affect the resources allocated to each group under fiscal policy. Lobbying also affect the burden of taxation imposed on each of the groups to finance fiscal policy. Moreover, we also determine the optimal taxation levied to finance the fiscal policy. Using element from game theory and Nash equilibrium shows that if both groups have the same utility from each dollar obtained from fiscal policy, then both groups will invest the same amount of resources in trying to obtain a larger proportion of the budget. The group with the larger needs, in equilibrium, will obtain the largest proportion of the budget and a higher probability of affecting fiscal policy. In the case where the politicians prefer the wealthier group, this group, in equilibrium, will have a higher expected utility than the other group. It is shown that is not always beneficial to increase the wealth of a certain group. Increasing the wealth of one of the groups may put this group in a worse position as it may decrease the probability of obtaining the funds from the government and decreasing the effectiveness this group has on affecting fiscal policy of the government. Therefore, groups that obtain funds from the government may not use them with accordance to what the government had wished for as this may decrease the probability of obtaining further funds in the future. Finally we show how the variance of the needs of the groups, i.e., the magnitude of the difference between the needs of the groups, affects the taxation levied on the different groups.

Chapter 8 analyzes the interaction between the inflation and growth within the Mankiw-Romer-Weil (1992) framework.Our results indicate that the inflation level has a significant negative effect on output in advanced capitalist economies, whereas inflation variability has a negative and significant effect on output in the long-run for all sub-samples. Our results also show that the variability effects are larger in terms of significance.

In the mid–1990s, eradication of persistent U.S. federal deficits won broad bipartisan support. In the same time frame, political pressures mounted to strengthen the Federal Reserve's explicit concern with price stability. Proposals considered at that time implied a much narrower focus on the part of Fed policymakers, and could be interpreted as targeting the price level rather than a negligible rate of inflation. The deficit-reduction and price-stability policies should be analyzed in combination, as reductions in the real interest rate triggered by lower deficits will have an impact on optimal monetary policy with anti-inflation and stabilization objectives.

Chapter 9 builds upon the analysis of Orphanides and Wilcox [2002] to evaluate optimal anti-inflation policy under a broader set of circumstances than considered in their work. We consider a monetary authority with two instruments: the funds rate (or rate of base money growth) and the discount rate, with the distinction that only movements of the latter are 'credible' alterations of the Fed's policy stance, reflecting reputational effects. The public forms expectations of inflation given realized inflation and the expected progress toward lower inflation, as evidenced by credible policy moves and the gradual eradication of the fiscal deficit.

The interaction between deficit reduction policy and the optimal monetary trajectory is analyzed, and the implications for the coordination of these strategies considered via stochastic simulations of the model. The impacts of a price level stabilization target on the Fed and a balanced-budget rule on the fiscal authorities are contrasted with their more flexible counterparts: an inflation target and restriction on deficit spending. Our results indicate that these more stringent political constraints on economic policy could have severe consequences on the ability of the monetary and fiscal authorities to mitigate adverse economic shocks.

In: Inflation, Fiscal Policy and Central Banks
Editor: Leo N. Bartolotti, pp. 1-29

ISBN 1-60021-122-4

Chapter 1

FISCAL POLICIES, EXTERNAL DEFICITS, AND BUDGET DEFICITS

Michel Normandin**
Department of Economics and CIRPÉE, HEC Montréal,
3000 Chemin de la Côte-Ste-Catherine, Montréal,
Québec, Canada, H3T 2A7

Abstract

This paper studies the effects of fiscal policies on external and budget deficits. From a tractable small open-economy, overlapping-generation model, the effects are measured by the responses of the external deficit to an increase in the budget deficit due to a tax-cut. The responses are positively affected by the birth rate and the degree of persistence of the budget deficit. Empirical results for the G7 countries over the post-1975 period reveal that the values of birth rate are small for all, but one, countries; but the responses of external and budget deficits are substantial and persistent for most countries. In particular, the fiscal policy has the most important effects on the external deficits for Canada, Japan, and the United States; somewhat smaller impacts for France, Germany, and the United Kingdom; and negligible effects for Italy.

JEL Classification: E62; F32; F41

Key Words: Agents' Superior Information; Birth Rate; Impact and Dynamic Responses; G7 Countries; Orthogonality Restrictions.

1 Introduction

This paper studies the effects of fiscal policies on external and budget deficits. More precisely, our analysis assesses the implications of reducing taxes. Conceptually, a tax-cut clearly leads to an increase of the budget deficit, but has ambiguous effects on the external deficit. For example, this fiscal policy augments the external deficit, as long as there is an

---

*E-mail address: michel.normandin@hec.ca.; Phone number: (514) 340-6841. Fax number: (514) 340-6469. I thank Mohammed Bouaddi for research assistance. I acknowledge financial support from Social Sciences and Humanities Research Council of Canada.

increase of consumption (of imported goods) induced by the increase of private after-tax incomes. However, the policy does not alter the external deficit, if private spendings are not affected by changes of means to finance public expenditures.

This controversy has motivated many empirical investigations. Some of these studies have estimated the influence of fiscal policies on external and budet deficits from reduced forms (Bernheim 1987; Roubini 1988; Anderson 1990; Evans 1990). The other analyses have tested the hypothesis that the means of financing public expenditures are neutral, from structural consumption models (Johnson 1986; Katsaitis 1987; Evans 1988; Leiderman and Razin 1988; Enders and Lee 1990; Haug 1990; Evans 1993; Evans and Hasan 1994) and current account specifications (Ahmed 1986, 1987; Hercowitz 1986; Sheffrin and Woo 1990; Otto 1992; Chen and Haug 1993; Ghosh 1995).

Unfortunately, these studies are plagued by severe problems. In particular, estimating reduced forms only allows one to verify the significance of the correlations between variables; it does not reveal the importance of the causal impacts of fiscal policies on the external deficit. Moreover, refuting the neutrality hypothesis from structural equations only implies that governments have the ability to affect the external deficit by changing the timing of taxes; it does not provide information on the importance of the effects of such a policy.

Recently, Normandin (1999) improves on earlier work by directly gauging the causal effects of fiscal policies on external and budget deficits. From a tractable small open-economy version of Blanchard (1985) overlapping-generation model, these effects are measured by the responses of the external deficit to an increase in the budget deficit due to a tax-cut. These responses increase as the birth rate increases. This occurs because a rise of the birth rate implies that the tax burden can be more easily shifted to future generations, so that current private consumption and external deficit augment. In addition, the responses increase as the persistence of the budget deficit increases. This arises because the persistence implies that an augmentation of the contemporaneous budget deficit signals future rises of this variable, and thus future tax reductions, so that these 'sunny days' lead to an increase of current consumption and external deficit.

This paper extends Normandin (1999) analysis in two crucial dimensions. First, the analysis is enlarged by studying the G7 countries. As a group, these countries account for 55 percent of the overall 1990 real gross domestic product of the 116 countries for which the data are available in the Penn World Tables (Mark 5.6a). This suggests that the inclusion of these countries is important to have a broad international perspective of the effects of fiscal policies on external and budget deficits. This constrasts with Normandin (1999) who considers exclusively Canada and the United States, which account for only 25 percent of the overall economic activity.

Second, the influences of fiscal policies are evaluated from both impact and dynamic responses. The impact responses give information on the instantaneous effects of a tax-cut. The dynamic responses document the delayed effects of such a policy. Thus, the joint analysis of impact and dynamic responses offers the considerable advantage of providing a complete assessment of the effects of fiscal policies on external and budget deficits through time. This constrasts with Normandin (1999) who focuses only on the impact responses.

Our analysis is performed on quarterly series for the G7 countries over the post-1975 period. Unit root tests reveal that the current account, budget deficit, net output, and nonhuman wealth are first-order integrated time series for almost all countries. Furthermore, cointegration tests indicate that there exists a single cointegration relation between the current account, the budget deficit, and the nonhuman wealth for most countries. It can be shown that these time-series properties provide empirical supports for the tractable small open-economy, overlapping-generation model, as long as the birth rate is strictly positive.

Combining the model with the notion of agents' superior information (relative to the econometrician) allows one to derive testable orthogonality restrictions. Furthermore, these restrictions are exploited to estimate the birth rate. Interestingly, the estimates confirm that the birth rate is always strictly positive. This implies that the neutrality hypothesis is rejected, so that fiscal policies alter the external deficit. Yet, the estimates reveal that the birth rate is numerically small. For example, the values of birth rate can be as low as 0.1 percent (per quarter) for all, but one, countries. This suggests that a tax-cut as only negligible effects on external deficit, unless the budget deficit exhibits a great degree of persistence. This is because the impact and dynamic responses of external deficit correspond to the value of the birth rate, in the absence of persistence.

Finally, combining the model with agents' superior information enables one to derive restricted vectors autoregressions. These processes capture the persistence of budget deficit, and are evaluated at the relevant values of birth rate to estimate the impact and dynamic responses of external and budget deficits following a tax-cut. Interestingly, these responses reveal that the budget deficit is persistently affected by the fiscal policy for all countries. Moreover, the responses indicate that the external deficit substantially and persistently increases for most countries. In particular, these responses often exceed the values of birth rate, to reach 1.36 currency units (e.g. dollars) at impact and 1.08 currency units after 20 quarters following a one-unit-currency tax-cut. Overall, the fiscal policy has the most important effects on the external deficits for Canada, Japan, and the United States; somewhat smaller impacts for France, Germany, and the United Kingdom; and negligible effects for Italy.

This paper is organized as follows. Section 2 presents the theoretical economic environment. Section 3 constructs and describes the data. Section 4 estimates the birth rate. Section 5 estimates the effects of fiscal policies on external and budget deficits. Section 6 concludes.

2 Theoretical Economic Environment

Blanchard (1985) overlapping generations model is amended to obtain a tractable small open economic environment. For this purpose, the behavior of individual and aggregate consumptions, the financing of government expenditures, as well as the determination of the current account and external deficit are derived. In contrast to Normandin (1999), the environment is completely described and fully solved.

2.1 Individual Consumption

In period t, each domestic consumer born at time s solves the following problem:

$$\max_{\{C_{s,t+j}\}} -\frac{1}{2}E_t \sum_{j=0}^{\infty}(C_{s,t+j} - \beta_s)^2(1+r)^{-j}(1-p)^j, \tag{1}$$

$$\text{s.t.} \quad (B_{s,t+1} + F_{s,t+1}) = (1+\eta)(B_{s,t} + F_{s,t} + W_{s,t} - T_{s,t} - C_{s,t}). \tag{2}$$

E_t represents the expectation operator conditional on information available in period t, $C_{s,t}$ is consumption, $W_{s,t}$ is a noninsurable stochastic labor income, $T_{s,t}$ is lump-sum taxes, $B_{s,t}$ is the purchases of one period bonds issued by the domestic government, and $F_{s,t}$ is the purchases of foreign one period bonds.

Also, the term $(1+\eta)$ represents the gross return on individual nonhuman wealth. To interpret this return, it is convenient to postulate the existence of insurance firms which make (receive) every period an annuity payment to (from) each consumer holding positive (negative) nonhuman wealth and inherit this wealth at consumer's death. Under the assumption that these firms face a zero-profit condition, Yaari (1965) shows that $(1+\eta) = (1+r)/(1-p)$. Here, $(1+r)$ corresponds to the gross return on one period bonds, while $(1-p)^{-1}$ is the gross annuity rate.

In addition, β_s is a bliss point, $(1-p)$ is the probability of being alive next period, and p is the birth rate. When $p = 0$, the domestic economy is described by an infinitely-lived representative consumer model. When $p = 1$, the domestic environment is represented by a sequence of static economies, i.e. each cohort is fully replaced in the subsequent period by a different cohort. The parameter p can also be interpreted as a measure of the imperfectness of intergenerational linkages. More precisely, domestic consumers are altruistic only when p is smaller than the actual domestic birth rate.

Equation (1) describes the preferences of the domestic consumer. These preferences are characterized by a quadratic period utility function. This specification allows one to simplify the exposition. Equation (2) corresponds to the budget constraint. This constraint involves a constant gross return. Again, this permits one to simplify the presentation. The consumer maximizes its utility subject to its budget constraint by choosing a path of expected consumption. The optimal path is given by the Euler equation:

$$E_t C_{s,t+j} = C_{s,t}. \tag{3}$$

This expression stipulates that the temporal trajectory of expected consumption is flat, i.e. consumption is a martingale. Also, the Euler equation (3) and the budget constraint (2) yield the individual consumption function:

$$C_{s,t} = \frac{\eta}{1+\eta}\left[(B_{s,t} + F_{s,t}) + E_t \sum_{j=0}^{\infty}(W_{s,t+j} - T_{s,t+j})(1+\eta)^{-j}\right]. \tag{4}$$

The function (4) is static for a sequence of static economies [$p = 1$, so that $(1+\eta) \to \infty$]. In contrast, (4) is dynamic when there is an infinitely-lived representative consumer [$p = 0$, so that $(1+\eta) = (1+r)$].

2.2 Aggregate Consumption

An aggregate variable is defined as $X_t = \sum_{s=-\infty}^{t} P_{s,t} X_{s,t}$. Here, $P_{s,t} = p(1-p)^{(t-s)}$ is the size in period t of the cohort born at time s, p is the number of individuals born each period (i.e. $P_{s,s} = p$), and $P = 1$ is the (normalized) total population. Following Gali (1990), the aggregation is performed by postulating that individual labor income and taxes are the same for all consumers. That is, $W_{s,t+j} = W_{t+j}$ and $T_{s,t+j} = T_{t+j}$, so that the aggregate labor income and taxes are $W_{t+j} = \sum_{s=-\infty}^{t} P_{s,t} W_{s,t+j}$ and $T_{t+j} = \sum_{s=-\infty}^{t} P_{s,t} T_{s,t+j}$. As in Obstfeld and Rogoff (1995, section 3), it is further assumed that domestic firms do not face capital installation costs and satisfy a zero-profit condition. In this case, aggregate labor income corresponds to the difference between aggregate output and aggregate investment expenditures; that is, $W_t = (Y_t - I_t)$.

Using these notions and the individual consumption function (4) yields the following aggregate consumption function:

$$C_t = \sum_{s=-\infty}^{t} P_{s,t} C_{s,t} = \frac{\eta}{1+\eta} \sum_{s=-\infty}^{t} P_{s,t} \left[(B_{s,t} + F_{s,t}) + E_t \sum_{j=0}^{\infty} (W_{s,t+j} - T_{s,t+j})(1+\eta)^{-j} \right],$$

$$= \frac{\eta}{1+\eta} \left[(B_t + F_t) + E_t \sum_{j=0}^{\infty} (W_{t+j} - T_{t+j})(1+\eta)^{-j} \right],$$

$$= \frac{\eta}{1+\eta} \left[(B_t + F_t) + E_t \sum_{j=0}^{\infty} (Y_{t+j} - I_{t+j} - T_{t+j})(1+\eta)^{-j} \right], \tag{5}$$

where C_t is the aggregate consumption and $(B_t + F_t)$ is the aggregate nonhuman wealth. The function (5) is static when $p = 1$ [i.e. $(1 + \eta) \to \infty$] and dynamic when $p = 0$ [i.e. $(1 + \eta) = (1 + r)$].

Moreover, using the notion that each consumer has zero nonhuman wealth at birth [i.e. $(B_{t+1,t+1} + F_{t+1,t+1}) = 0$] and the individual budget constraint (2) yields the following aggregate intertemporal budget constraint:

$$(B_{t+1} + F_{t+1}) = \sum_{s=-\infty}^{t+1} P_{s,t+1}(B_{s,t+1} + F_{s,t+1}) = (1-p) \sum_{s=-\infty}^{t} P_{s,t}(B_{s,t+1} + F_{s,t+1}),$$

$$= (1-p)(1+\eta) \sum_{s=-\infty}^{t} P_{s,t}(B_{s,t} + F_{s,t} + W_{s,t} - T_{s,t} - C_{s,t}),$$

$$= (1+r)(B_t + F_t + W_t - T_t - C_t) = (1+r)(B_t + F_t + Y_t - I_t - T_t - C_t). \tag{6}$$

Equation (6) reflects the idea that, in aggregate, the gross return on nonhuman wealth is $(1 + r)$, rather than $(1 + \eta)$. This is because the annuity payments represent pure transfers among consumers.

2.3   Financing of Government Expenditures

The public sector of the domestic country faces the following intertemporal budget constraint:

$$(B_{t+1} + B_{t+1}^*) = (1+r)(B_t + B_t^* + G_t - T_t), \tag{7}$$

$$= (B_t + B_t^*) + (1 + r)D_t. \tag{8}$$

The variable B_t^* is the value of foreign purchases of one period domestic bonds, G_t represents the domestic government stochastic expenditures on goods and services, and $D_t = \frac{r}{1+r}(B_t + B_t^*) + G_t - T_t$ corresponds to the definition of the budget deficit (which includes the service of the debt).

In this context, future aggregate taxes are obtained by applying recursive substitutions on (8):

$$T_{t+j} = \frac{r}{1+r}(B_{t+j} + B_{t+j}^*) + G_{t+j} - D_{t+j},$$

$$= \frac{r}{1+r}\left[(B_t + B_t^*) + (1+r)\sum_{k=0}^{j-1} D_{t+k}\right] + G_{t+j} - D_{t+j}, \tag{9}$$

where $j \geq 1$. Furthermore, the present value of aggregate taxes is given by:

$$\sum_{j=0}^{\infty} T_{t+j}(1+\eta)^j = \frac{r}{1+r}(B_t + B_t^*)\sum_{j=0}^{\infty}(1+\eta)^{-j}$$

$$+ \sum_{j=0}^{\infty}(G_{t+j} - D_{t+j})(1+\eta)^{-j} + r\sum_{j=1}^{\infty}(1+\eta)^{-j}\sum_{k=0}^{j-1} D_{t+k},$$

$$= \left(\frac{r}{1+r}\right)\left(\frac{1+\eta}{\eta}\right)(B_t + B_t^*) + \sum_{j=0}^{\infty}(G_{t+j} - D_{t+j})(1+\eta)^{-j} + r\sum_{j=0}^{\infty}D_{t+j}\sum_{k=j+1}^{\infty}(1+\eta)^{-k},$$

$$= \left(\frac{r}{1+r}\right)\left(\frac{1+\eta}{\eta}\right)(B_t + B_t^*) + \sum_{j=0}^{\infty}\left(G_{t+j} + \left(\frac{r-\eta}{\eta}\right)D_{t+j}\right)(1+\eta)^{-j}. \tag{10}$$

Substituting expression (10) in (5) allows one to rewrite the aggregate consumption function as:

$$C_t = \frac{\eta}{1+\eta}(B_t + F_t) - \frac{r}{1+r}(B_t + B_t^*) + \frac{\eta}{1+\eta}E_t\sum_{j=0}^{\infty}\left(Q_{t+j} + \left(\frac{\eta-r}{\eta}\right)D_{t+j}\right)(1+\eta)^{-j},$$

$$= \left[\frac{\eta}{1+\eta}(B_t + F_t) - \frac{r}{1+r}(B_t + B_t^*)\right] + \left[Q_t + \left(\frac{\eta-r}{\eta}\right)D_t\right] -$$

$$\left[-E_t\sum_{j=1}^{\infty}\left(\Delta Q_{t+j} + \left(\frac{\eta-r}{\eta}\right)\Delta D_{t+j}\right)(1+\eta)^{-j}\right], \tag{11}$$

where Δ is the first difference operator, $D_{t+j} = (\sum_{k=1}^{j}\Delta D_{t+k} + D_t)$, $Q_{t+j} = (\sum_{k=1}^{j}\Delta Q_{t+k} + Q_t)$, $Q_t = (Y_t - I_t - G_t)$ is the aggregate net output, and $[Q_t + ((\eta - r)/\eta)D_t]$ is the aggregate cash flow. The function (11) states that aggregate consumption is equal to the sum of the aggregate nonhuman income (the first set of brackets) and aggregate cash flow (the second set of brackets), minus the aggregate saving (the third set of brackets).

Here, the aggregate saving corresponds to expected future declines in aggregate cash flows. In addition, the measure of cash flow involves the term $((\eta - r)/\eta)$, which is the probability that consumers currently alive will not have to pay the future increases in taxes required to reimburse the contemporanous budget deficit. As before, the function (11) is static for a sequence of static economies $[p = 0$, so that $(1 + \eta) \to \infty]$. In addition, the tax burden is completely shifted to future generations [i.e. $((\eta - r)/\eta) \to 1]$. In contrast, (11) is dynamic when there is an infinitely-lived representative consumer $[p = 0$, so that $(1 + \eta) = (1 + r)]$. In this case, the consumer reimburses entirely the budget deficit [i.e. $((\eta - r)/\eta) = 0]$.

Finally, substituting expression (9) in (6) permits one to rewrite the aggregate intertemporal budget constraint as:

$$(B_{t+1} + F_{t+1}) = (1 + r)(B_t + F_t + Q_t + D_t - C_t) - r(B_t + B_t^*). \qquad (12)$$

2.4   Current Account and External Deficit

The external deficit is measured as the negative of the current account. For the domestic economy just described, the current account is defined as:

$$Z_t = [(F_{t+1} - F_t) - (B_{t+1}^* - B_t^*)]/(1 + r). \qquad (13)$$

Equation (13) corresponds to changes in net foreign asset positions. Also, substituting the aggregate intertemporal budget constraints (6) and (7) in (13) enables one to rewrite the current account as:

$$Z_t = \frac{r}{1 + r}(F_t - B_t^*) + Q_t - C_t, \qquad (14)$$

where $\frac{r}{1+r}(F_t - B_t^*)$ is the net income on foreign assets. Expression (14) corresponds to the portion of national ressources that is not absorbed by domestic agents.

Moreover, substituting the aggregate consumption function (11) in (14) and (12) yields:

$$Z_t = -\frac{p}{1 + r}(B_t + F_t) - \left(\frac{\eta - r}{\eta}\right)D_t$$
$$- \left[E_t \sum_{j=1}^{\infty}\left(\Delta Q_{t+j} + \left(\frac{\eta - r}{\eta}\right)\Delta D_{t+j}\right)(1 + \eta)^{-j}\right], \qquad (15)$$

and

$$(B_{t+1} + F_{t+1}) = (1 - p)(B_t + F_t) + (1 + r)\left(1 - \left(\frac{\eta - r}{\eta}\right)\right)D_t$$
$$- (1 + r)\left[E_t \sum_{j=1}^{\infty}\left(\Delta Q_{t+j} + \left(\frac{\eta - r}{\eta}\right)\Delta D_{t+j}\right)(1 + \eta)^{-j}\right]. \qquad (16)$$

Expressions (15) and (16) are the rules for the current account and nonhuman wealth. Again, these rules are static for a sequence of static economies $[p = 1$, so that $((\eta - r)/\eta) \to 1$ and $(1 + \eta) \to \infty]$. In this case, a one-currency-unit (e.g. one-dollar) tax-cut does not alter future nonhuman wealth, but implies a one-currency-unit decrease in the contemporanous current account. Consequently, this fiscal policy affects both the external and budget deficits. In contrast, the rules are dynamic when there is an infinitely-lived representative consumer [$p = 0$, so that $((\eta - r)/\eta) = 0$ and $(1 + \eta) = (1 + r)$]. In addition, a one-currency-unit tax-cut leads to a $(1 + r)$-currency-unit increase in future nonhuman wealth, but does not alter the current account. Thus, the fiscal policy only affects the budget deficit.

Finally, the rules (15) and (16) are rearranged as:

$$\hat{Z}_t \equiv Z_t + \frac{p}{1+r}(F_t + B_t) + \left(\frac{\eta - r}{\eta}\right)D_t, \tag{17}$$

$$= -E_t \sum_{j=1}^{\infty}\left(\Delta Q_{t+j} + \left(\frac{\eta - r}{\eta}\right)\Delta D_{t+j}\right)(1 + \eta)^{-j}, \tag{18}$$

and

$$(B_{t+1} \widehat{+} F_{t+1}) \equiv (B_{t+1} + F_{t+1}) - (1 - p)(B_t + F_t) - (1 + r)\left(1 - \left(\frac{\eta - r}{\eta}\right)\right)D_t, \tag{19}$$

$$= -(1 + r)E_t \sum_{j=1}^{\infty}\left(\Delta Q_{t+j} + \left(\frac{\eta - r}{\eta}\right)\Delta D_{t+j}\right)(1 + \eta)^{-j}. \tag{20}$$

Equations (17) and (19) define the adjusted current account, $\hat{Z}_t$, and the adjusted aggregate nonhuman wealth, $(B_{t+1} \widehat{+} F_{t+1})$. Expressions (18) and (20) are the rules for the adjusted variables. When $p < 1$, these rules are purely forward-looking since the adjusted variables are exclusively related to expected changes in future stochastic forcing variables. When $p = 0$, the single forcing variable corresponds to the aggregate net output. When $0 < p < 1$, the forcing variables also include the budget deficit. Equations (17) and (18) will be central to our analysis of the effects of fiscal policies on external and budget deficits.

3 Data

The quarterly seasonally adjusted measures are constructed for the G7 countries over the post-1975 period. As a group, these countries account for 55 percent of the overall 1990 real gross domestic product of the 116 countries for which the data are available in the Penn World Tables (Mark 5.6a). In contrast, Normandin (1999) considers exclusively Canada and the United States to account for only 25 percent of the overall economic activity.

3.1 Construction of the Data

The individual countries (samples) are Canada (1975-I to 2001-III), France (1975-I to 1998-IV), Germany (1975-I to 1998-IV), Italy (1975-I to 1998-IV), Japan (1977-I to 2001-III), the United Kingdom (1975-I to 1999-IV), and the United States (1975-I to 2001-III). Germany refers to West Germany and Unified Germany for the pre- and post-1990 periods. The measures are mainly computed from the International Financial Statistics (IFS) released by the International Monetary Funds (IMF), as well as the Main Economic Indicators (MEI) and the Quarterly National Accounts (QNA) published by the Organization for Economic Cooperation and Development (OECD).

Current Account and External Deficit

For each country, the current account (Z_t) is constructed as the product of the nominal current account in US dollars (source: IFS, IMF) and the nominal exchange rate of national currency units per US dollars (source: IFS, IMF), deflated by the all-item consumer price index (CPI) for the baseyear 1995 (source: MEI, OECD). For each country, the published series of current account are not seasonally adjusted. Thus, the current account is regressed (by OLS) on quarter dummies to remove seasonality. The external deficit is measured as the negative of the current account.

Budget Deficit

With the exception of Japan, the budget deficit (D_t) corresponds to the nominal budget deficit in national currency (source: IFS, IMF), normalized by the CPI. Because these data are not seasonally adjusted, the series are regressed on quarter dummies. For Japan, the budget deficit is the sum of the nominal government final consumption expenditures in national currency (source: QNA, OECD) and the nominal debt service in national currency (source: Japan Statistical Yearbook 2002) less the nominal total tax revenues in national currency (source: Revenue Statistics, OEDC), divided by the CPI. The published data on total tax revenues are annual. For this reason, this series is interpolated by using the Quadratic-Match Average Nonparametric Method available in Eviews.

Net Output

For each country, the net output (Q_t) is the difference between the nominal gross domestic product in national currency (source: QNA, OECD) and the sum of the nominal gross fixed capital formation in national currency (source: QNA, OECD) and the nominal government final consumption expenditures in national currency (source: QNA, OECD), divided by the CPI. The published data for Germany are not seasonally adjusted. Hence, the German series are regressed on quarter dummies.

Nonhuman Wealth

For each country, the nonhuman wealth $(B_t + F_t)$ is constructed as the weighted sum of the debt service and the net income on foreign assets. The weight corresponds to $(\frac{1+r}{r})$, with the calibration $r = 0.01$ (per quarter). For each country, the net income on foreign assets $[\frac{r}{1+r}(F_t - B_t^*)]$ is the nominal factor income in national currency (source: Time Series Query, World Bank), deflated by the CPI. Because the data on net factor income are annual, this series is interpolated by using the Quadratic-Match Average algorithm. For Japan, the debt service $[\frac{r}{1+r}(B_t + B_t^*)]$ is the nominal debt service in national currency (source: Japan Statistical Yearbook 2002), normalized by the CPI. For the other countries, the debt service is the sum of the nominal budget deficit in national currency (source: IFS, IMF) and the nominal total tax revenues in national currency (source: Revenue Statistics, OEDC) less the nominal government final consumption expenditures in national currency (source: QNA, OECD), divided by the CPI. Again, the series on total tax revenues are interpolated and the data on budget deficit are deseasonalized.

3.2 Description of the Data

Figure 1 displays the time series of current account, budget deficit, net output, and nonhuman wealth for each country. Visual inspection suggests that the current accounts and budget deficits exhibit volatilities which increase through time for most countries. Also, the net outputs and nonhuman wealth feature levels that increase through time for most countries. Overall, these characteristics suggest that the series are first-order integrated.

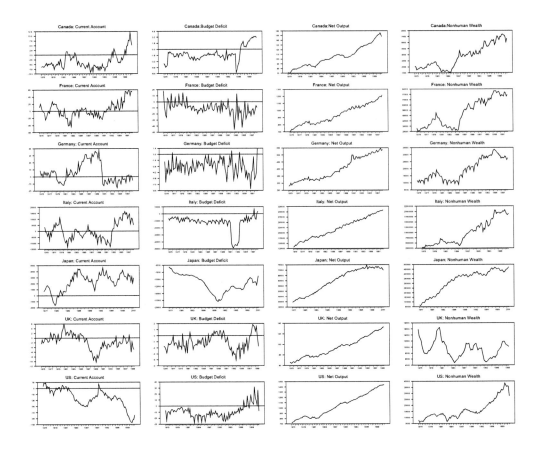

Figure 1: Data are in billions of real (baseyear 1995) national currencies.

Consequently, the tests developped by Dickey and Fuller (1979) [DF] and Phillips and Perron (1988) [PP] are performed to verify the presence of unit roots. In their basic form, these tests rely on a regression of the contemporaneous change of a series on the lagged level of this series. The null hypothesis of unit root cannot be rejected if the t-statistic indicates that the coefficient of the regression is not significantly different from zero. In practice, the regression is enriched by following the procedure outlined by Campbell and Perron (1991). For the DF and PP tests, a constant and a linear trend are also included in the regression if the associated estimates are individually significant at the 10 percent level. For the DF test, lagged changes of the series are further incorporated in the regression, where the relevant number (up to 15) of lags is selected by the Akaike information criterion. For the PP test, a triangular Bartlett window with a truncation parameter corresponding to the integer part of $\left[4 \times \left(\frac{T}{100}\right)^{2/9}\right]$ (where T is the sample size) is used to obtain a heteroscedasticity and autocorrelation consistent covariance matrix of the regression estimates (Newey and West 1987).

Table 1 reports the DF and PP tests for the levels of current account, budget deficit, net

Table 1: Tests of Unit Root: Levels

Countries	Tests	Variables			
		Z_t	D_t	Q_t	$(B_t + F_t)$
Canada	DF	-1.206^n	-2.711^t	-3.168^t	-2.622^t
	PP	-1.859^n	-2.781^t	3.653^n	-2.584^t
France	DF	-2.158^t	-3.265^t	-1.685^t	-2.127^t
	PP	-3.065^t	$-9.429^{t,a}$	-2.387^t	-2.150^t
Germany	DF	-1.626^n	$-4.059^{c,a}$	-1.867^t	-2.173^t
	PP	$-2.179^{n,b}$	$-8.059^{c,a}$	-2.598^t	-2.917^t
Italy	DF	-1.681^n	-2.461^c	$-4.584^{t,a}$	-2.584^t
	PP	$-2.259^{n,b}$	-2.461^c	$-4.406^{t,a}$	-2.491^t
Japan	DF	-3.270^t	-0.295^t	2.084^t	$-9.108^{t,a}$
	PP	-2.035^c	-0.498^t	-2.027^c	$-9.328^{t,a}$
UK	DF	-1.330^n	$-3.283^{c,b}$	1.154^c	$-4.051^{t,a}$
	PP	-3.353^t	$-4.096^{c,a}$	-1.721^t	$-2.968^{c,b}$
US	DF	-3.281^t	-1.004^n	7.715^n	-2.481^t
	PP	0.024^n	$-6.181^{t,a}$	6.341^n	0.843^n

output, and nonhuman wealth. Interestingly, the DF and PP tests almost always include the same sets of deterministic components. Also, both the DF and PP tests cannot reject the unit root hypothesis for 19 out of the 28 cases. In addition, either the DF or PP test cannot reject the null hypothesis for four series. Finally, both the DF and PP tests reject the presence of unit root for only five cases. These exceptions are the budget deficits for Germany and the United Kingdom, the net output for Italy, and the nonhuman wealth for Japan and the United Kingdom. Overall, these findings indicate that the unit root hypothesis is reasonable for almost all series.

Note: Entries are the t-statistics of the coefficients associated with the lagged values of the variables. The superscrits are x, y. $x = n, c$, and t when the regression includes no deterministic term, a constant, and a constant as well as a linear trend. $y = a$ and b when the coefficients are significant at the 1 and 5 percent levels. MacKinnon asymptotic critical values at the 1 and 5 percent levels are -2.56 and -1.94 for $x = n$; -3.43 and -2.86 for $x = c$; and -3.96 and -3.41 for $x = t$.

Table 2 presents the DF and PP tests for the changes of current account, budget deficit, net output, and nonhuman wealth. Again, the DF and PP tests incorporate the same deter-

Table 2: Tests of Unit Root: First Differences

Countries	Tests	Variables			
		ΔZ_t	ΔD_t	ΔQ_t	$\Delta(B_t + F_t)$
Canada	DF	$-6.317^{n,a}$	$-6.361^{n,a}$	$-7.315^{c,a}$	-2.622^{c}
	PP	$-12.736^{n,a}$	$-10.946^{n,a}$	$-7.012^{n,a}$	$-10.219^{n,a}$
France	DF	$-15.677^{n,a}$	$-16.155^{n,a}$	$-10.584^{c,a}$	$-10.207^{n,a}$
	PP	$-16.044^{n,a}$	$-32.509^{n,a}$	$-13.489^{c,a}$	$-10.194^{n,a}$
Germany	DF	$-12.710^{n,a}$	$-11.776^{n,a}$	$-4.600^{c,a}$	$-3.058^{n,a}$
	PP	$-12.710^{n,a}$	$-31.582^{n,a}$	$-14.589^{c,a}$	$-13.852^{n,a}$
Italy	DF	$-13.995^{n,a}$	$-6.566^{n,a}$	$-5.839^{c,a}$	$-7.234^{c,a}$
	PP	$-13.850^{n,a}$	$-10.828^{n,a}$	$-15.728^{c,a}$	$-10.134^{c,a}$
Japan	DF	$-3.528^{n,a}$	$-6.200^{t,a}$	$-10.252^{t,a}$	$-5.617^{t,a}$
	PP	$-11.862^{n,a}$	$-5.570^{n,a}$	$-14.438^{t,a}$	$-35.156^{n,a}$
UK	DF	$-9.967^{n,a}$	$-4.200^{n,a}$	$-11.393^{c,a}$	$-5.952^{n,a}$
	PP	$-14.118^{n,a}$	$-17.729^{n,a}$	$-11.453^{c,a}$	$-5.965^{n,a}$
US	DF	$-11.060^{n,a}$	$-14.229^{n,a}$	$-9.048^{c,a}$	$-2.366^{n,b}$
	PP	$-11.076^{n,a}$	$-24.169^{n,a}$	$-9.205^{c,a}$	$-7.922^{n,a}$

ministic terms for most of the cases. Moreover, both the DF and PP tests strongly reject the unit root hypothesis for 27 out of the 28 cases. The exception is that the DF test detects a unit root in the change of nonhuman wealth for Canada, while the PP test does not. In sum, these results confirm that the levels of current account, budget deficit, net output, and nonhuman wealth are generally first-order integrated, so that the changes of these series are stationary.

Note: Entries are the t-statistics of the coefficients associated with the lagged values of the variables. Δ represents the first difference operator. The superscrits are x, y. $x = n, c$, and t when the regression includes no deterministic term, a constant, and a constant as well as a linear trend. $y = a$ and b when the coefficients are significant at the 1 and 5 percent levels. MacKinnon asymptotic critical values at the 1 and 5 percent levels are -2.56 and -1.94 for $x = n$; -3.43 and -2.86 for $x = c$; and -3.96 and -3.41 for $x = t$.

Note: Entries are the number of cointegration relations at the 1 and 5 percent levels of significance.

For completeness, the tests developed by Johansen (1991) are performed to verify the

Table 3: Tests of Cointegration

Countries	Tests	Levels of Significance	
		1	5
Canada	Tr	0	1
	ME	0	0
France	Tr	1	2
	ME	1	2
Germany	Tr	1	1
	ME	1	1
Italy	Tr	1	2
	ME	1	2
Japan	Tr	1	2
	ME	2	2
UK	Tr	2	0
	ME	0	0
US	Tr	3	3
	ME	3	3

presence of cointegration relations between the levels of the series. In their basic form, these tests rely on a vector error correction model (VECM), where a vector containing the contemporaneous changes of the series is related to a vector including the lagged levels of the series. The appropriate number of cointegration relations is detected from statistics related to the trace [Tr] and the maximum eigenvalue [ME] of the coefficient matrix affecting the vector of the lagged levels of the series. In practice, the VECM is enriched by incorporating a vector of constants and vectors of lagged changes of the series. The relevant number (up to 15) of lags is determined by the Akaike information criterion.

Table 3 reports the Tr and ME tests for the cointegration relations between the levels of current account, budget deficit, and nonhuman wealth. Empirically, both the Tr and ME tests reject the no cointegration hypothesis for five out of the seven countries. In addition, either the Tr or ME test reject the null hypothesis for the other two cases. Finally, the Tr or ME test cannot reject the notion that there is a single cointegration relation for five countries. The exceptions are the United Kingdom with zero or two cointegration relations, and the United States with three cointegration relations. Overall, these findings indicate that the assumption of a single cointegration relation is reasonable for almost all countries.

To summarize, the test results reveal that the current account, budget deficit, net output, and nonhuman wealth are first-order integrated for almost all countries. Furthermore, there exists only one cointegration relation between the current account, the budget deficit, and the nonhuman wealth for most cases. Interestingly, these results provide an empirical support for our tractable theoretical economic environment, as long as the birth rate is strictly positive. Specifically, the environment predicts that the adjusted current account must be stationary. This is because equation (18) states that $\hat{Z}_t$ is a linear combination of ΔQ_t and ΔD_t, where these changes are always stationary. Moreover, equation (17) implies that $\hat{Z}_t = Z_t$ when $p = 0$, such that the current account should be stationary. However, this property never holds in the data, and as such it refutes the case of a null birth rate. Finally, equation (17) states that $\hat{Z}_t = \left[Z_t + \frac{p}{1+r}(F_t + B_t) + \left(\frac{\eta - r}{\eta} \right) D_t \right]$ when $p > 0$, which implies that their is a single cointegration relation between the current account, the budget deficit, and the nonhuman wealth. This property almost always holds in the data, so that it accords with a strictly positive birth rate.

4 Estimation of the Birth Rate

The birth rate is a key ingredient involved in the defintion (17) and the rule (18) of adjusted current account, which are central to the evaluation of the effects of fiscal policies on external and budget deficits. Here, two estimation methods for the birth rate are elaborated and applied. Both procedures exploit certain orthogonality restrictions. These restrictions can be derived when agents possess a richer information set than the econometrician. In contrast to Normandin (1999), the agents' superior information is fully detailed.

4.1 Agents' Superior Information

It is most plausible that agents' decisions rely on more information than just the history of forcing variables. In this spirit, the law of motion for forcing variables is specified as:

$$\begin{pmatrix} \Delta Q_t \\ \Delta D_t \\ \Delta H_t \end{pmatrix} = \begin{pmatrix} \pi_{11} & \pi_{12} & \pi_{13} \\ \pi_{21} & \pi_{22} & \pi_{23} \\ \pi_{31} & \pi_{32} & \pi_{33} \end{pmatrix} \begin{pmatrix} \Delta Q_{t-1} \\ \Delta D_{t-1} \\ \Delta H_{t-1} \end{pmatrix} + \begin{pmatrix} \nu_{q,t} \\ \nu_{d,t} \\ \nu_{h,t} \end{pmatrix},$$

or more compactly

$$W_t = \Pi_w W_{t-1} + V_t. \tag{21}$$

This law of motion assumes that the appropriate forcing variables are the net output and budget deficit. This is predicted by our theoretical economic environment when the birth rate is positive (see section 2). This is also consistent with the empirical time-series properties (see section 3).

The law of motion stipulates that the information set incorporates, not only past values of forcing variables, but also lagged values of a hidden variable H_t. This variable can be viewed as a composite of several exogenous variables. In addition, the hidden variable contains relevant extra information to improve forecasts of future forcing variables when it Granger-causes changes of net output or of budget deficit ($\pi_{13} \neq 0$ or $\pi_{23} \neq 0$). Finally, it is assumed that the hidden variable is observed and used by the economic agents, but is unknown or omitted by the econometrician. This implies that the agents' information set is superior to the econometrician's one.

In practice, the presence of the hidden variable makes it difficult to estimate the law of motion (21). Following Boileau and Normandin (2002, 2003), it is possible to use the rule (18) and the law of motion (21) to extract a law of motion that contains only variables that are observed by the econometrician. This occurs because the rule implies that agents fully reveal their expectations of future forcing variables through there forwarg-looking decisions. Then, an adequate law of motion is obtained by replacing the hidden variable by the adjusted current account. This yields a law of motion that is augmented by agents' superior information.

To derive the augmented law of motion, first the agents' expectations constructed from (21) are substituted in the rule (18) to yield:

$$\hat{Z}_t = \varphi_{zw} W_t, \tag{22}$$

where $\varphi_{zw} = -[e_1' + (\frac{\eta-r}{\eta})e_2']\Pi_w(1+\eta)^{-1}[I - \Pi_w(1+\eta)^{-1}]$, I is the identity matrix, $e_1 = (1 \quad 0 \quad 0)'$, $e_2 = (0 \quad 1 \quad 0)'$, and $e_3 = (0 \quad 0 \quad 1)'$. Second, the expression (22) is rewritten as:

$$X_{z,t} = \Upsilon_z W_t, \tag{23}$$

where $X_{z,t} = (\Delta Q_t \quad \Delta D_t \quad \hat{Z}_t)'$ and $\Upsilon_z = (e_1' \quad e_2' \quad \varphi_{zw})'$. Third, substituting (21) in (23) permits one to obtain a vector autoregression (VAR) for the adjusted current account:

$$\begin{pmatrix} \Delta Q_t \\ \Delta D_t \\ \hat{Z}_t \end{pmatrix} = \begin{pmatrix} \gamma_{11} & \gamma_{12} & \gamma_{13} \\ \gamma_{21} & \gamma_{22} & \gamma_{23} \\ \gamma_{31} & \gamma_{32} & \gamma_{33} \end{pmatrix} \begin{pmatrix} \Delta Q_{t-1} \\ \Delta D_{t-1} \\ \hat{Z}_{t-1} \end{pmatrix} + \begin{pmatrix} u_{q,t} \\ u_{d,t} \\ u_{z,t} \end{pmatrix},$$

or

$$X_{z,t} = \Gamma_z X_{z,t-1} + U_{z,t}, \tag{24}$$

where $\Gamma_z = \Upsilon_z \Pi_w \Upsilon_z^{-1}$ and $U_{z,t} = \Upsilon_z V_t$.

Note that the first two equations of (24) form the law of motion for forcing variables augmented by the adjusted current account. In this augmented law of motion, the feedbacks from lagged adjusted current account to contemporanous forcing variables reflect the effects of the lagged hidden variable on current forcing variables: $\gamma_{13} \neq 0$ and $\gamma_{23} \neq 0$ only if $\pi_{13} \neq 0$ and $\pi_{23} \neq 0$. This means that the existence of agents' superior information can be verified by applying Granger-causality tests on (24), since it exclusively contains variables that are in the econometrician's information set. Also, note that the last equation of (24) states that the innovation of adjusted current account is a function of the innovations of forcing and hidden variables: $u_{z,t} = \varphi_{zw} V_t$. This formulation is in accord with the notion that the adjusted current account completely captures the relevant information.

Given that the augmented law of motion contains all the relevant information, it is useful to estimate the unrestricted version of the VAR (24). In particular, this process allows one to derive a restricted VAR that involves the testable restrictions imposed by our theoretical economic environment. To do so, first the expectations constructed from the unrestricted VAR (24) are substituted in the rule (18) to yield:

$$\hat{Z}_t^m = \Theta_{zx} X_{z,t}, \tag{25}$$

where $\Theta_{zx} = -[e_1' + (\frac{\eta-r}{\eta})e_2']\Gamma_z(1+\eta)^{-1}[I - \Gamma_z(1+\eta)^{-1}]^{-1}$ is evaluated from the estimates of Γ_z and calibrated values of the birth rate p and the return r. The superscript m indicates that these variables are predicted by the model. Second, the expression (25) is rewritten as:

$$X_{z,t}^m = \Theta_z X_{z,t}, \tag{26}$$

where $X_{z,t}^m = (\begin{array}{ccc} \Delta Q_t & \Delta D_t & \hat{Z}_t^m \end{array})'$ and $\Theta_z = (\begin{array}{ccc} e_1' & e_2' & \Theta_{zx} \end{array})'$. Third, substituting (24) in (26) produces the restricted VAR for adjusted current account:

$$\begin{pmatrix} \Delta Q_t \\ \Delta D_t \\ \hat{Z}_t^m \end{pmatrix} = \begin{pmatrix} \phi_{11} & \phi_{12} & \phi_{13} \\ \phi_{21} & \phi_{22} & \phi_{23} \\ \phi_{31} & \phi_{32} & \phi_{33} \end{pmatrix} \begin{pmatrix} \Delta Q_{t-1} \\ \Delta D_{t-1} \\ \hat{Z}_{t-1}^m \end{pmatrix} + \begin{pmatrix} u_{q,t} \\ u_{d,t} \\ u_{z,t}^m \end{pmatrix},$$

or

$$X_{z,t}^m = \Phi_z X_{z,t-1}^m + U_{z,t}^m, \tag{27}$$

where $\Phi_z = \Theta_z \Gamma_z \Theta_z^{-1}$ and $U_{z,t}^m = \Theta_z U_{z,t}$.

For completeness, note that a similar procedure can be applied to obtain the restricted VAR for adjusted nonhuman wealth:

$$X_{(b+f),t}^m = \Phi_{(b+f)} X_{(b+f),t-1}^m + U_{(b+f),t}^m, \tag{28}$$

where $X_{(b+f),t}^m = (\begin{array}{ccc} \Delta Q_t & \Delta D_t & (\widehat{B_{t+1} + F_{t+1}})^m \end{array})'$, $\Phi_{(b+f)} = \Theta_{(b+f)} \Gamma_{(b+f)} \Theta_{(b+f)}^{-1}$, $U_{(b+f),t}^m = \Theta_{(b+f)} U_{(b+f),t}$, $\Gamma_{(b+f)}$ and $U_{(b+f),t}$ are the coefficient matrix and the innovations of the unrestricted VAR, $\Theta_{(b+f)} = (\begin{array}{ccc} e_1' & e_2' & \Theta_{(b+f),x} \end{array})'$, and $\Theta_{(b+f),x} = -(1+r)[e_1' + (\frac{\eta-r}{\eta})e_2']\Gamma_{(b+f)}(1+\eta)^{-1}[I - \Gamma_{(b+f)}(1+\eta)^{-1}]^{-1}$.

4.2   Orthogonality Restrictions

Under the null hypothesis that the actual and predicted adjusted current accounts are identical:

$$\hat{Z}_t = \hat{Z}_t^m, \tag{29}$$

certain orthogonality restrictions can be derived. To see this, first the expression (29) is rewritten by invoking the defintion $\hat{Z}_t = e_3' X_{z,t}$ and equation (25):

$$e_3' = \Theta_{zx} = -[e_1' + (\frac{\eta-r}{\eta})e_2']\Gamma_z(1+\eta)^{-1}[I - \Gamma_z(1+\eta)^{-1}]^{-1}, \tag{30}$$

or

$$e_3'[I - \Gamma_z(1+\eta)^{-1}] = -[e_1' + (\frac{\eta-r}{\eta})e_2']\Gamma_z(1+\eta)^{-1}. \tag{31}$$

The equation (31) imposes the three following linear restrictions: $\gamma_{31} = \gamma_{11} + (\frac{\eta-r}{\eta})\gamma_{21}$, $\gamma_{32} = \gamma_{12} + (\frac{\eta-r}{\eta})\gamma_{22}$, and $\gamma_{33} = \gamma_{13} + (\frac{\eta-r}{\eta})\gamma_{23} + (1+\eta)$.

Second, the variable $\epsilon_{z,t}$ is constructed as the following linear combination:

$$\epsilon_{z,t} = \hat{Z}_t - (1+\eta)\hat{Z}_{t-1} - \Delta Q_t - (\frac{\eta-r}{\eta})\Delta D_t. \tag{32}$$

This equation is then rewritten by using the first two equations of the unrestricted VAR (24) and the linear restrictions (31) to express the current variables $\hat{Z}_t$, ΔQ_t, and ΔD_t in (32) exclusively in terms of innovations:

$$\epsilon_{z,t} = u_{z,t} - u_{q,t} - (\frac{\eta-r}{\eta})u_{d,t}. \tag{33}$$

The expression (33) reveals that the linear restrictions (31) imply that the variable $\epsilon_{z,t}$ is orthogonal to the information dated before period t. Thus, the conditions (31) reflect the orthogonality restrictions.

Formally, the orthogonality restrictions (31) are jointly tested from a $\chi^2(3)$ distributed Wald test statistic. In practice, this statistic is easy to compute because it is numerically identical to the Wald statistic for the test that all the coefficients associated with the regression of $\epsilon_{z,t}$ on $\hat{Z}_{t-1}$, ΔQ_{t-1}, and ΔD_{t-1} are jointly insignificant.

4.3 Estimates of Birth Rate

The orthogonality restrictions (31) are useful to estimate the birth rate. One set of estimates is obtained by testing the restrictions from the following procedure.

Step 1. The variables $\epsilon_{z,t}$ and $\hat{Z}_t$ are constructed by using equations (32) and (17), the observations for Z_t, D_t, Q_t, and $(B_t + F_t)$, as well as the calibration $r = 0.01$ (per quarter) and a given value of birth rate p.

Step 2. The variable $\epsilon_{z,t}$ is regressed by Ordinary Least Squares (OLS) on the lagged variables $\hat{Z}_{t-1}$, ΔQ_{t-1}, and ΔD_{t-1}. Then, the probability value is calculated for the null hypothesis that the regression estimates are jointly insignificant.

Step 3. Steps 1 and 2 are performed for several values of birth rate, where $0 \leq p \leq 1$.

From this procedure, the relevant estimates of birth rate are the values of p for which the orthogonality restrictions hold. In addition, a second set of estimates of birth rate is directly obtained by applying the Generalized Method of Moments (GMM) for the orthogonality condition between $\epsilon_{z,t}$ and a constant, ΔQ_{t-1}, and ΔD_{t-1}, as well as from the calibrated value $r = 0.01$ (per quarter).

Table 4 reports the GMM estimates, $\hat{p}$, as well as the smallest values, $\underline{p}$, and largest values, $\bar{p}$, for which the orthogonality conditions are not rejected at the 1, 5, and 10 percent levels of significance. Figure 2 compares the probability values of the orthogonality test obtained from various values of birth rate to conventional levels of significance.

Empirically, there exist values of p for which the orthogonality conditions hold at the 10 percent level for several countries. However, exceptions are France, Italy, and Japan. Also, some values of p imply that the linear restrictions (31) are not rejected at the 5 percent level for all countries, except France. Interestingly, there exist values of p for which the

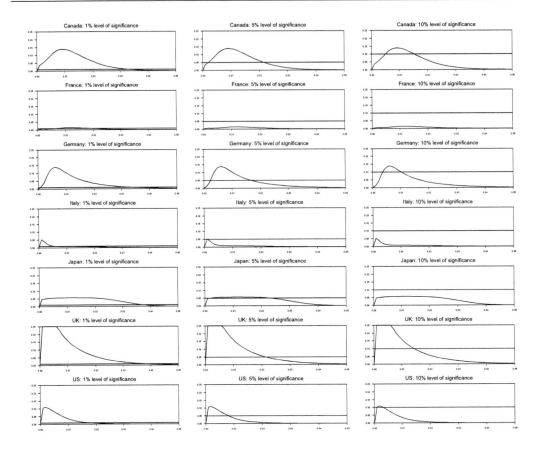

Figure 2: Orthogonality Restrictions. The horizontal lines correspond to the conventional levels of significance.

orthogonality restrictions are never refuted at the 1 percent level, without any exception. For this reason, our analysis relies on these latter values.

It is worth stressing that the values of $\underline{p}$ and $\bar{p}$ are always larger than zero and smaller than one. Under the interpretation that p is the birth rate, these results suggest that none of the selected country can be described by an infinitely-lived respresentative consumer model, nor by a sequence of static economies where each cohort is totally replaced in the subsequent period. Also, the values of $\underline{p}$ are systematically smaller than the birth rate, $\tilde{p}$, of 0.00525 per quarter (or 2.1 percent per year). Moreover, the values of $\bar{p}$ are always larger than $\tilde{p}$, except for Italy. Note that $\tilde{p}$ represents a meaningful benchmark: it corresponds to the birth rate required to ensure a constant population.

Under the interpretation that p is a measure of the imperfectness of intergenerational linkages, the findings suggest that some newborns are altruistically linked to their parents as long as the relevant values of p are $\underline{p}$, since these values are smaller than $\tilde{p}$. More precisely, the proportion of these newborns is given by $(\tilde{p}-\underline{p})/\tilde{p}$, which is substantial for all countries: it corresponds to 80.95%. In contrast, the proportion is only $(\tilde{p} - \bar{p})/\tilde{p} = 4.76\%$ for Italy and 0% for the other countries, when the relevant values of p are assumed to be $\bar{p}$.

Table 4: Estimates of Birth Rate

Countries	Levels of significance	$\underline{p}$	$\bar{p}$	$\hat{p}$
Canada	1	0.001	0.032	0.004
	5	0.003	0.021	(0.008)
	10	0.006	0.015	[0.142]
France	1	0.008	0.017	0.003
	5	—	—	(0.003)
	10	—	—	[0.008]
Germany	1	0.001	0.010	0.006^{b}
	5	0.003	0.016	(0.003)
	10	0.004	0.031	[0.260]
Italy	1	0.001	0.005	0.004
	5	0.001	0.001	(0.003)
	10	—	—	[0.684]
Japan	1	0.001	0.037	0.026^{a}
	5	0.003	0.022	(0.010)
	10	—	—	[0.037]
UK	1	0.001	0.036	0.002
	5	0.001	0.021	(0.002)
	10	0.001	0.014	[0.519]
US	1	0.001	0.016	0.002
	5	0.001	0.008	(0.003)
	10	0.001	0.003	[0.056]

Note: Entries are the estimates of the birth rate. $\underline{p}$ and $\bar{p}$ are the smallest and largest values of the birth rate for which the orthogonality restrictions are not rejected at the 1, 5, and 10 percent levels of significance. $\hat{p}$ represents the GMM estimates of the birth rate. The superscrits a and b indicate that the GMM estimates are significant at the 1 and 5 percent levels. Numbers in parentheses are the standard errors of the GMM estimates. Entries in brackets are the probability values associated with the J-test of overidentification restrictions.

Note: Entries are the probability values associated with the test that the lagged adjusted current account does not affect the current variables. $\underline{p}$ and $\bar{p}$ are the smallest and largest values of the birth rate for which the orthogonality restrictions are not rejected at the 1 percent level of significance,

Table 5: Tests of Granger-Causality

Countries	Variables	$\underline{p}$	$\bar{p}$	$\hat{p}$
Canada	ΔQ_t	0.723	0.417	0.511
	ΔD_t	0.709	0.713	0.729
France	ΔQ_t	0.813	0.769	0.948
	ΔD_t	0.997	0.977	0.991
Germany	ΔQ_t	0.092	0.796	0.756
	ΔD_t	0.336	0.438	0.337
Italy	ΔQ_t	0.691	0.909	0.953
	ΔD_t	0.181	0.621	0.565
Japan	ΔQ_t	0.323	0.071	0.065
	ΔD_t	0.587	0.629	0.546
UK	ΔQ_t	0.044	0.002	0.009
	ΔD_t	0.449	0.450	0.401
US	ΔQ_t	0.113	0.953	0.079
	ΔD_t	0.517	0.745	0.546

while $\hat{p}$ corresponds to the GMM estimates of the birth rate.

Note that the GMM estimates of p are numerically larger than zero and smaller than one. The estimates are not significantly different from zero for all countries, except for Germany and Japan. This means that most economies can be statistically described by an infinitely-lived respresentative consumer model. However, this conclusion is inconsistent with the time-series properties of the current account (see section 3). For this reason, our analysis assumes that the values of p are positive. Also, the GMM estimates are always significantly different from unity. This indicates that none of the country can be characterized by a sequence of static economies. Moreover, the estimates suggest that the proportions of altruistic newborns, $(\tilde{p} - \hat{p})/\tilde{p}$, are 61.90% for the United Kingdom and the United States, 42.86% for France, 23.81% for Canada and Italy, and 0% for Germany and Japan.

The GMM estimates are also numerically larger than the values of $\underline{p}$ and smaller than those of $\bar{p}$ for all countries, except for France. In fact, the estimates are never significantly different from the values of $\underline{p}$, with the exception of Japan. The estimates are significantly different from the values of $\bar{p}$, except for Germany, Italy, and Japan. In our analysis, the values of $\underline{p}$, $\bar{p}$, and $\hat{p}$ are used to verify the robustness of the results.

For completeness, Table 4 indicates that the overidentication restrictions related to the

GMM estimates are never rejected, except for France and Japan. This suggests that the orthogonality restrictions statistically hold for most countries, such that the actual and predicted adjusted current account are similar. Also, Table 5 presents the probability values of the test that $\hat{Z}_t$ does not Granger-cause ΔQ_t and ΔD_t (i.e. $\gamma_{13} = 0$ and $\gamma_{23} = 0$). To perform this test, the series $\hat{Z}_t$ is first constructed from equation (17), the values of $\underline{p}$, $\bar{p}$, and $\hat{p}$, as well as the calibration $r = 0.01$ (per quarter). Then, this series is used in the unrestricted VAR (24), which is estimated by OLS. The test results indicate that there are some feedback effects from the lagged adjusted current account to the contemporaneous net ouput for Germany when $p = \underline{p}$; for Japan when $p = \bar{p}$ and $p = \hat{p}$; for the United Kingdom when $p = \underline{p}$, $p = \bar{p}$, and $p = \hat{p}$; as well as for the United States when $p = \hat{p}$. As explained above, these findings are consistent with the presence of agents' superior information. Finally, the Schwarz information creterion reveals that a first-order unrestricted VAR, as stipulated in (24), is appropriate for almost all cases. Exceptions are France when $p = \hat{p}$ and the United States when $p = \bar{p}$, where in both cases a third-order VAR seems slightly preferable.

5   Estimation of the Effects of Fiscal Policies

The effects of fiscal policies are now evaluated. For this purpose, the impact and dynamic responses of external and budget deficits following a one-currency-unit tax-cut are analyzed. In contrast, Normandin (1999) studies only the impact responses.

5.1   Construction of the Responses

The effects of fiscal policies on external and budget deficits are documented from impact and dynamic responses. Conceptually, these responses are defined as:

$$R_{a,j} = -\Big(\frac{\partial A_{t+j}}{\partial \epsilon_{\tau,t}}\Big) = \Big(\frac{\partial A_{t+j}}{\partial \epsilon_{d,t}}\Big)\lambda. \tag{34}$$

Here, $R_{a,j}$ represents the impact response when $j = 0$ and dynamic responses if $j > 0$, while A_t is a generic variable. For example, the responses of external and budget deficits are obtained by using the definitions $A_t = -Z_t$ and $A_t = D_t$. Also, $\epsilon_{\tau,t}$ and $\epsilon_{d,t}$ correspond to positive shocks of taxes and of budget deficit, whereas λ is a scale parameter.

Equation (34) captures the responses of the variable A_t to an unexpected tax-cut. In addition, expression (34) states that these effects correspond to the responses of A_t to a positive shock of the budget deficit. To see this, note that $\epsilon_{d,t}$ captures the portion of the innovation of the budget deficit $u_{d,t}$ that is orthogonal to the innovations of net output $u_{q,t}$, where the net output is constructed from the government expenditures on goods and services. This ensures that the responses (34) represent the effects of an increase of the budget deficit that is exclusively due to a tax-cut, rather than to an increase of goverment expenditures. Finally, the parameter λ is chosen to scale to unity the impact response of budget deficit following a budget deficit shock. This eases the interpretation of (34), since it is equivalent to an experiment where the tax-cut is normalized to one currency unit.

Conceptually, the effects of fiscal policies are evaluated from our theoretical economic environment. In particular, these effects are derived by exploiting the definitions of adjusted current account (17) and nonhuman wealth (19), the rules of these adjusted variables (18) and (20), and the law of motion for forcing variables (21). Synonymously, the dynamic responses are constructed from the definitions (17) and (19), as well as the restricted VARs (27) and (28). Recall that the validity of the linear combinations involved in these definitions is supported by the results of unit root and cointegration tests (see section 3). Likewise, the relevance of the restricted VARs is confirmed by the test results of the orthogonality restrictions (see section 4). In this sense, assessing the effects of fiscal policies from our theoretical economic environment constitutes a relevant empirical exercise.

The responses of the levels of current account and nonhuman wealth are recovered from the definitions (17) and (19):

$$R_{z,j} = R_{\hat{z},j} - \frac{p}{1+r}R_{(b+f),j} - \frac{\eta-r}{\eta}R_{d,j}, \tag{35}$$

and

$$R_{(b+f),(j+1)} = R_{\widehat{(b+f)},(j+1)} + (1-p)R_{(b+f),j} + (1+r)\left(1 - \left(\frac{\eta-r}{\eta}\right)\right)R_{d,j}. \tag{36}$$

The responses of external deficit is simply the negative of $R_{z,j}$.

Furthermore, the responses of adjusted current account and nonhuman wealth are obtained from the restricted VARs (27) and (28):

$$R_{\hat{z},j} = [e_3'\Phi_{\hat{z}}^j\Theta_z\Lambda_z e_2]\lambda, \tag{37}$$

and

$$R_{\widehat{(b+f)},j+1} = [e_3'\Phi_{(b+f)}^j\Theta_{(b+f)}\Lambda_{(b+f)}e_2]\lambda. \tag{38}$$

Here, $\Omega_z = E(U_{z,t}^m U_{z,t}^{m\prime}) = \Lambda_z\Lambda_z'$ and $\Omega_{(b+f)} = E(U_{(b+f),t}^m U_{(b+f),t}^{m\prime}) = \Lambda_{(b+f)}\Lambda_{(b+f)}'$, where Λ_z and $\Lambda_{(b+f)}$ are lower triangular matrices with positive elements on their diagonals. These Cholesky decompositions yield orthogonalized shocks.

Finally, the responses of the level of budget deficit is derived from the restricted VAR (27):

$$R_{d,j} = \sum_{\kappa=0}^{j}[e_2'\Phi_{\hat{z}}^\kappa\Theta_z\Lambda_z e_2]\lambda. \tag{39}$$

Expression (39) exploits the notion that the responses of the level of budget deficit corresponds to the accumulation of the responses of the changes of this variable, since $D_{t+j} = \sum_{\kappa=0}^{j}\Delta D_{t+\kappa} + D_{t-1}$ and D_{t-1} is not affected by shocks occuring in period t.

The properties of the responses of external deficit are highlighted by performing the following simulation.

Step 1. The law of motion (21) is specified as:

$$\Pi_w = \begin{pmatrix} \pi_{11} & 0 & \pi_{13} \\ 0 & \pi_{11} & \pi_{13} \\ 0 & 0 & \pi_{11} \end{pmatrix}, \tag{40}$$

and

$$\Omega_w = E(V_t V_t') = I. \tag{41}$$

The parameter π_{11} corresponds to the eigenvalues, and thus, captures the degree of persistence of the forcing and hidden variables. Also, π_{13} reflects the degree of additional information used by agents.

Step 2. The restricted VARs for adjusted current account (27) and for adjusted nonhuman wealth (28) are constructed from the specification (40) and (41), for a given calibration of the parameters π_{11} and π_{13}, as well as of the birth rate p and the return $r = 0.01$.

Step 3. The simulated impact and dynamic responses of external deficit is measured by the negative of the responses of current account. To do so, the simulated responses are constructed recursively for $j = 0, 1, \ldots, 20$ from equations (35)–(39) and the notion that $R_{(b+f),0} = 0$, since the nonhuman wealth is a predetermined variable.

Step 4. Steps 1 to 3 are repeated for several calibrated values of p, π_{11}, and π_{13}. In particular, the birth rate is set to approach the cases where the economy is populated by an infinitely-lived representative consumer ($p = 0.001 \approx 0$) and by a sequence of one-period cohorts ($p = 0.999 \approx 1$). Also, the degree of persistence is fixed to capture oscillating ($\pi_{11} = -0.5$), smooth ($\pi_{11} = 0.5$), and nonpersistent ($\pi_{11} = 0.01$) dynamics. Finally, the last parameter is calibrated to take into account the presence ($\pi_{13} = -0.5$ and $\pi_{13} = 0.5$) and absence ($\pi_{13} = 0.01 \approx 0$) of agents' superior information.

Figure 3 displays the simulated responses of external deficit for the different calibrations. These responses exhibit three properties. First, the impact and dynamic responses are systematically larger when the birth rate is larger, for given degrees of persistence and agents' superior information. This arises because an increase in the birth rate implies that the tax burden can be more easily shifted to future generations. In this context, consumers perceive an increase in their cash flows, so that private consumption and external deficit augment. Also, the impact responses always converge to unity when the birth rate tends to one. This occurs because a sequence of static economies implies that the tax burden is completely shifted to future generations [i.e. $(\eta - r)/\eta \to 1$]. Conversely, the impact responses always equal zero when the birth rate is null. This is because consumers currently alive reimburse the budget deficit entirely [i.e. $(\eta - r)/\eta = 0$].

Second, the dynamic responses are always larger when the persistence parameter is larger, for given birth rate and degree of agents' superior information. This occurs because a smooth persistence implies that an increase of the contemporaneous budget deficit signals future rises of this variable, or synonymously, future tax reductions. In this case, consumers expect significant increases in their future cash flow, such that consumption and external deficit increase. To gauge the importance of this notion, it is useful to compare the dynamic responses for the cases where $\pi_{11} = 0.01$ and $\pi_{11} = 0.50$. In the absence of persistence ($\pi_{11} = 0.01$), the dynamic responses are flat and correspond to the value of the birth rate. In the presence of smooth persistence ($\pi_{11} = 0.50$), the dynamic responses sharply increase to reach a value that substantially exceeds that of the birth rate. More precisely, the responses are twice that of the birth rate, within six quarters after the fiscal policy. For example, for a birth rate equal to one, the external deficit rapidly increases by two currency units following an additional currency unit of budget deficit due to a tax-cut.

Finally, the responses do not seem to be affected by the degree of agents' superior information. That is, the responses are insensitive to changes in the value of π_{13}, for given

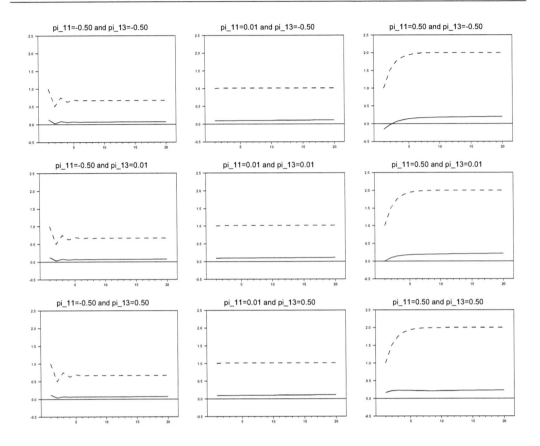

Figure 3: Simulated Responses. The solid (dashed) lines correspond to the simulated responses of external deficit with $p = 0.001$ ($p = 0.999$).

values of p and π_{11}.

5.2   Estimates of the Responses

To estimate the empirical responses for each country, the following procedure is performed.

Step 1. The variables $\hat{Z}_t$ and $(\widehat{B_{t+1} + F_{t+1}})$ are computed by using equations (17) and (19), the observations for Z_t, D_t, Q_t, and $(B_t + F_t)$, as well as the calibration $r = 0.01$ (per quarter) and a given value of birth rate p.

Step 2. The unrestricted VARs for adjusted current account and nonhuman wealth (24) are estimated by OLS. These processes are used to construct the restricted VARs for adjusted current account (27) and nonhuman wealth (28).

Step 3. The empirical impact and dynamic responses of external deficit are measured by the negative of the responses of current account (35). The empirical impact and dynamic responses of budget deficit are given by (39). These empirical responses are constructed recursively for $j = 0, 1, \ldots, 20$ from (35)–(39) and $R_{(b+f),0} = 0$.

Step 4. Steps 1 to 3 are performed for the GMM estimates of the birth rate, $\hat{p}$, as well as the smallest values, $\underline{p}$, and largest values, $\bar{p}$, for which the orthogonality conditions are not rejected at the 1 percent level of significance.

Figure 4 exhibits the empirical responses of external and budget deficits. Figure 5 presents the probability values that the responses of external deficit are equal to zero, one, and the birth rate. Recall that the impact responses are null and unity when the birth rates are equal to zero and one. Also, the dynamic responses correspond to the value of the birth rate when there is no persistence.

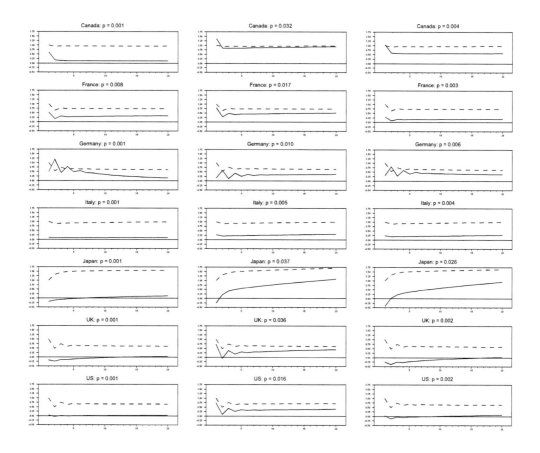

Figure 4: Empirical Responses. The solid (dashed) lines correspond to the empirical responses of external (budget) deficits.

Empirically, the responses of budget deficit are always numerically close to one and statistically significant. [For briefness, this last result is not reported.] This reveals that fiscal policies persistently affect the budget deficit. In addition, as explained above, the persistence of the budget deficit can lead to a substantial increase of the external deficit, so that the associated dynamic responses exceed the value of the birth rate.

In general, the responses of external deficit are numerically positive. Exceptions are Japan for the first five quarters after the shock when $p = \underline{p}$, and at impact when $p = \bar{p}$ and $p = \hat{p}$; the United Kingdom for the first 13 and 15 quarters when $p = \underline{p}$ and $p = \hat{p}$;

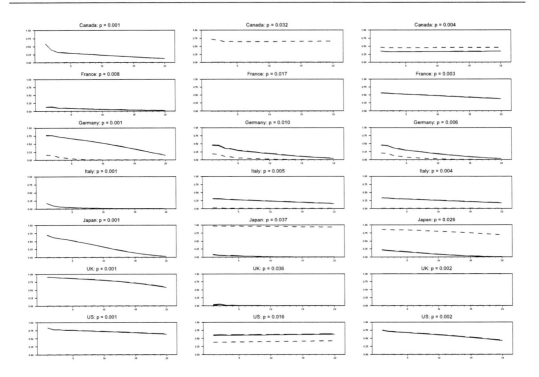

Figure 5: Probability Values. The solid (dashed) [dotted] lines correspond to the probability values that the responses of external deficit are equal to zero (the birth rate) [one].

and the United States for the second quarter when $p = \underline{p}$ and the first eight quarters when $p = \hat{p}$. Moreover, the responses are most of the time insignificantly different from zero (at the 10 percent level) when $p = \underline{p}$ and $p = \hat{p}$, but are often statistically positive when $p = \bar{p}$. Exceptions are France and Italy where the responses are statistically positive after one quarter when $p = \underline{p}$; Germany and Japan where the responses are significantly larger than zero after 14 and seven quarters when $p = \hat{p}$; as well as Italy and the United States where the responses are never significant when $p = \bar{p}$. Overall, these findings suggest that fiscal policies influence the external deficit, as long as $p = \bar{p}$. This is rationalized by the property stating that the responses increase as the birth rate increases, and the fact that $\bar{p}$ is always larger than $\underline{p}$ and $\hat{p}$.

The responses of external deficit are frequently numerically smaller than unity. Exceptions are Canada for the responses at impact when $p = \bar{p}$ and $p = \hat{p}$; Germany for the first quarter when $p = \bar{p}$; and Japan after 17 quarters when $p = \bar{p}$. Furthermore, the responses are systematically significantly different from one (at the 10 percent level) when $p = \underline{p}$, and are frequently statistically smaller than unity when $p = \bar{p}$ and $p = \hat{p}$. Important exceptions are Canada and Japan where the responses are never significantly different from one when $p = \bar{p}$ and $p = \hat{p}$; and the United States where the responses are always statistically equal to unity when $p = \bar{p}$. Thus, Canada, Japan, and the United States are the countries for which fiscal policies most strongly alter the external deficit, especially when $p = \bar{p}$. Again, this finding is explained by the concept that the responses are larger when the birth rate is larger, and the evidence that $\bar{p}$ is the largest estimate of the birth rate.

Finally, the responses of external deficit are numerically larger than the birth rate. Exceptions are Japan for the first six and two quarters after the shock when $p = \underline{p}$ and $p = \bar{p}$, and at impact when $p = \hat{p}$; the United Kingdom for the first 14 and 16 quarters when $p = \underline{p}$ and $p = \hat{p}$; and the United States for the second quarter when $p = \underline{p}$ and the first nine quarters when $p = \hat{p}$. In addition, the responses are most of the time insignificantly different from the value of the birth rate (at the 10 percent level) when $p = \underline{p}$ and $p = \hat{p}$, but are often statistically larger when $p = \bar{p}$. Exceptions are France and Italy where the responses are statistically larger than the birth rate after five and one quarters when $p = \underline{p}$; Germany and Japan where the responses are significantly larger than the birth rate after 15 and 10 quarters when $p = \hat{p}$; as well as Italy and the United States where the responses are never significantly different from the birth rate when $p = \bar{p}$. As shown above, the property that the responses are larger than the birth rate is due to the great persistence of the forcing variables, and in particular, the budget deficit.

In summary, fiscal policies subtantially and persistently affect the budget deficits of all countries. These policies are also likely to greatly influence the external deficits for Canada, Japan, and the United States. In particular, the effects of a tax-cut are enhanced by the large degree of persistence of the budget deficits for Canada and Japan. In contrast, a tax-cut has smaller impacts on the external deficits for France and Germany, mild influences for the United Kingdom, and only negligible effects for Italy.

6   Conclusion

This paper studied the effects of fiscal policies on external and budget deficits. To do so, it improves on previous analyses in two crucial dimensions. First, it enlarges the analysis by studying the G7 countries to have a broad international perspective of the effects of fiscal policies on external and budget deficits. Second, it evaluates both impact and dynamic responses to provide a complete assessment of the temporal effects of a tax-cut.

Our analysis is performed on quarterly series for the G7 countries over the post-1975 period. It is shown that the time-series properties of the current account, budget deficit, net output, and nonhuman wealth support the case where the birth rate is strictly positive. Interestingly, the estimates confirm that the birth rate is always strictly positive, but numerically small. Finally, the responses of external and budget deficits are substantial and persistent for most countries. In particular, the fiscal policy has the most important effects on the external deficits for Canada, Japan, and the United States; somewhat smaller impacts for France, Germany, and the United Kingdom; and negligible effects for Italy.

References

Ahmed, S. (1986) "Temporary and Permanent Government Spending in an Open Economy: Some Evidence for the United Kingdom," *Journal of Monetary Economics* **17**, pp. 197–224.

Ahmed, S. (1987) "Government Spending, the Balance of Trade and the Terms of Trade in British History," *Journal of Monetary Economics* **20**, pp. 195–220.

Anderson, P.S. (1990) "Developments in External and Internal Balances: A Selective and Eclectic Review," *BIS Economic Papers* no. **29**, Bank of International Settlements.

Bernheim, D.B. (1987) "Budget Deficits and the Balance of Trade," In: Summers, L.H. (Ed.), *Tax Policy and the Economy* **2**, National Bureau of Economic Research, Cambridge, pp. 1–31.

Blanchard, O.J. (1985) "Debt, Deficits, and Finite Horizons," *Journal of Political Economy* **93**, pp. 223–247.

Boileau, M., and M. Normandin (2002) "Aggregate Employment, Real Business Cycles, and Superior Information," *Journal of Monetary Economics* **49**, pp. 495–520.

Boileau, M., and M. Normandin (2003) "Labor Hoarding, Superior Information, and Business Cycle Dynamics," *Journal of Economic Dynamics and Control* **28**, pp. 397–418.

Campbell, J.Y., and P. Perron (1991) "Pitfalls and Opportunity: What Macroeconomists Should Know about Unit Roots," In: Blanchard, O.J., and S. Fischer (Eds.), *NBER Macroeconomics Annual,* MIT Press, Cambridge, pp. 141–201.

Chen, B., and A.A. Haug (1993) "The Twin Deficits Hypothesis: Empirical Evidence for Canada," Mimeo, York University.

Dickey, D.A., and W.A. Fuller (1979) "Distribution of the Estimators for Autoregressive Time Series with a Unit Root," *Journal of the American Statistical Association* **74**, pp. 427–431.

Enders, W., and B. Lee (1990) "Current Account and Budget Deficits: Twins or Distant Cousins?" *Review of Economics and Statistics* **72**, pp. 373–381.

Evans, P. (1988) "Are Consumers Ricardian? Evidence for the United States," *Journal of Political Economy* **96**, pp. 983–1004.

Evans, P. (1990) "Do Budget Deficits Affect the Current Account?" Mimeo, Ohio State University.

Evans, P. (1993) "Consumers are Not Ricardian: Evidence from Nineteen Countries," *Economic Inquiry* **31**, pp. 534–548.

Evans, P., and I. Hasan (1994) "Are Consumers Ricardian? Evidence for Canada," *Quarterly Review of Economics and Finance* **34**, pp. 25–40.

Gali, J. (1990) "Finite Horizons, Life Cycle Savings, and Time Series Evidence on Consumption," *Journal of Monetary Economics* **26**, pp. 433–452.

Gosh, A. (1995) "Capital Mobility Amongst the Major Industrialized Countries: Too Little or Too Much?" *Economic Journal* **105**, pp. 107–128.

Haug, A.A. (1990) "Ricardian Equivalence, Rational Expectations, and the Permanent Income Hypothesis," *Journal of Money Credit and Banking* **22**, pp. 305–326.

Hercowitz, Z. (1986) "On the Determination of External Debt: The Case of Israel," *Journal of International Money and Finance* **5**, pp. 315–334.

Japan Statistical Yearbook (2002) Statistics Bureau/Statistical Research and Training Institute, Ministry of Public Management, Home Affairs, Posts and Telecommunications, Japan.

Johansen, S. (1991) "Estimation and Hypothesis of Cointegration Vectors in Gaussian Vector Autoregressive Models," *Econometrica* **59**, pp. 1551–1580.

Johnson, D. (1986) "Consumption, Permanent Income, and Financial Wealth in Canada: Empirical Evidence on the Intertemporal Approach to the Current Account," *Canadian Journal of Economics* **19**, pp. 189–206.

Katsaitis, O. (1987) "On the Substituability Between Private Consumer Expenditure and Government Spending in Canada," *Canadian Journal of Economics* **20**, pp. 533–543.

Leiderman, L., and A. Razin (1988) "Testing Ricardian Neutrality with an Intertemporal Stochastic Model," *Journal of Money, Credit, and Banking* **20**, pp. 1–21.

Newey, N.K., and K.D. West (1987) "A Simple Positive Definite Heteroskedasticity and Autocorrelation Consistant Covariance Matrix," *Econometrica* **55**, pp. 703–708.

Normandin, M. (1999) "Budget Deficit Persistence and the Twin Deficit Hypothesis," *Journal of International Economics* **49**, pp. 171–193.

Obstfeld, M., and K. Rogoff (1995) "The Intertemporal Approach to the Current Account," In: Grossman, G., and K. Rogoff (Eds.), *Handbook of International Economics* **3**, North-Holland, Amsterdam, pp. 1731–1799.

Otto, G. (1992) "Testing a Present-Value Model of the Current Account: Evidence from US and Canadian Time Series," *Journal of International Money and Finance* **11**, pp. 414–430.

Phillips, P.C.B., and P. Perron (1988) "Testing for a Unit Root in Time Series Regression," *Biometrika* **75**, pp. 335–346.

Roubini, N. (1988) "Current Account and Budget Deficits in an Intertemporal Model of Consumption and Taxation Smoothing: A Solution to the 'Fedstein-Horioka' Puzzle?" *Working Paper* no. **2773**, National Bureau of Economic Research.

Sheffrin, S.M., and W.T. Woo (1990) "Present Value Tests of an Intertemporal Model of the Current Account," *Journal of International Economics* **29**, pp. 237–253.

Yaari, M. (1965) "Uncertain Lifetime, Life Insurance, and the Theory of the Consumer," *Review of Economic Studies* **32**, pp. 137–150.

In: Inflation, Fiscal Policy and Central Banks
Editor: Leo N. Bartolotti, pp. 31-59

ISBN: 1-60021-122-4
© 2006 Nova Science Publishers, Inc.

Chapter 2

DOES ONE MONETARY POLICY FIT ALL? THE DETERMINANTS OF INFLATION IN EMU COUNTRIES[*]

Melisso Boschi

University of Essex, UK and Ministry of Economy and Finance, Italy

Alessandro Girardi

University of Rome "Tor Vergata" and ISAE, Italy

Abstract

This chapter aims at assessing the long-run determinants and the short-run dynamics of inflation in each country belonging to the European Monetary Union (EMU). Our work complements the recent literature on this topic for the Euro Area as a whole. Detecting such determinants can be crucial in designing structural reforms acting as aside instruments of monetary policy in maintaining price stability. The empirical methodology consists of a re-interpretation of the structural cointegrating VAR approach, which allows for a structural long-run analysis of inflation determinants along with an accurate assessment of its short-run dynamics. The main conclusion emerging from the estimates is that not only the determinants of inflation differ in the countries belonging to the Euro Area, but also that cost-push factors have a considerable role in explaining inflation in most of the countries examined. As a policy implication, a tight monetary policy pursued in those countries whose inflation is mainly driven by costs would result in a contraction of economic activity without exerting relevant effects on price dynamics.

JEL no. C32, E00, E31, E37.

Keywords: Inflation, markup, EMU countries, long-run structural VARs, subset VEC models.

---

[*] The views expressed do not necessarily reflect those of the Ministry of Economy and Finance and of the Institute for Economic Studies and Analyses (ISAE) of Italy.

1   Introduction

On 1 January 1999 eleven European countries entered the third stage of the European Monetary Union. A new currency – the euro – replaced the national currencies, and a new institution – the Eurosystem, consisting of the European Central Bank (ECB) and the national central banks of those countries that adopted the euro – took on the responsibility for the monetary policy within the Euro Area. The single countries' governments remained in charge of the fiscal policy under the binding constraints of the Stability and Growth Pact.

In the new European institutional architecture designed by the Treaty of Maastricht, the Eurosystem has the main objective of maintaining the price stability in the Euro Area. More precisely, the single monetary policy of the ECB is carried out targeting the price stability of the Euro Area as a whole and, as such, it is common to all countries belonging to the EMU. The price stability is quantitatively defined as an annual inflation rate, referred to the Harmonized Index of Consumer prices (HICP), close to 2% in the medium-run. The ECB's monetary policy strategy is based on two pillars related to the temporal perspectives relevant for assessing the risks to price stability: the economic analysis aims to determine the short to medium-term determinants of price dynamics, while the monetary analysis focuses on longer-term horizons. The economic analysis focuses on the shocks hitting the European economy and produces projections of the main macroeconomic variables; the monetary analysis, exploiting the long-run link between money and prices, monitors the development of several monetary indicators, including the aggregate M3, its components, and counterparts, in particular the domestic credit and the different measures of excess liquidity (ECB, 2004).

By this strategy, the ECB fits one instrument to all countries, disregarding the country-specific determinants of prices long- and short-run dynamics. Nevertheless, the assessment of such determinants can be crucial in designing structural reforms acting as aside instruments of monetary policy in maintaining price stability. In this respect, a disaggregated analysis, conducted by estimating national models, can shed light on country-specific determinants of inflation and possibly identify those countries where cost-push factors have the most relevant role.

This chapter aims at assessing the long-run determinants and the short-run dynamics of inflation in each country belonging to the European Monetary Union (EMU). Our work is a complement of the recent literature on this topic for the Euro Area as a whole (Banerjee and Russel, 2002b; Bowdler and Jansen, 2004; Boschi and Girardi, 2005). With reference to the monetary policy strategy pursued by the ECB, the present analysis may be considered as contributing to the first "pillar," aiming to uncover the economic determinants of inflation.

The empirical methodology consists of a re-interpretation of the structural cointegrating VAR approach recently proposed by Garratt *et al.* (2003). This allows for a structural long-run analysis of inflation determinants along with an accurate assessment of its short-run dynamics. To this end, the Vector Error Correction (VEC) methodology (Johansen, 1995) is applied to a four-dimensional system including the labor productivity, the real exchange rate, the domestic inflation rate and the ratio between unit labor cost and price level. We use data ranging from the first quarter of 1984 to the last quarter of 1998 for each EMU member country, namely Austria, Belgium, Finland, France, Germany, Ireland, Italy, Netherlands, Portugal, and Spain. Luxembourg and Greece are not included, the first due to its negligible economic dimension, the second because it entered EMU later than the other countries.

The investigation consists of two stages. *First*, we disentangle the long-run determinants of inflation in each of the member countries of the EMU within the theoretical framework developed by Boschi and Girardi (2005), which is based on two long-run dynamic relationships (Juselius, 2002) relating inflation to the markup and the output gap respectively. This extends the model introduced by Banerjee *et al.* (2001). These long-run structural relationships between the variables of the model are embedded in an otherwise unrestricted VAR model and finally tested formally. *Next*, the estimated models are used to analyze the short-run behavior of inflation, highlighting the factors that drive its dynamics.

The main conclusions emerging from the estimates are that: *i*) the determinants of inflation differ in the countries belonging to the Euro Area; *ii*) cost-push factors have a considerable role in explaining inflation in most of the countries examined. A tight monetary policy pursued in those countries whose inflation is mainly driven by costs would result in a contraction of economic activity without exerting relevant effects on prices dynamics. This would be the consequence of higher financing costs for firms and a lower aggregate demand determined by an increasing interest rate. These are precisely the effects observed in the most recent years, when most of the European economies have been characterized by close to zero output rates of growth.

The paper is articulated as follows: Section 2 discusses some stylized facts on the convergence process of EMU member countries and their structural characteristics. Section 3 introduces the long-run theoretical framework. Section 4 describes the econometric methodology used, illustrating the long-run structural modeling approach and the parsimonious (subset) VEC procedure to analyze short-run dynamics. Section 5 illustrates the tests performed in order to check the statistical validity of the theoretical constraints on the long-run structure and reports both long- and short-run parameters estimates. Conclusion and References follow.

2   Stylized Facts

During the second stage of the EMU a progressive homogenization of national economic policies and structural features of several European countries took place, even though the Maastricht criteria were met only partially. Despite very dissimilar conditions in terms of deficit/GDP and debt/GDP ratios across member countries at the time of their entrance in the third stage of the EMU, an almost complete convergence in terms of interest and inflation rates occurred.

Figure 1 (dashed line) shows the reduction of the standard deviation of yield differentials between ten-year government bonds issued in the EMU member countries (with the exception of Greece) and the corresponding ten-year government bond issued in Germany, regarded to as a risk-free asset (Favero *et al.*, 1997), over the EMS years. During the eighties and the nineties, indeed, Germany was a meta-economic reference point for the other European countries. Although its central role may be less evident in recent years, Germany still weights for roughly one third of the euro area GDP. Moreover, the German monetary and fiscal policy strategies have inspired, to some extent, the EMU's institutional architecture.

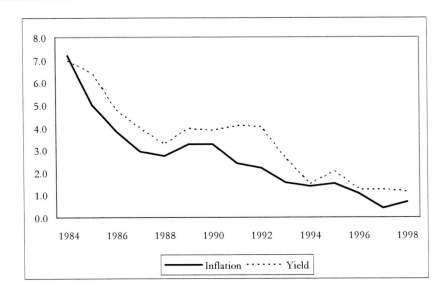

Figure 1 – Standard deviation of inflation and long-term interest rate differentials vis-à-vis Germany for EMU countries: 1984-1998. Percentage values.

Analogously, the dispersion of inflation differentials with respect to Germany decreased over time, mainly starting from the first years of the nineties (Figure 1, continuous line), suggesting that to some extent a convergence of price levels has occurred in Europe.

This is also shown in Figure 2, illustrating the dispersion of the relative price level at the beginning of the period of analysis (horizontal axis) and of the average inflation differential over the period 1984-1998 (vertical axis) for the EMU member countries with respect to Germany. It should be noted that countries exhibiting higher (lower) price levels as compared to the base country are characterized by lower (higher) inflation rates.

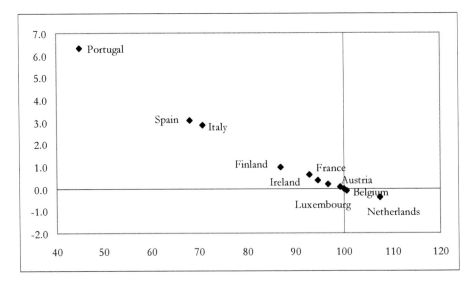

Figure 2 – Relative prices (horizontal axis) in 1984 and 1984-1998 average inflation rate differentials vis-à-vis Germany for EMU countries (vertical axis, percentage values).

The observed *nominal* convergence occurred in Europe during the mid-eighties and nineties was coupled by *real* convergence in several economies. Spain, Portugal and Ireland successfully restructured their economic systems through projects mainly financed by Cohesion Funds (see Basile *et al.*, 2001). Interestingly, the huge difference in GDP growth rates across EMU member countries was not accompanied by a relevant differentiation in terms of sector composition of their added value.

Table 1 reports the percentage share of each sector's added value for the ten countries analyzed over the sample period. Each country's average rate of growth is reported in the fourth column.

Table 1 – Distribution and average rate of growth of output ($1984q1$–$1998q4$).

	PRIMARY	SECONDARY	TERTIARY	AV. RATE OF GROWTH
Aus	3.26	33.66	63.08	2.40
Bel	2.22	31.05	66.73	2.33
Fin	5.80	33.26	60.93	2.50
Fra	3.64	29.02	67.34	2.13
Ger	1.54	35.67	62.79	2.11
Ire	8.57	35.94	55.49	5.72
Ita	3.78	32.76	63.46	2.06
Net	4.03	30.45	65.52	2.91
Por	7.06	31.53	61.41	3.25
Spa	6.44	32.44	61.12	2.95

Therefore, it is important to consider the structural features of these economies beyond such stylized facts, in order to uncover the main determinants driving inflation in EMU member countries.

3   Theoretical Framework

Inflation can be defined as the loss of purchasing power undergone by money over time: an increase in the general level of prices increases the number of monetary units required to buy a given good. The rate of growth of the prices level measures the rate of inflation.

Inflation can be classified according to its causes: *excess demand inflation, cost-pushed inflation,* and *imported inflation.*

The first type of inflation occurs when an increase of aggregate demand pushes the price level up because of the presence of an inelastic supply of goods and services, or in the extreme case of full employment. In monetary terms, the supply is higher than the demand for money. The economic agents will try and spend in goods and services the excess money balances, but since all production inputs are full employed, the increased aggregate demand will not result in increased supply but rather in a higher equilibrium level price. This is called excess demand inflation, or, more simply, demand inflation. According to the original cause of the excess money supply, we distinguish between financial and credit inflation. In the first case the excess money supply is caused by seigniorage, i.e. by the government issuing money in order to finance public expenditure; in the second case the excess money supply is determined by the excessive credit created by the financial system.

The second kind of inflation is originated by costs. Economic theory states that under perfect market competition equilibrium prices equal marginal costs. However, in practice a number of markets operate under imperfect or even monopolistic competition. In such market structures prices may well differ from marginal costs. Specifically, it is usually assumed that the mechanism of price formation be based on the markup, i.e. on the application of a proportional marginal profit on production costs. This pricing strategy implies that inflation may be determined by costs. For example, a sudden increase of oil price may be transmitted on prices through the markup.

Finally, in open economies, a further cause of inflation, referred to as "imported" inflation, is the nominal exchange rate devaluation. Inflation occurs because, in first instance, the exchange rate devaluation raises the local currency-denominated price of imported consumption goods and production inputs. Subsequently, the change in international relative prices will affect quantities, driving the economic system to a new equilibrium.

The main consequences of inflation are related to the change of relative prices. Relative prices change as a consequence of inflation and this causes uncertainty, distortions and income redistribution. An increase of inflation may exert a number of effects on the economy. *First*, given the nominal interest rate, it will reduce the real interest rate thus stimulating consumption to the detriment of saving and reducing the real burden of debt. *Second*, a raising inflation may reduce the international competitiveness of exporting firms, thus inducing them to reduce the markup.

In this Section the possible theoretical long-run path of the EMU countries' inflation is presented.[1] It consists of two dynamic steady-state relationships extending the scheme proposed by Banerjee *et al.* (2001) and Banerjee and Russell (2002 a).

The starting point of the analysis is the following system:

$$p_t - w_t = -\omega_1 \cdot OG_t - \omega_2 \cdot \phi_t - \omega_3 \cdot \Delta p_t - \omega_4 \cdot t \tag{1}$$

$$w_t - p_t = -\gamma_1 \cdot U_t + \gamma_2 \cdot \phi_t + \gamma_3 \cdot t \tag{2}$$

$$\Delta p_t = -\delta \cdot U_t \tag{3}$$

$$U_t = -\psi \cdot OG_t \tag{4}$$

where p_t indicates the logarithm of the price level, w_t the logarithm of nominal wages, OG_t an output gap measure, ϕ_t the logarithm of productivity, Δ the difference operator, and U_t the unemployment rate. The parameters are all positive. As in Banerjee *et al.* (2001), (1) and (2) represent the formulas for markup[2] and real wages, respectively, (3) identifies the Phillips curve, and (4) the Okun's law. The linear trend in (1) captures the possible effects of

[1] This Section and the subsequent draw extensively on Boschi and Girardi (2005).

[2] The presence of Δp_t in (1) implies that inflation may represent a cost to firms even in the long-run (e.g. because of the difficulties faced by price-setting firms in adjusting prices in an inflationary environment with incomplete information). Thus, an increase in costs may not be fully reflected in higher prices because the markup falls with higher inflation.

taxation and other costs (especially raw materials and energy) on the formation mechanism of markup. Analogously, the trend in (2) represents the possible influence of factors such as unemployment benefits and tax rates on the demand for real wages.

3.1   Cost-push Inflation

Substituting (4) in (2), OG_t can be deleted in (1) and (2) obtaining the relationship between markup and inflation:

$$(p_t - w_t) = \frac{(\omega_2 \cdot \gamma_1 \cdot \psi - \omega_1 \cdot \gamma_2)}{(\gamma_1 \cdot \psi - \omega_1)} \cdot \phi_t - \frac{\omega_3 \cdot \gamma_1 \cdot \psi}{(\gamma_1 \cdot \psi - \omega_1)} \cdot \Delta p_t - \frac{(\omega_4 \cdot \gamma_1 \cdot \psi - \omega_1 \cdot \gamma_3)}{(\gamma_1 \cdot \psi - \omega_1)} \cdot t \qquad (5)$$

In order to assure that labor and firms have stable income shares in the long-run, the coefficient of ϕ_t in (5) must be unitary. Assuming that firms maximize profits ($\omega_2 = 1$), this condition holds for any values of γ_2 if firms fix prices independently of demand ($\omega_1 = 0$) or if linear homogeneity is assumed ($\gamma_2 = 1$). Therefore, equation (5) becomes:

$$p_t - ulc_t = -\mu_1 \cdot \Delta p_t - \mu_0 \cdot t \qquad (6)$$

where $ulc_t = w_t - \phi_t$ indicates the unit labor cost and where $\mu_1 = (\omega_3 \cdot \gamma_1 \cdot \psi) / (\gamma_1 \cdot \psi - \omega_1)$ and $\mu_0 = (\omega_4 \cdot \gamma_1 \cdot \psi - \omega_1 \cdot \gamma_3) / (\gamma_1 \cdot \psi - \omega_1)$ are non-negative parameters. If $\mu_1 = 0$, the model (1)-(4) becomes analogous to the standard one proposed, for example, by Layard $et\ al.$ (1991) and Franz and Gordon (1993), where inflation does not represent a cost to firms.

In an open economy framework, equation (6) is modified to take into account the possible relevance of the import price on markup, as in de Brouwer and Ericsson (1998) and Banerjee $et\ al.$ (2001):

$$p_t - \delta \cdot ulc_t - (1 - \delta) \cdot pm_t = -\mu_1 \cdot \Delta p_t - \mu_0 \cdot t$$

or

$$-s_t - \beta_0 \cdot ppp_t = -\beta_1 \cdot \Delta p_t - b_0 \cdot t$$

where $s_t = ulc_t - p_t = (w_t - p_t) - \phi_t$ indicates the logarithm of labor income share, $ppp_t = (p_t^* + e_t - p_t) = (pm_t - p_t)$ is a competitiveness index, given by the logarithm of the real exchange rate, and $\beta_0 = (1 - \delta) / \delta$, $\beta_1 = \mu_1 / \delta$, $b_0 = \mu_0 / \delta$. If $\beta_0 > 0$, the external sector plays a role in the formation of domestic prices. Adding a stochastic residual, $\varepsilon_{mu,t}$, we obtain the first long-run condition to test:

$$-s_t - \beta_0 \cdot ppp_t + \beta_1 \cdot \Delta p_t + b_0 \cdot t = \varepsilon_{mu,t} \tag{7}$$

where $\varepsilon_{mu,t}$ is supposed to be stationary.

3.2   Demand Inflation

Generally, under this second approach inflation is studied through a relationship between price changes and a cyclical indicator (see, for example, Stock and Watson, 1999). From equations (4) and (3) this relationship can be represented as:

$$\Delta p_t = \beta_2 \cdot OG_t \tag{8}$$

where $\beta_2 = \psi \cdot \delta$ is a positive parameter. The potential output required to obtain OG_t is here estimated by means of a constant returns to scale production function[3] of labor (N_t) and capital stock (K_t), $Y_t = F(K_t, A_t \cdot N_t)$ (Binder and Pesaran, 1999) re-written as:

$$\frac{Y_t}{N_t} = A_t \cdot f(\kappa_t) \tag{9}$$

where $f(\kappa_t) = F(K_t, 1)$ is a function that satisfies the Inada conditions and $\kappa_t = K_t / (A_t \cdot N_t)$ indicates the capital stock per effective labor unit. Assuming that the logarithm of the technological progress index A_t is given by $\ln(A_t) = \varphi \cdot t + u_t$ where u_t is a mean-zero $I(1)$ process, equation (9) becomes (in logs):

$$\phi_t = \varphi \cdot t + \ln\left[f(\kappa_t) \right] + u_t$$

Binder and Pesaran (1999) show that the long-run path of productivity is determined mainly by the technological progress, i.e. $E[\Delta\phi_t] = \varphi$. Therefore, the variable OG_t is specified with a linear trend as a proxy of GDP and employment growth associated to the

---

[3] Alternatively, an algorithm for the extraction of trend from actual output or an explicit statistical model can be used (Clark *et al.*, 1996; Harvey and Jaeger, 1993).

technological progress.[4] The second long-run condition to test is obtained adding a stochastic residual, $\varepsilon_{pc,t}$, to (8)

$$\Delta p_t - \beta_2 \cdot \phi_t + b_1 \cdot t = \varepsilon_{pc} \tag{10}$$

where the output gap measure is $\phi_t - \varphi \cdot t$, $b_1 = \beta_2 \cdot \varphi > 0$ and ε_{pc} is supposed to be stationary.

4   Econometric Methodology

The econometric methodology is based on the VEC methodology (Johansen, 1995). This modeling approach allows to describe in detail both long-run relationships and short-run dynamic interdependencies existing among (a small set of) variables. More specifically, the approach used in this study consists of two steps. In the first step, the empirical investigation is driven by the theoretical specification of the long-run equilibrium paths. This is consistent with the idea that economic theory is able to highlight the long-run equilibrium relationships among variables, but it is less informative about their short-run dynamics (Garratt *et al.*, 2003). In the second step, the dynamic structure of the model is specified according to the statistical properties of the short-run parameters.

4.1   The Structural Cointegrating VAR Model

The long-run relationships presented in Section III are approximated by log-linear equations and embedded in a VEC model:

$$\Delta \mathbf{y}_t = \mathbf{a} + \sum_{j=1}^{m-1} \mathbf{\Gamma}_j \cdot \Delta \mathbf{y}_{t-j} + \mathbf{A} \cdot \mathbf{\varepsilon}_{t-1} + \mathbf{\Phi} \cdot \mathbf{d}_t + \mathbf{u}_t \tag{11}$$

$$\mathbf{u}_t \sim N\left(\mathbf{0}, \mathbf{\Sigma}_u\right) \tag{12}$$

This model allows to take jointly into account both the short-run dynamics among the variables collected in the vector $\mathbf{y}_t = [s_t, \; ppp_t, \; \Delta p_t, \; \phi_t]'$, and the long-run structure represented by the vector of residuals $\mathbf{\varepsilon}_t$ of cointegration relations:

$$\mathbf{b} \cdot t + \mathbf{B}' \cdot \mathbf{y}_t = \mathbf{\varepsilon}_t \tag{13}$$

---

[4] Under the assumption that the share of employed workers on population is stationary, as in Garratt *et al.* (2003), (labor) productivity may represent a measure of per-capita output.

In (11) Γ_j's are matrices of autoregression coefficients, $\mathbf{A}$ is a matrix collecting the adjustment coefficients of short-run dynamics to long-run paths, $\mathbf{a}$ is a vector of intercepts, $\mathbf{d}_t$ is a vector of dummy variables whose parameters are in matrix $\boldsymbol{\Phi}$, and $\mathbf{u}_t$ is a vector of residuals distributed according to (12). Equation (13) summarizes the $r < k$ equilibrium relationships that are supposed to hold in the economy: matrix $\mathbf{B}$ collects the parameters defined in (7) and (10), vector $\mathbf{b}$ contains b_0 and b_1 (i.e. the slopes for linear deterministic trends – these are restricted to belong to the cointegration space in order to avoid quadratic trends in the level variables), and $\boldsymbol{\varepsilon}_t$ contains the residuals $\varepsilon_{mu,t}$ and $\varepsilon_{pc,t}$.

All four variables in $\mathbf{y}_t$ are considered endogenous *a priori*, while their possible exogeneity will be verified *ex post*.

In order to exactly-identify the cointegrating matrix $\mathbf{B}$, r contemporaneous restrictions on each cointegration relationship are imposed. Out of these r^2 restrictions, r are normalizations necessary to rotate the cointegration space in the directions represented by the equilibrium conditions. The *structural* relationships (7) and (10) provide the remaining $r^2 - r$ constraints plus an additional one needed in order to obtain an over-identified model. Thus, the system (13), solved with respect to the parameters collected in $\mathbf{b}$ and $\mathbf{B}$, becomes:

$$\begin{bmatrix} b_0 \\ b_1 \end{bmatrix} \cdot t + \begin{bmatrix} -1 & -\beta_0 & \beta_1 & 0 \\ 0 & 0 & 1 & -\beta_2 \end{bmatrix} \cdot \mathbf{y}_t = \begin{bmatrix} \varepsilon_{mu,t} \\ \varepsilon_{pc,t} \end{bmatrix} \tag{14}$$

The above theoretical framework can be verified through a LR test of the overall constraints imposed in (14).

If $r = 1$, the above framework can also serve as a procedure to discriminate among competitive theories. If inflation is interpretable exclusively from a supply-side point of view, imposing an additional constraint to the $r^2 = 1$ exactly-identifying ones (14) becomes

$$b_0 \cdot t + \begin{bmatrix} -1 & -\beta_0 & \beta_1 & 0 \end{bmatrix} \cdot \mathbf{y}_t = \varepsilon_{mu,t} \tag{15}$$

From a demand-side perspective, (14) becomes:

$$b_1 \cdot t + \begin{bmatrix} 0 & 0 & 1 & -\beta_2 \end{bmatrix} \cdot \mathbf{y}_t = \varepsilon_{pc,t} \tag{16}$$

with two additional constraints.

4.2   The Subset VEC Model

The short-run dynamics is modeled using a parsimonious (subset) VEC model, obtained dropping those parameters of the matrices $\mathbf{A}$, Γ_j and $\boldsymbol{\Phi}$ with p-values lower than a threshold, according to the Sequential Elimination of the Regressors Testing Procedure

(SER/TP) proposed by Brüggemann and Lütkepohl (2001). Specifically, the statistically significant parameters of **A** give useful information about how the economy moves around the long-run equilibrium path. Moreover, the rows of **A** containing only zeroes allow to identify possible (weakly) exogenous variables. This model reduction process has two further implications. Firstly, the impulse response functions (and their confidence intervals) may differ, even markedly, from those derived from an unrestricted model (Brüggemann and Lütkepohl 2001). Secondly, dropping the statistically irrelevant variables can improve the quality of the forecasts generated by the model (Clements and Hendry, 2001, p. 119).

5   The Estimated Structural VEC Models

5.1   Preliminary Analysis

Prior to the estimation of the model (11)-(13), the unit root tests have been performed on the time series over the period $1984q1$-$1998q4$. The sample span refers to a macroeconomic framework characterized by an acceleration of the harmonization process of domestic economic policies towards the EU commitments and a progressive liberalization of capital and trade movements. The first few years of the European Monetary System (EMS) are left out because of the turbulence caused by adjustment to the new monetary system. This choice also allows excluding the absorption process of the oil shocks occurred in the seventies, whose effects were particularly severe for small open economies, heavily dependent on foreign energy net suppliers. In order to avoid an arbitrary distinction between the variables of each country model, as suggested by Sims (1980), all of them are modeled as endogenous *a priori*, but their possible weak exogeneity is subsequently tested.[5]

5.1.1   Data Sources and Variables Construction

The elaborations have been performed using the econometric packages J–Multi 3.30 for the unit root tests and the construction of the VEC models, and Pc–Fiml 10.3 for the preliminary analysis and the diagnostic tests. Quarterly non-seasonal adjusted data are from OECD (Statistical Compendium CD–Rom, 2004/2) and IMF (IFS CD–Rom, October 2004). The log level price, p_t, is the consumer price index, the log real unit labor cost, s_t, is the ratio of real wages over productivity, the productivity, Φ_t, is given by the logarithm of the ratio of total output over the total number of employed workers.

The foreign variables in $ppp_t = e_t + p_t^* - p_t = (e_{0t} - e_t) + p_t^* - p_t$ are given by:

$$p_t^* = \sum_{i=1}^{16} w_i \cdot p_{it} \text{ and } e_t^* = \sum_{i=1}^{16} w_i \cdot e_{it}$$

where i denotes the i-th country in the group including the Euro Area member countries, the remaining G7 countries not belonging to the Euro Area, the EMU member countries, and

---

[5] This decision can also be motivated from a statistical point of view since the erroneous treatment of endogenous variables as weakly exogenous can produce inefficient estimates.

Switzerland. The star, *, denotes the variables of the rest of the world (RoW). The nominal effective exchange rate is given by difference between $e_{0t} = \log(\text{national currency/US dollar})$ and $e_t^* = \log(\text{RoW currency/US dollar})$. The weights w_i, shown in Table 2, are given by the country i's share of world trade, where the latter is defined as the sum of imports and exports.

5.1.2   Unit Root Tests

The employed econometric methodology allows for series integrated at most of order 1. Testing for unit roots is a way of checking for the absence of $I(2)$ variables in our sample, as this might produce poor results when coupled with standard VEC modelling (see Haldrup, 1998). Therefore, we have run ADF tests on each series, both in levels and differenced, with an optimal regression lag determined according to the BIC criterion with a maximum lag of four. The critical values are taken from Davidson and MacKinnon (1993). The results, reported in Table 3, suggest that all variables are indeed integrated of order one. The only exceptions are the levels of Δp_t for Italy and the Netherlands, and of s_t for Spain, for which the null hypothesis of a unit root is rejected respectively at the 10% and the 5% levels of significance, and the first difference of $\Delta\phi_t$ for Ireland and Spain, for which the null is rejected at the 5% level of significance.

5.1.3   Model Specification and Dummy Variables

Table 4 reports a brief description of each model's main features. The sample period is $1984q1$–$1998q4$ for all models. The number of lags has been selected according to the BIC criterion. In order to obtain a satisfactory fit of the model to the data, especially with regard to the residuals normality, dummy variables $dXXY$ have been introduced. $dXXY$ is a series $0,0,\ldots,1,0,\ldots$, where XX indicates the year and Y the quarter. These dummy variables are grouped in three main categories according to the source of shock: idiosyncratic shocks (I), EMS shocks (EMS), and 1995 Mexican crisis shock (M).

5.1.4   Cointegration Rank

The cointegration rank r has been determined using the trace test and the maximum eigenvalue test. Table 5 reports eigenvalues as well as the trace (upper part) and the maximum eigenvalue test (lower part) results. Both tests have been corrected for the number of degrees of freedom. Critical values are taken from Osterwald and Lenum (1992).

The trace test results point to two long-run relationships for Austria and the Netherlands, while only one relationship is detected in all other models. These results are confirmed by the maximum eigenvalue test with the only exception of the Netherlands for which no long-run relationships exist according to the second test. We follow Johansen (1992) in accepting the trace test results in order to avoid inconsistency problems possibly arising with the maximum eigenvalue test. The rest of the analysis thus sets $r = 2$ in the Netherlands's model.

Table 2 – Matrix of bilateral flow trade weights.

	AUS	BEL	CAN	DEN	FIN	FRA	GER	IRE	ITA	JAP	NET	POR	SPA	SWE	SWI	UK	USA
AUS	.0000	.0291	.0082	.0104	.0083	.0600	.5237	.0050	.1121	.0297	.0394	.0066	.0225	.0198	.0347	.0408	.0496
BEL	.0095	.0000	.0060	.0094	.0072	.2042	.2388	.0095	.0580	.0244	.1879	.0078	.0290	.0238	.0159	.1050	.0635
FIN	.0136	.0363	.0086	.0431	.0000	.0589	.1852	.0086	.0443	.0528	.0542	.0085	.0258	.1456	.0903	.1270	.0973
FRA	.0131	.1161	.0090	.0118	.0075	.0000	.2337	.0122	.1300	.0356	.0658	.0171	.0933	.0180	.0250	.1169	.0952
GER	.0697	.0905	.0091	.0263	.0136	.1574	.0000	.0113	.1117	.0539	.1136	.0139	.0462	.0318	.0450	.1035	.1025
IRE	.0057	.0372	.0092	.0120	.0075	.0814	.1318	.0000	.0367	.0468	.0600	.0046	.0223	.0199	.0171	.3613	.1466
ITA	.0339	.0544	.0125	.0129	.0073	.1920	.2701	.0094	.0000	.0317	.0614	.0134	.0648	.0164	.0377	.0919	.0900
NET	.0146	.1509	.0060	.0172	.0109	.1113	.3135	.0111	.0566	.0296	.0000	.0084	.0293	.0279	.0212	.1153	.0762
POR	.0100	.0409	.0048	.0159	.0081	.1520	.2029	.0064	.0760	.0202	.0559	.0000	.2215	.0188	.0211	.1000	.0456
SPA	.0118	.0422	.0064	.0097	.0081	.2432	.1926	.0093	.1185	.0305	.0506	.0689	.0000	.0148	.0151	.1053	.0730

Note. Partner countries are reported in columns. The weights are averages over the period 1994-1996. The weights sum to unit by row. Each country's own trade is set to zero. Source: OECD.

Table 3 – ADF unit root test.

	AUS	BEL	FIN	FRA	GER	IRE	ITA	NET	POR	SPA
s_t	-2.16 (4)*	-1.86 (0)*	-3.03 (4)**	-2.40 (1)**	-1.40 (0)*	-2.24 (0)**	-1.79 (2)*	-1.79 (1)*	-0.94 (0)*	-3.62 (4)**
q_t	-1.15 (1)*	-1.07 (1)*	-0.86 (1)*	-1.93 (1)**	-2.31 (1)**	-2.40 (1)**	-1.63 (1)*	-1.03 (1)*	-2.42 (1)*	-1.76 (1)*
Δp_t	-1.58 (3)*	-2.47 (3)*	-1.72 (2)*	-2.39 (4)*	-2.28 (2)	-2.78 (3)**	-3.29 (1)**	-2.70 (3)*	-2.34 (3)**	-2.54 (3)**
ϕ_t	-1.83 (4)**	-2.45 (4)**	-3.00 (4)**	-1.27 (0)**	-2.67 (2)**	-2.50 (2)*	-1.16 (0)**	-2.82 (3)**	-2.32 (1)**	-1.24 (1)**
Δs_t	-6.10 (2)*	-6.13 (0)*	-7.72 (0)*	-5.94 (0)*	-4.62 (0)*	-8.99 (0)*	-4.25 (0)*	-8.14 (0)**	-4.22 (1)*	-3.50 (0)**
Δq_t	-5.49 (0)*	-5.15 (0)*	-5.06 (0)*	-5.16 (0)*	-5.54 (0)*	-4.99 (0)*	-5.17 (0)*	-6.08 (0)*	-5.18 (0)*	-5.01 (0)*
$\Delta^2 p_t$	-13.3 (2)*	-8.70 (0)*	-9.10 (1)*	-8.03 (1)*	-7.82 (2)*	-7.88 (2)*	-8.62 (0)*	-11.5 (2)*	-6.91 (2)*	-8.20 (2)*
$\Delta \phi_t$	-4.35 (3)*	-7.99 (0)*	-5.11 (2)**	-7.73 (0)*	-6.25 (0)*	-3.13 (0)*	-3.75 (1)*	-7.25 (0)*	-11.3 (0)*	-2.98 (0)*

Table 4 – Models' specification.

Country	Lags	Sample period	Dummy variables	
AUS	4	1985q1–1998q4	d871	*shock* to the labor market (I)
			d952, d953	*shock* to the real exchange rate (M)
BEL	5	1985q2–1998q4	d924	*shock* to the real exchange rate (EMS)
			d952, d953	*shock* to the real exchange rate (M)
FIN	4	1985q1–1998q4	d924	*shock* to the real exchange rate (EMS)
FRA	2	1984q3–1998q4	d924	*shock* to the real exchange rate (EMS)
			d952, d953	*shock* to the real exchange rate (M)
			d861, d983	*shock* to the inflation (I)
			d862	*shock* to the productivity (I)
GER	2	1984q3–1998q4	d871, d872	*shock* to the productivity (I)
			d911, d912	*shock* to the labor market (I)
			d923, d924	*shock* to the real exchange rate (EMS)
			d952, d953, d961	*shock* to the real exchange rate (M)
IRE	4	1985q1–1998q4	d924	*shock* to the real exchange rate (EMS)
			d972	*shock* to the labor market (I)
ITA	2	1984q3–1998q4	d923, d924	*shock* to the real exchange rate (EMS)
			d951, d952, d953	*shock* to the real exchange rate (M)
			d972	*shock* to the labor market (I)
NET	4	1985q1–1998q4	d924	*shock* to the real exchange rate (EMS)
			d951, d952	*shock* to the real exchange rate (M)
			d973, d981	*shock* to the labor market (I)
POR	3	1984q4–1998q4	d844, d851, d911	*shock* to the labor market (I)
			d924	*shock* to the real exchange rate (EMS)
			d953, d954	*shock* to the real exchange rate (M)
SPA	2	1984q3–1998q4	d924	*shock* to the real exchange rate (EMS)
			d953	*shock* to the real exchange rate (M)

5.1.5 The Specification of the Long-run Structure

In the models of Austria and Netherlands the two cointegrating relationships seem to be identified by the long-run structural theoretical relationships (15) and (16). In all other countries prices appear to be determined in the long-run by the equation (15), excepting for the model of Portugal whose inflation is determined exclusively by demand-side factors. For sake of completeness, the last three columns of Table 6 display the LR test results for the specification of the relationship (second column) alternative to the one discussed at length in the following Subsection regarding those countries' models with rank $r = 1$. The central columns of Table 6 report the estimated parameters (indicated by a star, *) of each model's "best" specification.

Table 5 – Cointegration rank.

EIGENVALUES

AUS	BEL	FIN	FRA	GER	ITA	IRE	NET	POR	SPA
0.67	0.52	0.47	0.54	0.45	0.50	0.44	0.41	0.48	0.49
0.48	0.30	0.30	0.21	0.34	0.25	0.35	0.36	0.26	0.27
0.15	0.16	0.24	0.11	0.18	0.13	0.19	0.26	0.17	0.19
0.07	0.02	0.11	0.02	0.00	0.08	0.08	0.04	0.06	0.06

TRACE TEST

H_0	H_1	5%	1%	AUS	BEL	FIN	FRA	GER	IRE	ITA	NET	POR	SPA
$r=0$	$r \geq 1$	62.99	70.05	114.8	70.52	77.59	65.92	70.35	75.68	69.71	74.46	69.15	72.75
$r \leq 1$	$r \geq 2$	42.44	48.45	50.93	30.46	41.57	21.06	35.49	41.78	29.48	44.48	31.72	33.57
$r \leq 2$	$r \geq 3$	25.32	30.45	13.14	10.69	21.66	7.54	11.41	17.06	12.43	19.38	14.63	15.37
$r \leq 3$	$r = 4$	12.25	16.26	4.04	0.88	6.35	0.94	0.06	5.10	4.55	2.47	3.76	3.37

MAXIMUM EIGENVALUE TEST

H_0	H_1	5%	1%	AUS	BEL	FIN	FRA	GER	IRE	ITA	NET	POR	SPA
$r=0$	$r = 1$	31.46	36.65	63.81	40.06	36.01	44.86	34.86	33.89	40.22	29.98	37.42	39.19
$r \leq 1$	$r = 2$	25.54	30.34	37.79	19.77	19.92	13.52	24.08	24.72	17.05	25.10	17.09	18.19
$r \leq 2$	$r = 3$	18.96	23.65	9.10	9.82	15.31	6.60	11.36	11.96	7.89	16.91	10.87	12.01
$r \leq 3$	$r = 4$	12.25	16.26	4.04	0.88	6.35	0.94	0.06	5.10	4.55	2.47	3.76	3.37

Table 6 – The specification of the long-run structure

Specification		t	s_t	q_t	Δp_t	ϕ_t	χ^2(gdl)	stat	[prob]
Bel	(16)	*			1	*	(2)	17.26	[0.00]
Fin	(16)	*			1	*	(2)	13.94	[0.00]
Fra	(16)	*			1	*	(2)	32.27	[0.00]
Ger	(16)	*			1	*	(2)	27.25	[0.00]
Irl	(16)	*			1	*	(2)	16.73	[0.00]
Ita	(16)	*			1	*	(2)	23.69	[0.00]
Por	(15)	*	−1				(3)	25.11	[0.00]
Spa	(16)	*			1	*	(2)	17.13	[0.00]

5.2 The Estimated Long-run Structure

For each model, the chosen long-run structural specification is shown in Table 7, where the estimated coefficients and their corresponding standard errors are reported.

The statistics of the LR test for the over-identifying restrictions have a χ^2 distribution with a number of degrees of freedom depending on the number of restrictions. The probabilities associated to the statistics' realizations are reported in square brackets.

The signs of the estimated parameters are consistent with the economic theory and statistically significant. Moreover, LR test results do not reject the over-identifying restrictions. To summarize, all countries with high rates of growth are characterized by demand-side inflation (see Table 1). A significant exception is Ireland whose long-run structure is more similar to that of the countries belonging to the "core Europe", i.e. Germany, Austria and the Netherlands, whose specification of the markup is almost identical.

In order to better compare the estimated long-run structure, Table 8 reports each model's net markup (first three columns) as long as the estimated coefficients μ_0 (fourth column) and μ_1 (fifth column) derived from the estimation of the structure reported in Table 7. Consistently with the economic theory, inflation is an extra cost to firms in all economies whose prices are determined according to equation (15), excepting for Finland. Unlike other countries, in Austria, Germany, the Netherlands, and Ireland, whose economic structure is rather similar, the import price level pm_t does not appear to be a determinant of the net markup. Specifically, in Belgium, Finland, and Spain the markup is determined in the same proportion by pm_t and ulc, while in Italy and France the unit labor cost has a bigger influence on the markup than the import prices. The economic structure of France, in particular, looks very similar to that of the core Europe's countries being characterized by a proportion of ulc_t over pm_t of 8 as determinants of the markup. The fourth column of Table 8 shows how the exogenous component of inflation, captured by the slope of the linear time trend, is small and ranging between 0% for Ireland and Italy, and 1.5% for Germany and Spain. It is advisable to notice that the exogenous component of German inflation coincides with the minimum inflation rate compatible with the German economic structure benchmarked by the Bundesbank (see Sinn and Reutter, 2000). Finally, the fifth column of Table 8 shows the variation of markup induced by an annual increase of 1% (corresponding to a 0.25% increase on a quarterly basis) in inflation. The highly heterogeneous results can be summarized noticing that inflation represents an high cost to those countries whose prices are determined to a lesser extent by imports prices, i.e. Germany, Austria, Netherlands, and Ireland, where the reduction of markup ranges from 3% to 7%. In all other countries, inflation does not represent such a high cost, being the markup contraction comprised between 0% of Finland and 1% of Spain.

The markup/inflation trade-off estimated for France, 0.4%, is quite similar to the 0.7% obtained by Banerjee and Russell (2002), while the values for Germany (1.2%) and Italy (2%) are quite different. This may be due to a number of reasons, including the different sample periods, the treatment of seasonality, the specification of the deterministic part of the cointegration space and the measurement of variables.

Table 7 – Estimates of equations (15) and (16).

ε_t	t	s_t	$\mathbf{b} \cdot t + \mathbf{B}' \cdot \mathbf{y}_t$ PPP_t	Δp_t	ϕ_t
			Austria		
$\varepsilon_{mu,t}$	0.0013	−1.0000		11.4410	
	(0.0003)			(1.8844)	
$\varepsilon_{pc,t}$	0.0013			1.0000	−0.2507
	(0.0002)				(0.0418)
			$\chi^2(2)$ 1.81 [0.41]		
			Belgium		
$\varepsilon_{mu,t}$	0.0054	−1.0000	−0.5515	4.2497	
	(0.0012)		(0.1291)	(1.6379)	
			$\chi^2(1)$ 2.53 [0.11]		
			Finland		
$\varepsilon_{mu,t}$	0.0012	−1.0000	−1.0606		
	(0.0005)		(0.0763)		
			$\chi^2(2)$ 5.26 [0.07]		
			France		
$\varepsilon_{mu,t}$	0.0014	−1.0000	−0.1407	1.9751	
	(0.0003)		(0.0339)	(0.8569)	
			$\chi^2(1)$ 2.82 [0.09]		

Table 7 – Continued

ε_t	t	s_t	ppp_t	Δp_t	ϕ_t
			Germany $\mathbf{b}\cdot t+\mathbf{B}'\cdot\mathbf{y}_t$		
$\varepsilon_{mu,t}$	0.0037	−1.0000		12.0290	
	(0.0010)			(4.3173)	
$\chi^2(2)$ 0.21 [0.90]					
			Ireland		
$\varepsilon_{mu,t}$	0	−1.0000	0	29.3130	0
				(6.6052)	
$\chi^2(3)$ 7.51 [0.06]					
			Italy		
$\varepsilon_{mu,t}$		−1.0000	−0.6481	4.2779	
			(0.0594)	(0.6866)	
$\chi^2(2)$ 1.15 [0.56]					
			Netherlands		
$\varepsilon_{mu,t}$	0.0025	−1.0000		12.0390	
	(0.0006)			(2.2240)	
$\varepsilon_{pc,t}$	0.0019			1.0000	−1.0000
	(0.0001)				
$\chi^2(3)$=1.94 [0.58]					

Table 7 – Continued

ε_t	t	s_t	PPP_t	Δp_t	ϕ_t
			Portugal		
$\varepsilon_{pc,t}$	0.0020			1.0000	−0.3461
	(0.0006)				(0.1136)
			$\chi^2(2)=4.98[0.08]$		
			Spain		
$\varepsilon_{mu,t}$	0.0080	−1.0000	−1.0589	7.8374	
	(0.0007)		(0.1085)	(2.1699)	
			$\chi^2(1)=0.84 [0.36]$		

$\mathbf{b} \cdot t + \mathbf{B}' \cdot \mathbf{y}_t$

Table 8 – Net markup, trade-off between markup and inflation, extra-costs.

	NET MARKUP			EXTRA-COSTS	MARKUP/INFLATION
	p_t	ulc_t	pm_t	$\mu_0 \cdot 400$	μ_1
AUS	1	−1		0.52%	−11.44
BEL	1	−0.64	−0.36	1.40%	−2.74
FIN	1	−0.48	−0.52	0.24%	
FRA	1	−0.88	−0.12	0.48%	−1.73
GER	1	−1		1.48%	−12.03
IRE	1	−1			−29.31
ITA	1	−0.61	−0.39		−2.60
NET	1	−1		1.00%	−12.04
SPA	1	−0.49	−0.51	1.56%	−3.81

As for the four biggest European economies, namely Germany, France, Italy, and Spain whose aggregate GDP is over 80% of the Euro Area's GDP, and for Belgium and Finland, the absence of cost-push inflation points to an excess of production capacity. Regarding Ireland, the estimated long-run structure is at odds with the sustained economic growth characterizing the economy over the sample period. This may be due to the presence of a number of export-oriented multinational firms. As for the remaining countries, whose long-run structures include the Phillips curve, the results are heterogeneous. Table 9 reports the potential, i.e. not augmenting inflation, annual rate of growth of output and employment derived from equation (16).

Table. 9 – Potential output growth.

Austria	Netherlands	Portugal
2.08 %	0.76 %	2.32 %

The lowest value refers to the Netherlands, implying that its economy is characterized by full employment, as also indicated by the estimated value of the productivity coefficient in equation (16). Notice the high value of potential growth of Portugal, possibly due to the slow transition of the Portuguese economy from the prevalence of the primary sector to the secondary and tertiary sectors. This is witnessed by the large share of the agricultural sector on the Portuguese economy (over 7%) when compared to that of the other European countries.

The long-run structure of Austria and Netherlands, whose models include two cointegration relationships, may be better described by embedding the second long-run restriction into the first one, thus obtaining a new stationary relationship (since a linear combination of two stationary relationships is stationary itself). This leads to a single long-run relationship between the output gap and the net markup. Table 10 reports the effect on the net markup of an annual one percent increase in the output gap.

Table 10 – Markup and output gap

Austria	Netherlands
–0.72%	–3.01%

Table 10 clearly shows that the markup is anti-cyclical, consistently with Gali (1994) according to which private firms do set prices depending on demand. This can be justified by the two following argumentations. The first line of reasoning relies on the increase of the marginal costs faced by firms due to the employment of production inputs in a period of economic expansion. The second one considers the pressure exerted on wages and other costs by an increase of aggregate demand.

5.3 The Estimated Short-run Structure

In this Section we discuss the dynamic properties of each country's estimated VEC model. Table 11 reports the main diagnostic tests for the single equations.

The statistical fit of the inflation equation is satisfactory in almost all models. This supports the choice of the theoretical framework used for the analysis of the price dynamics in the EMU countries. The only exception is Spain whose equation of productivity growth shows the lowest standard error. The residuals do not appear to be serially correlated in 33 (38) equations at the 5% (1%) level of significance. The models of Netherlands and Portugal, whose single equations residuals are serially correlated, do not present autocorrelation at a system-wide level (not reported). This supports the choice of the number of lags for each model. The results of the autocorrelation tests on the squared residuals are even more satisfactory. Autocorrelation is rejected for all equations at the standard 5% level excepting the equation of Δq_t in the model of Finland, where autocorrelation is rejected at the 4% level. Finally, the residuals of all equations of 5 out of 9 models appear to be normally distributed, while in the remaining 4 models non-normality emerges only for the equations of the competitiveness index and, in the model of Spain, for the Δs_t equation. At a system-wide level, only the models of Netherlands and Spain show non-normal residuals.

Table 11 – Diagnostic tests of the dynamic models.

		AUS	BEL	FIN	FRA	GER	IRE	ITA	NET	POR	SPA
σ_u	Δs_t	0.0082	0.0081	0.0172	0.0051	0.0083	0.0080	0.0065	0.0079	0.0120	0.0057
	Δq_t	0.0201	0.0176	0.0150	0.0155	0.0136	0.0271	0.0167	0.0188	0.0186	0.0166
	$\Delta^2 p_t$	0.0033	0.0038	0.0039	0.0023	0.0041	0.0039	0.0028	0.0036	0.0064	0.0044
	$\Delta \phi_t$	0.0081	0.0077	0.0166	0.0052	0.0072	0.0058	0.0061	0.0055	0.0104	0.0028
A		$F_{(4,31)}$	$F_{(4,27)}$	$F_{(4,42)}$	$F_{(4,39)}$	$F_{(4,36)}$	$F_{(4,34)}$	$F_{(4,39)}$	$F_{(4,29)}$	$F_{(4,34)}$	$F_{(4,43)}$
	Δs_t	1.12	0.86	*2.93*	*3.31*	1.83	2.50	1.41	1.13	2.71	0.64
	Δq_t	1.95	0.32	1.49	1.29	1.37	1.24	1.96	0.68	1.21	0.57
	$\Delta^2 p_t$	1.37	0.30	2.59	2.58	0.80	0.82	0.41	2.59	0.22	*2.66*
	$\Delta \phi_t$	0.26	0.54	*3.30*	1.97	1.12	1.61	1.18	**5.28**	**5.64**	0.63
N		$\chi^2(2)$	$\chi^2(2)$	$\chi^2(2)$	$\chi^2(2)$	$\chi^2(2)$	$\chi^2(2)$	$\chi^2(2)$	$\chi^2(2)$	$\chi^2(2)$	$\chi^2(2)$
	Δs_t	0.17	5.17	1.14	1.43	3.88	*7.15*	1.93	0.10	4.23	**21.09**
	Δq_t	**16.49**	2.70	7.22	2.88	1.20	**9.55**	4.19	**16.78**	5.62	2.01
	$\Delta^2 p_t$	*6.44*	2.15	0.18	0.00	0.57	0.81	3.43	3.09	4.77	1.93
	$\Delta \phi_t$	0.15	1.53	0.42	0.88	5.29	**9.48**	2.74	1.35	5.95	4.29
AS		$F_{(4,27)}$	$F_{(4,23)}$	$F_{(4,38)}$	$F_{(4,35)}$	$F_{(4,32)}$	$F_{(4,30)}$	$F_{(4,35)}$	$F_{(4,25)}$	$F_{(4,30)}$	$F_{(4,39)}$
	Δs_t	0.33	0.94	0.47	0.55	0.15	0.49	0.51	0.20	0.27	0.44
	Δq_t	0.24	0.33	*2.73*	0.39	0.96	0.19	0.74	0.23	0.25	0.60
	$\Delta^2 p_t$	0.69	0.17	0.59	0.09	0.98	0.48	2.40	0.78	0.23	1.83
	$\Delta \phi_t$	0.21	0.36	1.08	0.23	0.27	0.40	0.59	0.08	0.53	0.43

Note. Statistics in bold (italics) indicate statistical significance at the 5% (10%) level.

The dynamic properties of the single models are analyzed conditioning on the elimination of the statistically insignificant short-run coefficients through the SER/TP approach developed by Brüggemann and Lütkepohl (2001). The models are estimated with a 3SLS procedure. The parsimonious models are obtained setting a threshold significance level of $t = 1.60$ for the short-run parameters and following the BIC criterion.[6]

Table 12 reports the restrictions determined for vector **a** (column two), matrix **A** (column three), matrices $\mathbf{\Gamma}_j$ (column four), and matrix **Φ** (column five) for each model (11), as well as the LR test statistics (column seven) which are χ^2 distributed, with the number of degrees of freedom given by the number of total short-run restrictions (column six). All LR statistics are well below the 5% and 10% level critical values, therefore showing how the data do not reject the imposed restrictions.

Table 12 – Short-run restrictions.

	NUMBER OF RESTRICTIONS				χ^2	STATISTICS	5% C.V.	10% C.V.
	a	**A**	$\mathbf{\Gamma}_j$	**Φ**				
Aus	1	3	22	11	37	36.53	52.19	48.36
Bel	2	1	41	11	55	37.53	73.31	68.80
Fin	0	1	18	12	31	24.61	44.99	41.42
Fra	1	2	10	19	32	18.51	46.19	42.59
Ger	2	1	5	30	38	32.72	53.38	49.51
Ire	2	1	21	10	34	15.38	48.60	44.90
Ita	2	1	9	18	30	13.67	43.77	40.26
Net	1	3	34	21	59	35.60	77.93	73.28
Por	1	2	13	12	28	15.60	41.34	37.92
Spa	1	0	4	9	14	7.69	23.68	21.06

Table 13 shows the speed of adjustment coefficients along with the corresponding standard errors of each model. From the analysis of the coefficients of matrix **A** emerges that 33 out of 48 (lagged) cointegration residuals are statistically significant. This finding points to the existence of a strong adjustment effect running from the ε terms to the first differenced variables. Conversely, an adjustment mechanism for the real exchange rate cannot be detected. This implies that the real exchange rate can be considered as a candidate to be one of the common trends of the system. The weakly exogeneity of the real exchange rate characterizes all models, excepting those of Spain, Austria, and Finland. Specifically, the equations describing inflation dynamics are influenced by all cointegration errors determined in the previous Subsection.

---

[6] The choice is justified by the opinion that it is preferable to maintain the coefficients with uncertain significance rather than deleting them. Therefore, we adopt a "conservative" strategy, in the terminology of Krolzig and Hendry (2001).

Table 13 – Speed of adjustment coefficients and their associated standard errors.

	ε_{t-1}	Δs_t	Δppp_t	$\Delta^2 p_t$	$\Delta\phi_t$
AUS	$\varepsilon_{mu,t-1}$	0.205 (0.046)	0.146 (0.045)	−0.072 (0.011)	−0.119 (0.048)
	$\varepsilon_{pc,t-1}$			−0.529 (0.095)	
BEL	$\varepsilon_{mu,t-1}$	0.092 (0.019)		−0.055 (0.012)	0.028 (0.005)
FIN	$\varepsilon_{mu,t-1}$	0.217 (0.068)	0.327 (0.072)		−0.216 (0.073)
FRA	$\varepsilon_{mu,t-1}$	0.166 (0.029)		−0.094 (0.024)	
GER	$\varepsilon_{mu,t-1}$	0.021 (0.006)		−0.011 (0.002)	0.015 (0.003)
IRE	$\varepsilon_{mu,t-1}$	0.088 (0.019)		−0.014 (0.004)	−0.077 (0.017)
ITA	$\varepsilon_{mu,t-1}$	0.172 (0.028)		−0.052 (0.009)	−0.059 (0.024)
NET	$\varepsilon_{mu,t-1}$	0.057 (0.017)		−0.083 (0.007)	
	$\varepsilon_{pc,t-1}$	−0.548 (0.112)		−0.142 (0.044)	0.382 (0.076)
POR	$\varepsilon_{pc,t-1}$			−0.558 (0.066)	0.408 (0.111)
SPA	$\varepsilon_{mu,t-1}$	0.062 (0.014)	0.100 (0.043)	−0.086 (0.011)	0.004 (0.001)

Focusing on supply-side error corrections, which are included in nine out of ten cases, the absolute value of the speed of adjustment coefficient of the equation of $\Delta^2 p_t$ is systematically lower than the corresponding coefficient of Δs_t in all models, excepting those of the Netherlands and Spain. This suggests that if inflation is cost-pushed, the supply-side disequilibrium is corrected mainly through adjustments occurring in the labor market rather than as a consequence of monetary policy decisions.

6   Conclusion

By adopting a single currency, the EMU countries waived their monetary policy, which has since been taken on by the European Central Bank.

Maintaining price stability within the Euro Area is the main task of the ECB, which has quantified it as an average inflation rate ranging from 0% to 2% in order to minimize the inflation costs related to redistribution effects, uncertainty and market distortions. The main goal of the present study is to assess the validity of the choice of monetary policy as the right instrument to maintain price stability.

We consider all main countries belonging to the Euro Area, namely Austria, Belgium, Finland, France, Germany, Ireland, Italy, Netherlands, Portugal, and Spain. The sample period goes form the first quarter of 1984 to the fourth quarter of 1998, including a time horizon characterized by a relatively stable macroeconomic framework where oil shocks are absorbed by the system, the constraints implied by the exchange rate arrangements are binding and the financial system is progressively being liberalized.

The econometric strategy, based on the estimation of a VEC model for each country, develops in two successive phases: in the first phase the long-run paths of the EMU countries' economies are specified; in the second phase the dynamic properties of the single models are analyzed.

The long-run structure includes two economic relationships linking, through a dynamic equilibrium, inflation to the markup and the output gap respectively, thus allowing for a distinction between cost-pushed and demand-pushed inflation.

The coefficient estimation is conditioned on the execution of unit root tests on all variables. *A priori* all variables are treated as endogenous in each VAR model, while their weak exogeneity is tested *ex post* in order to avoid imposing an arbitrary distinction upon them. The cointegration rank is determined according to the trace test and the maximum eigenvalue test.

The specification of cost-pushed inflation expresses the markup as a function of the real unit labor cost, the import prices, and the linear trend as a way to capture the influence of national structural factors.

The specification of demand-pushed inflation relies on a version of the Phillips curve featuring the inflation rate as a function of the unemployment rate, and the Okun's law, with the unemployment depending on the output gap. Moreover, the productivity is included as a further explanatory variable, while a linear trend is intended to *proxy* the growth of output and employment due to technological progress.

Both the cointegration relationships are supported by the data in the models of Austria and the Netherlands, in the model of Portugal only the demand-side long-run relationship holds, while in the rest of the countries the supply-side relationship holds.

For those economies characterized by cost-pushed inflation, the net markup is calculated showing that inflation represents a cost to firms due to the corresponding loss of competitiveness. The above loss is higher in those economies where inflation is not affected by import prices. The first important result is that demand-pushed inflation is detected in those countries characterized by a sustained output growth, the only exception being Ireland, whose long-run structure includes only a cost-push determination of inflation.

An excess of production capacity, i.e. an insufficient level of aggregate demand, therefore characterizes all other countries, whose long-run structure does not include a demand-pushed inflation equation.

The second part of the paper presents a short-run dynamic analysis of the parsimonious VEC models. The statistically insignificant coefficients, i.e. those to which corresponds a value of the t statistics lower than the threshold value of 1.60, are deleted. The LR test results suggest that the data do not reject the parsimonious specification of all models. Almost the 70% of the speed of adjustment coefficients related to the error correction terms are statistically significant, thus confirming the presence of strong feedback mechanisms running from the error correction terms to the first differenced variables.

The above results suggest that the ECB should take into account that the actual determinants of inflation differ in the single countries belonging to the Euro Area, and that the best objective of monetary policy is the only demand-pushed inflation. A tight monetary policy pursued in those countries whose inflation is mainly driven by costs would result in a contraction of economic activity without exerting relevant effects on price dynamics. This would be the consequence of higher financing costs for firms and a lower aggregate demand determined by an increasing interest rate. These are precisely the effects observed in the most recent years, when most of the European economies have been characterized by close to zero output rates of growth. In 2003 the ECB has redesigned its strategy setting a rate of interest of 2% as its main objective, but there is still room for a modification of the monetary policy strategy capable of considering the different factors driving inflation in EMU countries.

References

Banerjee, A., Cockerell, L., & Russell, B. (2001). An I(2) analysis of inflation and the markup. *Journal of Applied Econometrics*, **16**, 221–240.

Banerjee, A., & Russell, B. (2002a). The relationship between the markup and inflation in the G7 economies and Australia. *Review of Economics and Statistics*, **83**, 377-384.

Banerjee, A., & Russell, B. (2002b). A markup model for forecasting inflation in the Euro Area. European University Institute *Working Paper*, 2002/16.

Basile, R., de Nardis, S., & Girardi A. (2001). Regional inequalities and cohesion policies in the european union. *Working Paper ISAE*, **23**.

Binder, M., & Pesaran, H. M. (1999). Stochastic growth models and their econometric implications. *Journal of Economic Growth*, **4**, 139-183.

Boschi, M., & Girardi, A. (2005). Euro Area inflation: Long-run determinants and short-run dynamics. ISAE Working Paper, 60. Forthcoming *Applied Financial Economics*.

Bowdler, C., & Jansen, E. S. (2004). A markup model of inflation for the Euro Area. ECB *Working Paper*, **306**.

Brüggemann, R., & Lütkepohl, H. (2001). Lag selection in subset VAR models with an application to a U.S. monetary system. In R. Friedmann, L. Knüppel, & L. Lütkepohl (Eds.), Econometric Studies: A Festschrift in Honour of Joachim Frohn. Münster: LIT Verlag.

Clark, P., Laxton, D., & Rose, D. (1996). Asymmetry in the U.S. output-inflation nexus. *IMF Staff Papers*, **43**, 216-251.

Clements, M. C., & Hendry, D. F. (2001). *Forecasting non–stationary economic time series*. London: MIT Press.

Davidson, R., & Mackinnon, J. (1993). *Estimation and inference in econometrics*. Oxford: Oxford University.

de Brouwer, G., & Ericsson, N. R. (1998). Modeling inflation in Australia. *Journal of Business and Economic Statistics*, **16**, 4, 433-449.

European Central Bank (2004). The monetary policy of the ECB. Frankfurt: European Central Bank.

Favero, C. A., Giavazzi, F., & Spaventa, L. (1997). High Yields: The spread on German interest rates. *Economic Journal*, **107**, 956-985.

Franz, W., & Gordon, R. J. (1993). German and American wage and price dynamics. *European Economic Review*, **37**, 719-762.

Gali, J. (1994). Monopolistic competition, business cycles, and the composition of aggregate demand. *Journal of Economic Theory*, **63**, 73–96.

Garratt, A., Lee, K., Pesaran, H. M., & Shin, Y. (2003). A long–run structural macroeconometric model of the UK. *Economic Journal*, **113**, 412–455.

Haldrup, N. (1998). An econometric analysis of I(2) variables. *Journal of Economic Surveys*, **12**, 595–650.

Harvey, A. C. & Jaeger, A. (1993). Detrending, stylized facts and the business cycle. *Journal of Applied Econometrics*, **8**, 231-247.

Johansen, S. (1992). Determination of the cointegration rank in the presence of a linear trend. *Oxford Bulletin of Economics and Statistics*, **54**, 383–397.

Johansen, S. (1995). Likelihood–based inference in cointegrated vector autoregressive models. Oxford: Oxford University Press.

Juselius, K. (2002). Wage, price, and unemployment dynamics and the convergence to purchasing power parity in the Euro Area. Mimeo, University of Copenhagen.

Krolzig, H. M., & and Hendry, D. F. (2001). Computer automation of general to specific model selection procedures. *Journal of Economic Dynamics and Control*, **25**, 6-7, 831-866.

Layard, R., Nickell, S. J., & Jackman, R. (1991). Unemployment: macroeconomic performance and the labor market. Oxford: Oxford University Press.

Osterwald–Lenum, M. (1992). A note with quantiles of the asymptotic distribution of the maximum likelihood cointegration rank test statistics. *Oxford Bulletin of Economics and Statistics*, **54**, 461–472.

Sims, C. A. (1980). Macroeconomics and reality. *Econometrica*, **48**, 1–48.

Sinn, H. W., & Reutter, M. (2000). The minimum inflation rate for Euroland. *CESifo Working Paper*, **377**.

Stock, J. H., & Watson, M. W. (1999). Forecasting Inflation. *Journal of Monetary Economics*, **44**, 293–335.

In: Inflation, Fiscal Policy and Central Banks
Editor: Leo N. Bartolotti, pp. 61-81

Chapter 3

THE EUROSYSTEM'S OPEN MARKET OPERATIONS: FIRST EXPERIENCE WITH THE MARCH 2004 CHANGES TO THE MONETARY POLICY OPERATIONAL FRAMEWORK[*]

Doris Decker[1] and Natacha Valla[2][†]
[1]European Central Bank
[2]European Central Bank, Banque de France
and Institut d'Etudes Politiques de Paris.

Abstract

The design of a central bank's monetary policy operational framework is likely to affect short-term interest rates and credit institutions' bidding behaviour. Within the euro area, from mid-1999 until 2003, the Eurosystem witnessed several episodes of instable bidding behaviour from credit institutions in periods of imminent expectations of interest rate changes -the so called "overbidding" and "underbidding" phenomena. This paper gives a brief overview on the Eurosystem's operational framework for monetary policy and its performance since its inception six years ago. Despite some instability in bidding behaviour, the operational framework has overall proved very robust and has catered for an efficient transmission of the monetary policy stance. In this paper, a particular attention is given to the changes to the Eurosystem's monetary policy operational framework that were introduced in March 2004, with a view to provide an assessment of the experience under the new framework until December 2004.

JEL Classification: E43, E52

---

[*]This paper has been presented at the conference "Monetary Policy Implementation: lessons from the past and challenges ahead" held in Frankfurt on January 20/21, 2005. We are very grateful for substantial input provided by M. Enciò. We also thank D. Blenck, N. Cassola, G. Camba-Méndez, H.-J. Klöckers, H. Pill, F. Papadia, C. Rogers, T. Välimäki and seminar participants for their comments. All remaining errors are ours. The views expressed in this paper are those of the authors and not necessarily those of the ECB.

[†]E-mail address: natacha.valla@banque-france.fr. Corresponding author. Postal address for correspondence: Banque de France, 41-1422 DGEI-SEPMF, F-75049 Paris Cedex 1

1   Introduction

The design of a central bank's monetary policy operational framework is likely to affect short-term interest rates and credit institutions' bidding behaviour. Within the euro area, from mid-1999 until 2003, the Eurosystem witnessed several episodes of unstable bidding behaviour from credit institutions in periods of imminent expectations of interest rate changes -the so called "overbidding" and "underbidding" phenomena.

This paper gives a brief overview on the Eurosystem's operational framework for monetary policy and its performance since its inception six years ago. [1] Despite some unstability in bidding behaviour, the operational framework has overall proved very robust and has catered for an efficient transmission of the monetary policy stance. In this paper, a particular attention is given to the changes to the Eurosystem's monetary policy operational framework that were introduced in March 2004, with a view to provide an assessment of the experience under the new framework until December 2004.

The paper is organised as follows. Section 2 describes the main components of the Eurosystem's operational framework and briefly reviews the framework's performance since its inception. Section 3 reviews the major episodes of unbalanced bidding and explains the changes to the operational framework that were decided in January 2003 and became effective as of March 2004. Section 4 reviews the experience gained so far with the new operational framework by comparing the developments in the period March 2004-December 2004 (i.e. the experience under the new monetary policy operational framework) to the time of the old framework (mostly focussing on the period since June 2000, when the variable rate tender regime was started). Section 5 concludes.

2   The Main Components of the Eurosystem's Operational Framework for Monetary Policy and Its General Performance Since Its Inception

2.1   The Main Components of the Eurosystem's Operational Framework for Monetary Policy

It is generally useful to distinguish the ECB's monetary policy strategy from the Eurosystem's operational framework. The former describes how the relevant information on the economy is organised to provide a foundation for monetary policy decisions, the outcome of which is a certain level of short-term interest rates that is considered adequate in terms of the ECB's objective of achieving price stability. In order to achieve this objective, the ECB has at its disposal a set of monetary policy instruments and procedures. [2] This set forms the

---

[1] For the sake of simplicity, the terms "ECB" and "Eurosystem" are used interchangeably throughout this paper.

[2] See also "The implementation of monetary policy in the euro area - General documentation on Eurosystem monetary policy instruments and procedures", February 2004 and $\tilde{A}$ ^{a} " $\pm$ ^{a} ¨$\phi\!\!\!/\!\!\!B$$-\pm$¥ β $\pm$ ¨ ^{a} ¤› $\Box$, 2004.

operational framework for monetary policy, which is used by the ECB to steer the short-term market interest rates. The desired level of interest rates is signalled to the financial markets through the rates of the main refinancing operations and the standing facilities. So far, the former has been either the minimum bid rate of variable rate tenders or the rate applied to fixed rate tenders.

The main components of the Eurosystem's monetary policy operational framework are the open market operations, the standing facilities, and the minimum reserve system.

Open market operations play an important role in the monetary policy of the Eurosystem for the purposes of steering interest rates, managing the liquidity situation in the market and signalling the stance of monetary policy. While in principle more types of instruments are available to the Eurosystem, recourse is made at present to main refinancing operations (MROs), to longer-term refinancing operations (LTROs), and to fine-tuning operations (FTOs):

• MROs are regular liquidity-providing reverse transactions with a weekly frequency. Until March 2004, MROs had a maturity of two weeks, so that two operations of this type were outstanding at any point in time. Since March 2004, the maturity has been reduced to one week. MROs are the most important open market operations, signalling the stance of monetary policy, playing a key role in the steering of interest rates and managing the liquidity situation in the market. They provide the bulk of refinancing to the financial sector. A broad range of monetary policy counterparties can participate to MROs.

• LTROs are liquidity-providing reverse transactions with a monthly frequency and a maturity of normally three months. In these operations, the Eurosystem does not, as a rule, intend to send signals to the market and therefore normally acts as a rate taker.

• FTOs are executed on an ad hoc basis with the aim of managing the liquidity situation in the market and steering interest rates, in particular in order to smooth the effects on interest rates caused by unexpected liquidity fluctuations in the market. FTOs are primarily executed as reverse transactions, but can also take other forms.

Standing facilities aim to provide and absorb overnight liquidity, signal the general stance of monetary policy and bound overnight market interest rates. Two standing facilities are available to eligible counterparties on their own initiative, subject to their fulfilment of certain operational access conditions. Counterparties can use the marginal lending facility to obtain overnight liquidity from the national central banks against eligible assets. The interest rate on the marginal lending facility normally provides a ceiling for the overnight market interest rate. Furthermore, counterparties can use the deposit facility to make overnight deposits with the national central banks. The interest rate on the deposit facility normally provides a floor for the overnight market interest rate.

Finally, the Eurosystem's minimum reserve system applies to credit institutions in the euro area and primarily pursues the aims of stabilising money market interest rates and creating or enlarging a structural liquidity shortage. The reserve requirement of each institution is determined in relation to elements of its balance sheet. In order to pursue the aim of stabilising interest rates, the Eurosystem's minimum reserve system enables credit institutions to make use of so-called "averaging provisions". Compliance with the reserve requirement is determined on the basis of the institutions' average daily reserve holdings over the maintenance period. Institutions' holdings of required reserves are remunerated at the rate of the Eurosystem's main refinancing operations (fixed rate of the operation until June 2000, marginal rate of the variable rate tender after June 2000). From January 1999 until February 2004, the reserve maintenance period lasted one month, always starting on the 24th calendar day of each month and ending on the 23rd calendar day of the following month (also regardless of whether these days were TARGET operating days or not).

2.2   The Framework's General Performance Since Its Inception

The main objective of the Eurosystem's operational framework for monetary policy is the steering of short term interest rates. Specific emphasis is put on the overnight rate, the starting point of the yield curve. In Chart 1, the graph of the EONIA and the ECB policy rate (the fixed rate in fixed rate tenders or the minimum bid rate in variable rate tenders) reveals that the overnight rate has tracked the ECB policy rate rather closely within the corridor formed by the rates applied on the standing facilities (deposit facility and marginal lending facility). In this regard, the framework has had considerable success.

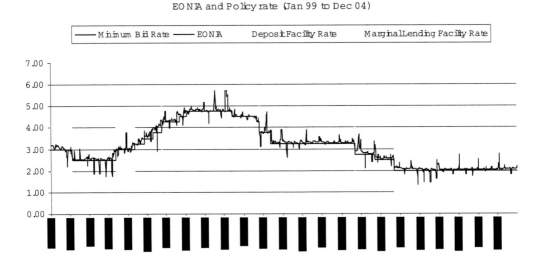

Figure 1: Chart 1: EONIA and ECB policy rate, 1999-2004

Source: ECB.

As is visible from Chart 2, occasional spikes occurred at the end of the maintenance period. However, this feature was not unexpected.

The volatility of the EONIA can be described for example, by the standard deviation of the spread between the EONIA and the ECB policy rate (EONIA spread), which stood at

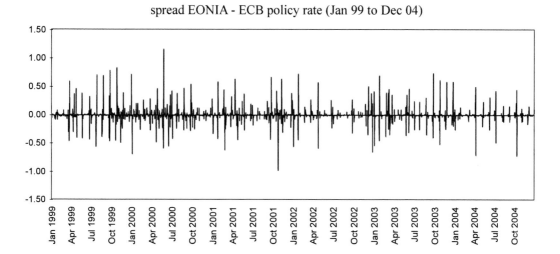

Figure 2: Chart 2: The spread between the EONIA and the ECB policy rate, 1999-2004

Source: ECB.

18 basis points from 1999 until December 2004. Another measure of EONIA volatility is the standard deviation of the daily changes in the EONIA spread which was 12 basis points. It appears overall that during each reserve maintenance period, the EONIA remained quite stable.

The volatility of the EONIA is mainly attributable to two factors: first, events of unstable bidding behaviour by counterparties, and, second, end of reserve maintenance period volatility, when credit institutions have to adjust the level of their reserve holdings. This volatility has never spilled-over to longer maturities and was therefore not of relevance for the transmission of monetary policy through the economy.

In sum, the Eurosystem's framework for monetary policy implementation has generally been assessed positively since the launch of the euro in 1999. The volatility of short-term money market rates has, on average, been low in the euro area in comparison with European national money markets prior to January 1999. This is also true by international standards. The low degree of volatility has been fostered by the use of averaging provisions by the minimum reserve system, with little need for the ECB to conduct fine-tuning operations. Moreover, credit institutions have had only limited recourse to the standing facilities, indicating that the money market has been working efficiently. The small and fairly stable spread between the ECB's main refinancing rate and the short-term money market rates has also demonstrated the ECB's ability to closely steer short-term interest rates in line with its intentions.

Also, the operational framework has been robust when faced with exceptional challenges, like Y2K, the transition to the millennium year 2000, the terrorist attacks of 11 September 2001 or the euro cash changeover in January 2002.

Still, some strains emerged when high expectations of changes in the key ECB interest rates translated into unstable bidding by credit institutions in the MROs, namely episodes of "overbidding" and of "underbidding". The occurrence of overbidding was eliminated when the ECB Governing Council decided, in June 2000, to switch from the fixed rate tender to variable rate tenders. Subsequently, however, the problem of underbidding led the ECB Governing Council in January 2003 to decide on changes to the operational framework that became effective from March 2004. The next section reviews these events.

3   Measures to Improve the Monetary Policy Operational Framework

3.1   Episodes of Unstable Bidding under the Old Framework

A central bank's monetary policy operational framework is likely to affect short-term interest rates and credit institutions' bidding behaviour. Within the euro area, between mid-1999 and 2003, the Eurosystem witnessed several episodes of unstable bidding behaviour from credit institutions in periods of imminent expectations of interest rate changes. Such unstable bidding is composed of two types of instability, namely episodes of "overbidding" and of "underbidding".[3]

Overbidding refers to the phenomenon of credit institutions submitting high and even continuously increasing bids to MROs, such that the ratio between allotment and bid amounts falls to very low levels. Overbidding occurred under the regime of fixed rate tenders, when there were expectations of an imminent interest rate hike by the ECB. Due to such expectations of an increase in interest rates, the short-term money market rates stood at a level clearly above the fixed tender rate.

Several episodes of overbidding occurred in particular in the second half of 1999 and the first half of 2000, when the Eurosystem conducted the MROs through a fixed rate tender procedure in an environment of strong expectations of interest rate increases. Over that period, the allotment ratio fell to extremely low levels, dropping to as low as 0.87% on 31 May 2000. In addition to a general downward trend, this allotment ratio was volatile, implying that it was difficult for participants in the MROs to predict the amount of liquidity they would actually receive. During the overbidding period, when the corresponding market rates tended to be above the fixed tender rate, credit institutions faced difficulties in forecasting precisely the rather volatile allotment ratio and, accordingly, the risk of receiving significantly more or less liquidity in the tender than desired. Furthermore, some credit institutions felt uncomfortable to bid for amounts that exceeded the collateral they had available.

As these issues could not be addressed under a fixed rate tender system, the ECB changed the tender procedure and adopted in June 2000 the variable rate tender procedure

---

[3]See also the article "Changes the the Eurosystem's operational framework for monetary policy", published in the ECB Monthly Bulletin in August 2003.

with a minimum bid rate. The minimum bid rate in the variable rate tender plays the key role of signalling the monetary policy stance, a role which was previously performed by the rate in fixed rate tenders. This change successfully eliminated overbidding episodes.

However, under the variable rate tender regime, occasional episodes of underbidding occurred. Underbidding refers to the situation in which credit institutions submit an aggregate amount of bids which is less than the one needed to allow for a smooth fulfilment of reserve requirements in the period until the next MRO is conducted. Its consequence is that the ECB can not allot its benchmark allotment amount.

The Eurosystem has experienced nine episodes of underbidding in the "old" operational framework, eight of these occurring under the regime of variable rate tenders with a minimum bid rate in place since June 2000.[4] In all but one episode, the underbidding occurred in an environment of strong expectations of an imminent reduction in the key ECB rates, of which eventually five materialised. On several occasions, underbidding in one MRO was followed by allotments in the remaining MROs of the reserve maintenance period that did not allow credit institutions to compensate fully for the under-fulfilment of reserve requirements during the week after the underbidding occurred. In this context, credit institutions faced the risk of running short of liquidity at the end of the maintenance period and, as a consequence, had to take recourse to the marginal lending facility. All cases triggered significant temporary volatility in the short-term money market rates.

Overall, underbidding typically resulted in tight liquidity conditions in the euro money market and probably also affected market uncertainty about the liquidity conditions that would prevail over the remainder of the maintenance period. Shorter-term interest rates were driven up and volatility of the overnight interest rates rose. Moreover, in situations where the key ECB rates were actually reduced, the temporary upward movement of the overnight rate associated with underbidding created a source of noise, at least temporarily, in the signalling of the monetary policy stance.

3.2   The Rationale for Changes to the Monetary Policy Operational Framework

When considering implementing some reforms to its operational framework, the ECB drew experience from the delicate situation for liquidity management arising in case of underbidding, as the ECB found itself in the following trade-off situation. On the one hand, any shortfall in liquidity created by interest rate speculation on the side of counterparties could not immediately be compensated for, as incentives for bidding "smoothly" over the maintenance period needed to be preserved. On the other hand, the resulting temporary volatility in money market rates was undesirable. Overall, all the episodes of unstable bidding showed that no instrument was easily available to the Eurosystem to prevent these occasional tensions. Indeed, the occasional occurrence of unstable bidding behaviour by counterparties,

---

[4]The underbidding episodes under the variable rate tender regime in the old framework are presented in Annex 1.

and the related volatility in short-term money market rates were endogenous features of the "old" operational framework.

The possibility of changes in the key ECB rates during the reserve maintenance period, which affected short-term interest rates and credit institutions' bidding behaviour in MROs, was mainly due to the following elements of the old framework:

- The reserve maintenance period starting on the 24th calendar day of each month and ending on the 23rd calendar day of the subsequent month;

- The two-week maturity of the weekly MROs.

The definition of reserve maintenance periods that prevailed at that time implied that changes in the key ECB interest rate could occur in the course of a maintenance period. Indeed, the assessment by the Governing Council of the monetary policy stance did not coincide with the start of the maintenance period.[5] If the Governing Council decided to change the MRO minimum bid rate and the rates applied on the standing facilities, the new rates would come into force immediately, i.e. they were applied already at the next MRO being announced and to the standing facilities on the following day. As a consequence, rate change expectations within the prevailing reserve maintenance period implied that overnight interest rates may have deviated from the rates used by the ECB to signal its monetary policy stance, even if neutral liquidity conditions were expected for the end of the reserve maintenance period. The resulting spreads between the ECB's main refinancing rate and the corresponding money market rates, therefore, gave credit institutions incentives for excessive bidding in case of rate increase expectations or disincentives to participate in the MROs in case of rate cut expectations.

Moreover, the two-week maturity of the weekly MROs implied that at least the last MRO of each reserve maintenance period overlapped with the subsequent period. Therefore, expectations of an interest rate change to take place in the subsequent reserve maintenance period could also destabilise bidding at the end of the prevailing maintenance period. In conclusion, these features of the old operational framework made the expectations of a change in the key ECB interest rates occurring within one or even two maintenance periods particularly relevant for credit institutions' bidding in MROs.

In order to neutralise the impact of interest rate change speculation within a maintenance period, the ECB, therefore, considered to change the timing of the reserve maintenance period, and to shorten the maturity of the MROs, as described below.

---

[5] As of 8 November 2001, the ECB Governing Council had decided that it would, as a rule, assess the stance of the ECB's monetary policy and change interest rates only at its first meeting of each month, which is usually the first Thursday.

3.3   The Decided Changes

3.3.1   The Changes

On 23 January 2003, the ECB Governing Council decided on the following two measures to improve the efficiency of the operational framework for monetary policy, also taking into account the feedback received from a public consultation: [67]

- The timing of the reserve maintenance period was changed so that it always starts on the settlement day of the MRO following the Governing Council meeting at which the monthly assessment of the monetary policy stance is pre-scheduled. Furthermore, as a rule, the implementation of changes to the standing facility rates should be aligned with the start of the new reserve maintenance period.

- The maturity of the MROs was shortened from two weeks to one week.

Given the technical and legal preparatory work - by counterparties and by the Eurosystem - required for the implementation of these measures, they were scheduled to come into effect in March 2004. In this respect, the Eurosystem implemented the necessary changes to the minimum reserve regulation and the regulation on consolidated balance sheet, and to the calendars of the tender operations, of the maintenance period, and of the freezing of minimum reserves. Furthermore, in order to minimise disruption to the timetable of LTROs, the link between the maintenance period and LTRO allotment days was discontinued. In the old framework, LTROs were allotted on the first Wednesday of each reserve maintenance period. From February 2004 onwards, LTROs were normally allotted on the last Wednesday before the end of the month.

A transitional reserve maintenance period, from 24 January 2004 to 9 March 2004, phased in the new monetary policy operational framework.

In sum, the following positive features were attributed to the changes that were decided for the Eurosystem's monetary policy operational framework. The measures were expected to help remove expectations of interest rate changes during any particular maintenance period, given that changes in the ECB's key interest rates would only apply, in general, to the forthcoming reserve maintenance period and that liquidity conditions would no longer spill over from one reserve maintenance period to the next. Consequently, within a maintenance period, the overnight rate would normally no longer be affected by rate change expectations. Hence, the overnight rate would, due to the generally neutral liquidity management policy of the ECB, tend to remain close to the minimum bid rate. This was expected to eventually

---

[6]On 7 October 2002, the ECB launched a public consultation that was addressed to all credit institutions in the euro area and to banking and financial market associations. The Eurosystem received a strong response to this public consultation, highly representative of the euro area banking community. Comments were received from 17 banking and financial market associations (five pan-European associations and 12 national associations representing eight countries). There were also 42 replies from individual credit institutions, including both large EONIA panel banks and small institutions.

[7]In addition to the above mentioned two measures, the ECB also asked the market participants whether to suspend the longer-term refinancing operations. However, since these operations appear to continue to serve the liquidity management needs of the Eurosystem's counterparties, they were not suspended.

prevent speculative considerations from disrupting the bidding behaviour of credit institutions in MROs and, moreover, support the signalling of the monetary policy stance provided by the minimum bid rate in the MROs.[8]

3.3.2   Additional Communication

In addition to these changes to the operational framework, the ECB decided to systematically provide its forecast of the average autonomous factors and its calculation of the benchmark allotment amount on each day it announces or allots an MRO with a view to eliminating misperceptions in the market as to whether or not the allotment decisions in MROs targeted balanced liquidity conditions.[9] Previously, the ECB only published its forecast of the average autonomous factors on MRO announcement days, on the basis of which the market could calculate a proxy of the benchmark allotment. The additional information now made explicitly clear to the market whether or not the ECB's allotment decisions in MROs aim at balanced liquidity conditions. Prior to this, when credit institutions observed a deviation between the MRO allotment amount and the benchmark amount that they had calculated, there was uncertainty as to whether the deviation was actually due to the ECB deliberately pursuing a non-neutral liquidity target, or whether it was simply due to updates of the autonomous factors forecast, which were not published at that time. This had occasionally led to misinterpretations of the ECB's allotment decisions.

3.3.3   Risks Associated with the Changes

Concerning the risks associated with these changes, it was noted that the change in the timing of the maintenance period would imply a more variable length of the reserve maintenance periods.

More importantly, the shortening of the maturity of the MRO would imply an increased turnover of central bank refinancing. All other things equal, the allotment amounts of the MROs would double. It was not excluded that some credit institutions could face difficulties to adjust their bids to the higher weekly turnover in MROs, especially with regards to the collateral.

Furthermore, since the last MRO of the maintenance period would always be allotted eight days before the end of the maintenance period (i.e. a period longer than the on average around half a week in the old framework), there could be a higher probability of the accumulation of large aggregate liquidity imbalances at the end of the period, leading to greater volatility in interest rates. In this respect, it should however also be stressed that the

---

[8]It is noted that also in the new operational framework, "technical" underbidding may in principle still occur, i.e. for reasons other than expectations of interest rate changes. This means essentially stochastic factors, such as technical failures at an individual bank or the "co-ordination" problem, which can also affect the total bid amount.

[9]The published benchmark allotment is rounded to EUR 500 million.

Italian tax collection,[10] which has typically been a significant source of unexpected fluctuations in autonomous factors, would in the new framework occur before the last MRO of the maintenance period. Anyway, fine-tuning operations would always be available to the ECB to cope with unbalanced liquidity conditions.

Whether these risks have materialised is assessed in the following section that reviews the first experience with the new framework.

4 First Experience with the New Monetary Policy Operational Framework

This section describes the experience with the changes to the Eurosystem's monetary policy operational framework that became effective in March 2004.[11] It reviews in turn the interest rate conditions in the overnight euro money market, the bidding behaviour of counterparties in the MROs as well as the tender outcomes, and the ECB's liquidity management.

4.1 Interest Rate Conditions in the Overnight Euro Money Market

4.1.1 Evolution of the Spread between the EONIA and the Minimum Bid Rate ("Overnight Spread")

Conditions in the overnight market, when assessed from the point of view of EONIA developments, became remarkably stable when the March 2004 changes came into force. Leaving aside EONIA developments on the very last day of each maintenance period, the overnight spread became significantly lower and stable after March 2004. As shown in Chart 1, money markets enjoyed about half a year of very low interest rates, with an EONIA hovering some 2-4 basis points above the minimum bid rate on normal days.[12]

At the end of the Summer 2004, however, the EONIA started to experience end-of-period deviations from the minimum bid rate which gradually intensified and changed in nature over time. By the end of 2004, the usual final day interest rate spikes started to spill over to several days prior to the end of the maintenance periods. The overnight spread started to widen earlier than the last couple of days of the maintenance period, thereby potentially affecting bidding behaviour in all MROs within the maintenance period and contaminating other money market maturities and segments (e.g. derivatives).

Chart 3 shows the overnight spreads that have prevailed on average on each successive day of a period. A first average is computed for the "pre-March 2004" sample, i.e. June

---

[10]Italian government deposits are the most fluctuating autonomous factor, with a large impact of the monthly tax collection by the government.

[11]The period covered in this section ends in December 2004. See also the article "Initial Experience with the Cnages to the Eurosystem's Operational Framework" for Monetary Policy Implementation published in the ECB Monthly Bulletin in February 2005.

[12]Excluding the last day of the maintenance period, or days affected by specific factors such as end-of-month or quarter effects.

2000-February 2004. A second average is shown for the maintenance periods since March 2004.[13]

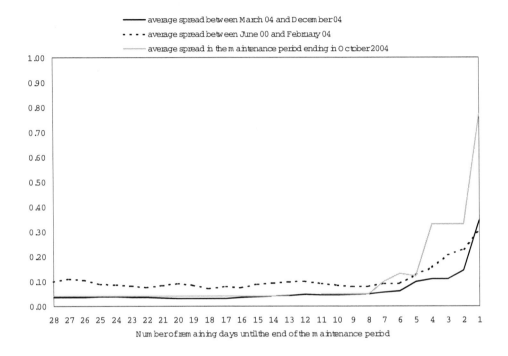

Chart 3: Spread between the EONIA and the minimum bid rate ("overnight spread") within a maintenance period [14]

Source: ECB, percentages, daily data.

Chart 3 suggests that, except for the last day of the maintenance period, the average overnight spread has declined under the new framework all along the maintenance period, including during the days between the last MRO and the end of the maintenance period. However, this evidence should be treated with due caution given that the sample covering the new framework represents only few observations and is probably affected by the fact that three maintenance periods ended with a fine-tuning operation aiming at rebalancing liquidity conditions.

4.1.2   Volatility of the Overnight Rate

In parallel to the increase in the overnight spread observed during the last quarter of 2004, developments in the volatility of the overnight rate also seemed to have changed.

These changes started with the maintenance period ending on 11 October 2004, as can be seen also from the atypically high overnight spread observed at the end of that period

---

[13]The maintenance period ending on October 2004 has also been singled-out in Chart 3. It is commented further below.

(singled-out in Chart 3). Regarding volatility developments, unusual intra-day movements of the overnight rate have been observed towards the end of the maintenance periods ending on 11 October, 8 November and 7 December 2004.

However, overall the volatility of the overnight rate remained low in the new framework. An analysis of the daily evolution of the realised volatility of the overnight interest rate, defined as the sum of high-frequency intra-daily squared returns1 is shown in Chart 4, which displays the log realised volatility of the intra-day overnight rate and its moving average over 21 business days, i.e. around one month.[15] Overall, the realised volatility of the overnight interest rate follows a downward trend, which was more pronounced after the launch of the new operational framework in March 2004. Volatility was lower on average after March 2004. After August 2004 volatility increased again albeit from a low level, and still remains below the levels reached under the old framework.

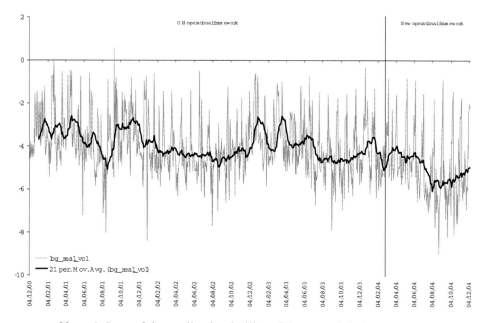

Chart 4: Log of the realised volatility of the overnight interest rate

Source: Reuters, ECB's calculations, 5-minutes intraday data, 4 December 2000-7 December 2004.

Nevertheless, evidence on the overnight spread as well as on the evolution of the intraday overnight rate volatility suggests that overnight rate developments can be split in two distinct "phases" under the new framework: an initial period of quiet market conditions with low levels of spreads which prevailed until the end of the Summer 2004, and a sequence of consecutive maintenance periods with heightened interest rate volatility and increases in

---

[15]This analysis has been conducted by Alain Durré and Stefano Nardelli, ECB, DG Economics. The (log) realised volatility of the overnight interest rate is defined as follows: $\ln(RV_d) = \ln (\sum_h r_{d,h}^2)$, where $r_{d,h}^2 = (_d r_{h+1} -_d r_h)$ is the 5-minute return for the 5-minute interval h ($h \in [9 : 00, ..., 17 : 55]$) on a particular day d.

overnight spreads. In response to these money market developments, fine-tuning operations have been carried out on the last day of the maintenance period, with a view to offsetting large expected liquidity imbalances. The fine-tuning episodes are reviewed in section 4.3 below.

4.1.3   Have the Effects of Interest Rate Expectations Been Eliminated?

The March 2004 changes have been designed to eliminate the adverse effects of interest rate expectations on the counterparties' demand for liquidity within the reserve maintenance period. Having neutralised the effects of interest rate expectations on the path of liquidity demand within each maintenance period, it was thought that banks would have no (or fewer) incentives to front - or backload reserves, thereby also stabilising the flows being traded in the secondary euro money market.

At the current stage, it is fair to say that the answer to this question remains uncertain. If indeed liquidity volumes demanded at regular MROs have not behaved abnormally since March 2004 – in particular no underbidding episode took place in relation to interest rate expectations - all MROs took place in an environment of an unchanged monetary policy stance where the minimum bid rate has been kept constant at 2% by the Governing Council of the ECB. During this time, interest rate expectations also remained broadly flat across maintenance periods. However, in the very last months of the period under review, banks may have started to show an aversion towards liquidity uncertainty, which could have possibly led to renewed frontloading.

4.2   Bidding Behaviour of Counterparties in the MROs and Tender Outcomes

This section compares the bidding behaviour of counterparties in MROs and the tender outcomes before and after the changes to the framework were implemented in March 2004.

4.2.1   Benchmark Allotment Amount and Total Bid Amount

Chart 5 reveals a significant change in the behaviour of the total bid amount in comparison to the benchmark allotment. [The rest of the paragraph should be redrafted] The ratio total bid amount / benchmark allotment (a proxy for the bid-to-cover ratio at the ECB's MROs) has been on a declining trend between the inception of variable rate tenders with minimum bid rate in June 2000 and the implementation of the changes in March 2004 (represented by the vertical red line in the Chart). Within this period, the liquidity deficit gradually broadened, reflecting a strong increase in the demand for banknotes since the beginning of 2002. By contrast, since March 2004, total bids gradually diverged away from the benchmark allotment amount.

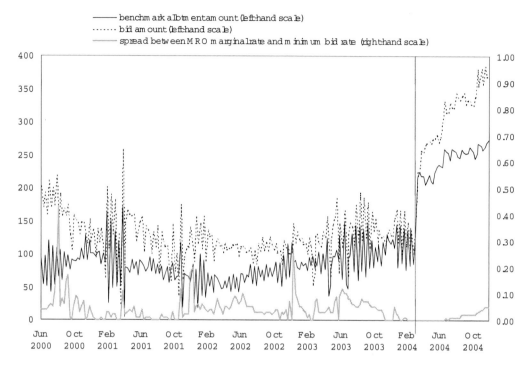

Chart 5: Benchmark allotment and total bid amount

Source: ECB, weekly data (left-hand scale: EUR billion; right-hand scale: percentages).

After March 2004, when the size of MRO allotments sharply increased, bid amounts quickly adapted to the new average scale of benchmark amounts. Gradually, the total MRO bid amount even increased to levels steadily above the allotment amount, and it stood in December 2004 at an all-time high of around EUR 400 billion. Only one case of "technical underbidding" occurred during the transition on 23 March 2004, when the total amount of bids fell short of the benchmark amount by EUR 5 billion.

Overall, the gradual divergence between the bid and allotment amounts suggests that the higher turnover of collateral implied by the shortening of the MRO maturity has, to date, not caused any major difficulty associated with collateral constraints.

4.2.2   Did the Smoother Allotment Path Help Counterparties to Bid?

The introduction of symmetric and non-overlapping MROs with one-week maturity reduced the imbalance between the size of consecutive MROs (see also Chart 5). Before the March 2004 changes, the average weekly change in the benchmark allotment had an absolute value of ca. EUR 33 billion. By December 2004, this figure had been reduced to EUR 7 billion. This smoother path of liquidity provision can be attributed to the fact that the MRO maturity is now always aligned with the horizon of the liquidity target on which the benchmark allotment is based – i.e. the day before the settlement of the next MRO. [16]

Intuitively, it should be the case that the reduced short-term fluctuations in the benchmark allotment amount contribute to a stabilisation of credit institutions' bidding in MROs. As shown in Chart 6, the bid-to-cover ratio, has been quite volatile under the "old" framework. Between January 2000 and February 2004, the average weekly change in the bid-to-cover ratio was 0.65. It decreased to 0.06 in the period since March 2004, suggesting that the risk of misalignment between the scale of bids and the allotment size has diminished under the new framework.

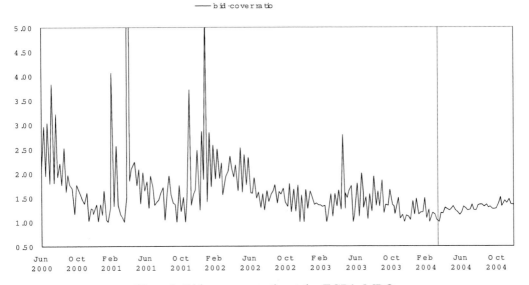

Chart 6: Bid-to-cover ratio at the ECB's MROs

Source: ECB, weekly data.

4.2.3 The Evolution of Tender Rates and the "Tender Spread"

To some extent, developments in the overnight spread described above mirror those of the so-called "tender spread", defined as the spread between the marginal rate prevailing at MRO tenders and the minimum bid rate. The tender spread remained remarkably small and stable between March and June 2004 (zero basis point), following which it started to gradually increase to 7 basis points by mid-December 2004. [17]

---

[16]Prior to March 2004, the two-week maturity of the MROs was always longer than the horizon of the liquidity target. Therefore, the relationship between the volumes of the two outstanding MROs turned-out to be complex and occasionally led to sharp fluctuations across weekly benchmark allotments.

[17]Note that the observed widening of the tender spread is not inconsistent with the fact that the total bid amount has accelerated relative to the rate of growth of the benchmark allotment, leading to the increased bid-to-cover ratio presented in Chart 6.

One may put forward the following factors behind the gradual increase in the tender spread in the most recent period. First, there may have been an increase in banks' preferences for frontloading reserve holdings, as a reaction to higher (first perceived, and then actual), end-of-period uncertainty. Second, banks may have developed – wrongly - the perception of a tightening bias in the ECB's liquidity management. These perceptions may be due to the fact that the first fine-tuning intervention conducted by the ECB under the new framework happened to be a liquidity absorbing operation. However, there does not seem to be strong empirical support to the perceptions of asymmetric ECB preferences. Indeed, these perceptions were not well founded.

4.3 The ECB's Liquidity Management: Early Responses and Challenges Ahead

The higher end-of-period uncertainty that has prevailed towards the end of 2004 under the new framework stems from the increased likelihood of large liquidity imbalances accumulated after the allotment of the last MRO of a reserve maintenance period. These potentially large end-of-period imbalances are related to the fact that under the new framework, the allotment of the last MRO always takes place eight days ahead of the last day of the reserve maintenance period. By contrast, in the previous framework, the last allotment took place between two and eight days (and given the frequency, four on average) before the end of the period. All other things equal, this has increased the volatility of the overnight rate in the last week of the maintenance period.

The distribution of accumulated autonomous factor errors after the last MRO has therefore widened. Chart 7 compares the distribution of errors accumulated after the last MRO of the maintenance period, under the old and new framework respectively. Each distribution corresponds to an accumulation over four (the average horizon under the old framework) and eight (the current horizon) days.

The two distributions presented in Chart 7 measure the precision with which last MRO allotments of the maintenance period can be calibrated. The standard deviation of the accumulated autonomous factor forecast error over eight calendar days is normally around EUR 7 billion, while it stays around EUR 3 billion over four working calendar days. All in all, higher uncertainty about end-of-period liquidity imbalances may imply wider and earlier fluctuations of the overnight rate away from the minimum bid rate after the last MRO allotment of the maintenance period. The potential for higher overnight rate volatility may also be amplified by the increased transparency in the publication of both autonomous factors forecasts and the benchmark allotment, which make it easier for counterparties to follow the path of liquidity imbalances in "real time".

Money markets needed to be monitored very closely in order to detect any unexpected development associated with the implementation of the changes to the operational framework. In response to the higher end-of-period uncertainty and its effect on money market developments, fine-tuning operations on the last day of the maintenance period have been

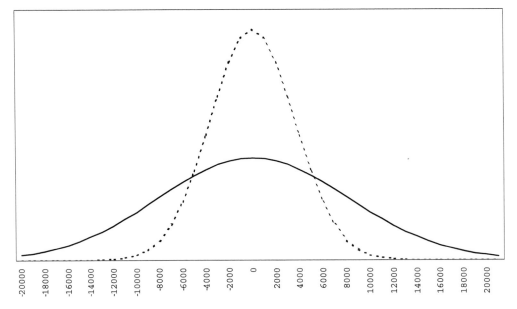

—— accum m ula ted enrors over 8 calendar days
· · · · accum u la ted enrors over 4 calendar days

Chart 7: Distribution of accumulated autonomous factor forecast errors

Source: ECB, EUR billion, daily data, 8 January – 8 December 2004.

carried-out at three occasions after the changes to the operational framework became effective.[18]   Indeed, large expected liquidity imbalances that resulted from changes in the Eurosystem's forecast of autonomous factors needed to be offset.[19]

All three fine-tuning operations conducted in 2004 after the changes were carried out irrespective of the sign of the liquidity imbalance: on 11 May and 7 December 2004, liquidity-absorbing fine-tuning operations were conducted, while on 8 November 2004 a liquidity-providing fine-tuning operation was carried out. The operations restored balanced liquidity conditions at the end of the maintenance period. Indeed, from the moment the possible recourse to a fine-tuning operation was announced by the ECB one day before the end of the period, the overnight rate stabilised at a level closer to the minimum bid rate.

When taking the decision to conduct a fine-tuning operation on 8 November, a liquidity imbalance of EUR 6.5 billion was expected, which was less than what had been expected at the end of some previous maintenance periods when the ECB did not conduct fine-tuning operations. This reflects the fact that the ECB, possibly taking into account its first experience with the new framework and its preference for smooth money market conditions throughout the maintenance period, acted in a way that addressed more effectively

---

[18]As of 31 December 2004. On 18 January 2005, the last day of the maintenance period, another liquidity providing fine tuning operation was conducted to rebalance liquidity conditions in the euro money market.

[19]On several occasions, forecasts had, for example, to be corrected due to unforeseen developments in banknotes in circulation.

liquidity imbalances at the end of the reserve maintenance periods. This way to address such liquidity imbalances has evolved gradually and may have benefited from experience in successive maintenance periods. Before the changes to the framework were implemented in March 2004, the end-of-period liquidity imbalances and the resulting volatility in the overnight rate were normally rather moderate, and the ECB never carried out a fine-tuning operation after the last MRO allotment in response to them. This was consistent with the idea that some volatility in the overnight rate at the end of the maintenance period can enhance credit institutions' incentives to bid in MROs, as they seek to reduce their interest rate risk. Owing to the initial concerns expressed by some credit institutions that the higher collateral turnover brought about by the shorter MRO maturity could increase the risk of underbidding, it was considered important not to reduce incentives to bid.

As the analysis of bidding behaviour in the previous section suggests, it turned out that both bid amounts and bid rates showed that incentives to bid steadily increased after the changes to the framework. Therefore, there seems to be little, if any, need to enhance incentives to bid by allowing excessive volatility in the overnight rate at the end of the period. In addition, some tentative evidence has emerged that such volatility, which can reach elevated levels (as seen in October 2004), can be somewhat disruptive to interbank money market liquidity and to the smooth operation of the associated derivative markets. Hence, on several occasions in the autumn of 2004 the ECB address more effectively liquidity imbalances at the end of the maintenance period via fine-tuning operations.

5   Conclusion

This paper reviewed the overall performance of the Eurosystem's operational framework for monetary policy since its inception, addressing in particular the changes to the framework that were implemented in March 2004 as well as the experience gained so far with the adapted framework.

Overall, although the new framework had not, as of December 2004, been directly tested against expectations of interest rate changes, its seems pretty immune to unstable bidding behaviour and tender developments of the kind experienced before the changes, namely the episodes of underbidding (as well as of overbidding under the fixed rate tender regime).

The paper shows that the transition to the new regime proved smooth and conducive to stable money market conditions and appropriate tender developments at MROs. Counterparties quickly adapted to the increased allotment amounts in the weekly MROs, thereby dispelling fears that collateral constraints may become an issue. In this respect, the main goal of the changes implemented in March 2004, namely preventing bidding behaviour in the MROs from being destabilised by expectations of interest rate changes, has so far proven successful.

The stable bidding behaviour has also been accompanied by an overall narrowing of the spread between the interbank overnight rate and the minimum bid rate during the maintenance period. In addition, it led to an overall decline in the volatility of the overnight interest rates.

The new framework, however, showed to be vulnerable to the increased scope for end-of-period liquidity imbalances brought about by errors in forecasting autonomous factors in the last week of each maintenance period. Indeed, the reaction of the overnight rate to these imbalances has been amplified, bringing about undue intra-day interest rate volatility and widening the spreads between the minimum bid rate on one side, and tender, overnight, and other short-term money market rates on the other side, towards the end of the maintenance period.

As a result, the ECB countered liquidity imbalances at the end of the reserve maintenance period more effectively via fine-tuning operations conducted on the last day of the maintenance period. These fine-tuning operations contributed to contain the average volatility of the overnight rate.

Annex 1: Main Episodes of Underbidding under the "Old" Framework[20]

In the following, the main episodes of underbidding experiences by the Eurosystem in the old operational framework are described.

In the underbidding episode of 13 February 2001, the overnight rate crept upwards as a result of a shortage of bids by counterparties in the MRO allotted on that day. Although the ECB satisfied all the bids, the operation sfell short of the neutral liquidity allotment by around 23 billion as a considerable number of counterparties had expected that overnight rates would drop below the market rates in the days to come and therefore reckoned that borrowing from the market would be cheaper than from the ECB. Although the ECB allotted a record amount in the subsequent MRO, it did not cover the full liquidity needs. This implied for the credit institutions a substantial recourse to the marginal lending facility at the end of the maintenance period.

After the bids had fallen short by 28 billion of the intended allotment volume in the MRO conducted on 10 April 2001, the spread between the overnight and the minimum bid rate increased substantially, since most market participants did not expect the ECB to step in to restore normal liquidity conditions before the end of the maintenance period. The recourse to the marginal lending facility was, after the previous underbidding episode, the second highest ever.

The underbidding episode of 9 October 2001 took place in an environment of expectations of a reduction of the key ECB interest rates. As the liquidity deficit that consequently accumulated in the following week was only partially offset by the relatively high allotment in the subsequent MRO, credit institutions had to take substantial recourse to the marginal lending facility in order to fulfil their reserve requirements. Until the end of the maintenance period, the overnight rate was driven substantially upward towards the marginal lending facility rate.

---

[20]Most of these cases are described in the article "Changes to the Eurosystem's operational framework for monetary policy", ECB Monthly Bulletin, August 2003, p. 41-54.

In the episode of 6 November 2001, despite the underbidding, the credit institutions did not have to resort to the marginal lending facility in order to fulfil their reserve requirements, mainly due to the allotment amounts in the remainder of the maintenance period and other liquidity factors. The overnight rate, which had edged upwards on the day of the announcement of the underbid MRO, returned closer to the minimum bid rate level a few days later.

The underbidding episode of 3 December 2002 should be analysed in conjunction with the episode of 17 December 2002, as they both impacted on liquidity conditions in the same reserve maintenance period. While the episode of 3 December 2002 took place in an environment of expectations of interest rate reductions and resulted in a fairly marginal underbidding amount, the one on 17 December 2002 appeared atypical as it did not seem to be related to expectations of reductions in the key ECB interest rates. Indeed, the spread between the two-week swap rate and the tender rate was positive at the time of bid submission. Anecdotal evidence suggests that underbidding on 17 December 2002 was related to the reluctance of credit institutions to participate in an MRO with maturity on 31 December 2002, which was considered to be a particularly unattractive day for the settlement of the tender. This episode was even more special as it occurred in the last MRO of the maintenance period, implying that the related liquidity deficit could not be offset before the end of the maintenance period, unless the ECB conducted a liquidity-providing fine-tuning operation. Actually, on this specific occasion, the ECB conducted a fine-tuning operation on the settlement day of the underbid MRO with a view to reducing the liquidity shortage. The allotment amount reflected a balance between the ECB's aim to restore normal liquidity conditions, while at the same time preserving incentives for credit institutions to bid sufficiently in MROs.

In the underbidding episode of 3 March 2003, very large reserve deficits accumulated after the announcement of underbidding of the size of 42 billion. The overnight rate remained above the former minimum bid rate, even after the expected decrease in interest rates had materialised. In order to facilitate liquidity management without generating a considerable difference between the sizes of the two outstanding MROs, the ECB decided the following week to conduct an additional MRO with a maturity of one week in parallel to the regular MRO. As a result, liquidity conditions were perceived as satisfactory and credit institutions only had to take a small net recourse to the marginal lending facility.

Finally, the last case of underbidding in the old operational framework occurred on 3 June 2003. Again, underbidding took place in an environment of strong expectations of interest rate decreases. As, however, underbidding turned out to be less significant than initially expected, overnight rates fell after the tender result was announced. Apart from the very end of the maintenance period, the overnight rate presented a pattern similar to that observed in the underbidding episode of 3 December 2002.

In: Inflation, Fiscal Policy and Central Banks
Editor: Leo N. Bartolotti, pp. 83-99

ISBN 1-60021-122-4
© 2006 Nova Science Publishers, Inc.

Chapter 4

CENTRAL BANK CONTRACTS WITH MULTIPLE PRINCIPALS

Juan Cristóbal Campoy* and Juan Carlos Negrete†
Departamento de Fundamentos del Análisis Económico,
Facultad de Economía y Empresa, Universidad de Murcia,
30100 Espinardo, Murcia (Spain).

Abstract

This paper analyzes how the inflation bias to discretionary monetary policy is affected when we extend the basic principal-agent framework to allow for the existence of two principals, namely, the government and an interest group which design Wash inflation contracts. We begin by considering an scenario where the interest group has an output objective that exceeds the government's. We show that, in this case, a deflation bias arises. Then, we analyze a setting where the interest group's dislike of deviations of inflation from its objective is higher than the government's. In this context, we conclude that a deflation bias also occurs but it is smaller than the one arising in the first scenario.

KeyWords: Central bank, discretionary monetary policy, inflation bias.

JEL: E58, F41

1 Introduction

Up until the appearance of the seminal papers by Kydland and Prescott (1977) and Barro and Gordon (1983a), monetary policy was considered as exogenous in macroeconomic analysis. The debate focused on whether this policy should be implemented following rules, as the one proposed by Friedman, or leaving it to the discretion of central banks. The natural response appeared to be the second alternative since, after all, following a rule seems to be one of the actions available to discretionary policymakers. The two seminal papers just mentioned provided the first modern analysis to this issue. They showed that economic

---
*E-mail address: juancris@um.es; Telf: 0034-968363822. Fax: 0034-968363758.
†E-mail address: jcnegret@um.es; Telf: 0034-968363760. Fax: 0034-968363758.

outcomes could be improved if policymakers are able to credibly commit to certain aspects of their future policies. This new approach produced new insights into the analysis of institutional reforms since it emphasizes two important aspects: first, the incentives that central banks face when implementing their monetary policies; and, second, that policy outcomes are obtained as the result of the interactions between monetary authorities and a private sector that cannot be systematically fooled[1].

More specifically, Kydland and Prescott (1977) and Barro and Gordon (1983a) pointed out that discretionary monetary policy faces a time inconsistency problem, namely, it tends to generate an inefficiently high level of inflation with no gain in terms of output. This outcome is accounted for in a sequential setting where the private sector knows that, if expectations on inflation are sufficiently low, the policymaker will tend to carry out a monetary surprise with the aim of making output exceed the natural level. Therefore, the private sector will increase its expectations on inflation to the point where such a systematic surprise becomes too costly for the monetary authorities. As a result, the time consistent (or the subgame perfect) equilibrium is characterized by an "inflation bias"[2].

Both of these papers made it clear that a key element that originates this problem is the policymaker's inability to credibly commit to the socially optimal inflation rate. However, these authors did not address the critical issue of how monetary authorities could obtain credibility. This task was taken up by an active line of investigation which has followed two different routes, namely, the "reputation" approach and the "institutional design" approach[3]. An important feature shared by the arrangements belonging to both approaches is that they make it more costly for the central banks to generate inflation. Therefore, the expectations on this variable are lowered and, as a result, the inflation bias is reduced or even eliminated.

The reputation approach was pioneered by Barro and Gordon (1983b). They considered a dynamic context where a central banker who carries out a monetary surprise is "punished" by the private sector since it will rise its expectations on inflation[4]. By contrast, the institutional design approach aims at proposing monetary institutions that provide central banks with the right incentives to deal with the inflation bias. Within this approach, Rogoff (1985) showed that this bias can be partially reduced by delegating monetary policy to an independent central bank governor who dislikes inflation more than society. However, this arrangement implies a suboptimal stabilization of output. By contrast, Walsh (1995a) showed that the government can set the central banker's remuneration contingent upon realized inflation -a linear inflation contract- in such a way that the inflation bias is completely eliminated and output is stabilized optimally. Therefore, this mechanism achieves a higher social welfare than Rogoff's[5]. Svensson (1997) argued that an equivalent favorable out-

---

[1]This approach contrast with the previous literature which assumed that the government was able to continually manipulate the public's beliefs so as to obtain electoral advantages (see, for instance, the classical article by Nordhaus [1975]).

[2]Finn Kydland and Edward Prescott won the 2004 Nobel Prize in Economics for their contribution on the time inconsistency problems and for their work on real business cycle models.

[3]Such a classification can be found, for instance, in Persson and Tabellini (2000) and in Walsh (2003).

[4]However, this approach has been criticized on the following grounds (see Waller [1995] and Persson and Tabellini [2000]). To begin with, the number of trigger strategies that sustain this outcome is infinite and it is not clear which one will be selected. Besides, this mechanism requires the assumption that the private sector can manage to coordinate on the punishment strategy. Finally, this approach lacks normative implications, passing on to the private sector the entire responsibility of dealing with the inflationary bias.

[5]Bernanke (2004) has stated that, over the past 25 years, the papers by Kydland and Prescott (1977), Rogoff

come can be achieved if the central bank is assigned a loss function with a specific inflation target smaller than the one which is socially optimal.

Now, even though Walsh's proposal was originally termed as the "contract approach", the mechanisms put forward by Rogoff (1985) and Svensson (1997) can also be interpreted as a contract that the government (the principal) designs and offers to the central bank (the agent)[6]. In fact, all these three monetary institutions belong to the so-called "incentive theory" which deals with settings where a principal is required to delegate a certain task to an agent. The central concern is how the principal can best motivate the agent to perform the task as the former would prefer.

On the other hand, these three arrangements have in common that the central bank's objective function is characterized by the sum total of two terms: (a) the first one, represents the society's preferences on inflation and output stabilization; (b) and the second term refers to the value that the monetary authorities attach to a financial reward received from the government. However, these three proposals differ in the functional form of the second term of this objective function.

This literature generally considers that the government is the only principal. However, a key assumption underpinning this literature is that the monetary authorities are self-interested utility maximizers. As a result, this approach implicitly opens the possibility that the central banker may respond to incentive schemes offered by other potential principals. After all, monetary policy decisions can be influenced through a variety of channels, namely, lobbying, press criticism and so forth. Besides, the incentives of the central bank can also be non-pecuniary, since the monetary authorities' performance influences their reputation.

The aim of this paper is to analyze how the inflation bias to discretionary monetary policy is affected when we extend the basic principal-agent framework to allow for the existence of two principals with different macroeconomic objectives. We consider a common agency problem in which the central bank (the agent) enters into two contracts. One with the government and another one with another principal that, throughout the paper will be labelled generically as "the interest group". In other words, a common central bank selects its monetary policy under the influence of competing principals.

Our paper is related to the work by Dixit and Jensen (2003) who also adopt a multiple-principal framework. However, instead of considering a closed economy, their analysis develops in the context of a monetary union where the principals are the member governments and the agent is the common central bank. In this setting, they show that when principals try to influence the common central bank's monetary policy by offering competing Walsh contracts, a deflation bias emerges[7]. However, in contrast with Dixit and Jensen (2003), we consider scenarios where the principals have different preferences over macroeconomic stabilization.

(1985) and Walsh (1995a) have been the most influential ones in monetary policy.

[6]The interpretation of Rogoff's arrangement as a "quadratic contract" appears in Walsh (1995a), Beetsma and Jensen (1998) and Jensen (2000). The interpretation of Svensson's institution as a contract appears in Persson and Tabellini (2000). On the other hand, this contract approach has been proposed as a commitment technology for the international coordination of monetary policy (Persson and Tabellini [1995], Jensen [2000], Negrete [2000] and Campoy and Negrete [2006]).

[7] Chortareas and Miller (2004) also adopt a multiple-principal framework. However, as Campoy and Negrete (2006) have shown, the contracts proposed by these authors are not derived from optimazing behavior.

This framework is inspired in several real life situations. Society is not homogeneous in the sense that there are different sectors whose economic objectives may not be necessarily coincident. This feature opens the door to the possibility of the formation of interest groups who may try and lobby the central bank. In fact, the government in some countries is made up of representatives of several parties with very different preferences over economic outcomes. For instance, some Cabinet members may be more inflation averse than others. In this case, the economic priorities of the "consensus" central banker may be considered far from ideal by some government components who may try to influence the monetary authorities' decisions. On the other hand, as in the case of the European Monetary Union, when a supranational institution implements the common monetary policy of different countries, a subgroup of member states could be tempted to try to persuade the central bank for a change in the common monetary policy. In fact, asymmetries in the economies of the member countries may lead to non-synchronized business cycles. As a result, if the common central bank is implementing a tight monetary policy which favors member countries with full employment, a subgroup of states whose economies are in a recession may try to push the monetary authorities for a reduction in interest rates.

Among the private interests strongly affected by monetary policy, perhaps the most directly and persistently affected is the financial services sector. Private bankers bear the initial impact of open market policy, and central bankers around the world have long been concerned with private bankers' adjustment to and opinion of monetary policy actions. Therefore, within the financial services sector the banking industry is probably the most affected by monetary policy (Havrilesky [1994]). Therefore it is no surprise that there may exist lobbies that can back up anti-inflationary monetary policies.

Taking into account this reality, we study two scenarios. First, we consider the possibility that the interest group's desired level of output is higher that the government's; and second, we study an scenario where the former is more concerned over the stabilization of inflation than the latter. In both cases, we assume that the government and the interest group simultaneously offer the central bank take-it-or-leave-it Walsh contracts. Both principals choose these incentives schemes in a non-cooperative fashion so that Nash equilibria are reached. The central bank then selects its policy instrument to maximize its overall utility, taking as given the contract offers proposed by the interest group and government.

We show that, in both settings, the competing inflation contracts cannot prevent a deflation bias from arising. This result is obtained since both the government and the interest group care about the costs of the transfer paid to the central bank. Therefore, as we will show below, each principal tries to save this costs by manipulating its contract with the aim of shifting its share of the total transfer to its counterpart. In doing so both principals impose a negative externality to one another which results in suboptimality low rate of inflation.

The rest of the paper is organized as follows. Section 2 presents the model. Section 3 studies how the inflation bias is affected when an interest group offers the central bank an aditional inflation contract which competes with the one designed by the government We analyze two scenarios. To wit , the case where the interest group's output objective is greater than the geovernment's and the setting where the former's concern over inflation is greater that the latter's. Finally, Section 4 concludes.

2 The Model

Our framework is based on the standard stochastic model which have been widely used in the literature on credibility in monetary policy (see, for instance, Walsh [2003, chapter 8]). However, we extend this setup so as to include an additional principal, namely, an interest group. Formally, the working of the economy is summarized by the following equations:

$$y = \overline{y} + \alpha(\pi - \pi^e) - \varepsilon, \tag{1}$$
$$U_G = -[\beta\pi^2 + (y - y_G)^2] - \phi(A - b\pi), \tag{2}$$
$$U_{CB} = -[\beta\pi^2 + (y - y_G)^2] + \xi[(A - b\pi) + (C - d\pi)], \tag{3}$$
$$U_{IG} = -[\lambda\pi^2 + (y - y_{IG})^2] - \psi(C - d\pi), \tag{4}$$

where $\overline{y}$, α, β, ϕ, $\xi > 0$; and subscripts, "G", "CB", and "IG", respectively, stand for "Government", "Central Bank" and "Interest Group". Equation (1) shows that the economy possesses a Lucas supply function, so that the difference between output (y) and the natural level $(\overline{y})$ depends on the deviations of inflation (π) from its expected value (π^e) and on a supply shock (ε) with zero mean and finite variance (σ_ε^2). Expectations are rational, that is, $\pi^e = E\{\pi\}$, where $E\{.\}$ is the expectations operator. There is a potential stabilizing role for monetary policy since nominal wages are determined before the realization of the supply shock is observed and remain fixed during the period of analysis.

Expression (2) represents the utility function of the government or society. The first term states that society dislikes deviations of inflation and output from optimal levels, normalized to zero and y_G, respectively. Now, as it is standard in the literature on credibility in monetary policy, we define:

$$k \equiv y_G - \overline{y} > 0$$

The positive sign of k means that the governments' output objective is higher than the natural level[8]. Therefore, a monetary surprise involves a gain in terms of output. As a consequence, the classical time consistency problem in monetary policy is present, which results in an "inflation bias".

In order to tackle this problem, the government delegates the conduct of monetary policy to an independent central banker whose utility function appears in (3). This agent has the social preferences over stabilization of output and inflation (i. e., the first terms in (2) and (3) coincide). However, their behavior can be influenced by a transfer payment $((A - b\pi)$ in (2) and $(3))$. In this sense, in a setting where the government is the only principal, Walsh (1995a) showed that this incentive scheme can be designed so that the inflation bias is eliminated without any loss in terms of output stabilization. This transfer payment can be interpreted as the central banker's income (or their budget) and is made up of two components: a fixed part (A) and a penalization on inflation $(-b\pi)$. However, as explained in Persson and Tabellini (1993) and Walsh (1995a), the penalization can also be interpreted as a non-pecuniary reputation penalty. As Walsh (1995a) and Bernanke (2004) have stated, performance contracts are best treated as a metaphor rather than a literal proposal for central bank reform. Even if the financial reward received by the monetary authorities while they

---

[8]The suboptimality of the natural level of output stems from the existence of market failures, distortions, imperfections or rigidities in the economy.

are in office is unlikely to depend directly on the realized rate of inflation, central bankers take into account many others aspects of their job, including their professional reputations, the prestige of the institutions in which they serve and the probability that they will be reappointed. Walsh (1995a) describes this mechanism as a useful fiction for deriving the optimal incentive structure. Besides, Walsh (1995b, 2002) shows how the properties of a linear inflation contract can be mimicked by a dismissal rule under which the central banker is fired if inflation ever rises above a critical level.

Parameters ϕ and ξ represent, respectively, the weight that the government and the central banker put on the financial reward, relative to the social loss in terms of stabilization of both inflation and output. Since both of these parameters are positive, the agent values positively the transfer payment associated to the contract and, conversely, the government values it negatively. The assumption that the transfer is costly to the government has also been considered in Walsh (1995a).[9]

However, in contrast with Walsh (1995a), the central banker's utility function in (3) includes an additional financial reward ($C - d\pi$), which is an incentive scheme offered by a second principal which throughout will be labelled as "the interest group". The objective function of this second principal appears in (4) and has the same structure as that of the government. Therefore it is made up of two components. The first one expresses the interest group's dislike of the deviations of inflation and output from some desired levels. The second component is the transfer paid by the interest group to the common agent, namely, the central bank. Parameter ψ stands for the valuation that the interest group puts on the financial reward relative to the loss in terms of the deviations of inflation and output from their desired levels. Since this parameter is positive, it implies that the incentive scheme is costly to the interest group.

We assume that the government and the interest group have different preferences over macroeconomic stabilization. In other words, the first term in their utility function (i.e., in (2) an (4) is different). More specifically, in Subsection 3.1 we consider the the case where the interest group output's objective is higher that the government's (i.e., $y_{IG} > y_G$); and in Subsection 3.2 we analyze the scenario where the former has a greater dislike of deviations of inflation from the desired level (i.e., $\lambda > \beta$).

The interactions between the government, the central banker, the private sector and the interest group are modelled by making use of a multi-stage game. The sequence of events is as follows:

1) The central banker is offered, simultaneously, two incentive schemes. One is proposed by the government and the second one by the interest group. Both principals design the contracts in a non-cooperative fashion.

2) The private sector observes both incentive schemes and then forms its expectations on inflation.

3) The realization of the output shock becomes common knowledge.

---

[9]See Walsh (1995a, footnote 10). On the other hand, Candel and Campoy (2004) show that the inflation bias is not eliminated when the following conditions apply: (a) the transfer (pecuniary incentives) is costly to the government; (b) the fixed part of the contract is exogenously given and (c) the central bank values the pecuniary incentives but there are also important non-pecuniary motives that lead the central banker accept the contract, i.e., the pecuniary participation constraint does not hold.

4) The central banker selects the inflation rate[10].

Throughout the paper, different equilibria will be obtained and evaluated making use of quadratic loss functions as the ones in $(2) - (4)$, which are standard in the literature on credibility in monetary policy. On the other hand, Dixit and Lambertini (2003a,b) and Woodford (2003, chapter 6) have shown that this type of objective functions build on microeconomic foundations, since they can be obtained starting from the utility function of a representative agent[11].

3   The Results

In this section we analyze the effects on the inflation bias that result from the strategic interactions between the governments, the interest group, the private sector and the central bank. In subsection 3.1 we study the case where both principals have different output objectives but the same weight to inflation; and in Subsection 3.2 we consider a setup in which they only disagree over the weight to inflation stabilization.

3.1   Different Desired Levels of Output

We begin by analyzing the case where the inflation objectives for the interest group and the government coincide but the former's output objective is greater than the latter's. Formally, with reference to (2), (3) and (4) we assume that $\lambda = \beta$ and $y_{IG} > y_G$. In this scenario, we study how the inflation bias is affected if both principals have the ability to design and offer the central bank Walsh inflation contracts. Therefore, setting $\lambda = \beta$ into (3) and (4) we have that the objective functions of the government, the central bank and the interest group are, respectively:

$$
\begin{aligned}
U_G &= -[\beta\pi^2 + (y - y_G)^2] - \phi(A - b\pi), & (5) \\
U_{CB} &= -[\beta\pi^2 + (y - y_G)^2] + \xi[(A - b\pi) + (C - d\pi)], & (6) \\
U_{IG} &= -[\beta\pi^2 + (y - y_{IG})^2] - \psi(C - d\pi). & (7)
\end{aligned}
$$

We look for a subgame perfect equilibrium. Therefore, we solve by backward induction the game outlined in Section 2, for the particular case considered in this subsection.

In the last stage of the game, once the private sector has set up its expectations on inflation,the central banker observes the realization of the shock (ε) and then responds to the incentives embedded in the contracts offered by the two principals. It does so by selecting the value for π that solves the following program:

$$
\begin{aligned}
\max_{\{\pi\}} \quad & -\left(\beta\pi^2 + (y - y_G)^2\right) + \xi[(A - b\pi) + (C - d\pi)] \\
s.t. \quad & y = \overline{y} + \alpha(\pi - \pi^e) - \varepsilon.
\end{aligned}
$$

---

[10]The central bank's information advantage about the realization of the shocks in relation to the private sector stems from the fact that, in practice, monetary policy decision can be modified more often than nominal wages.

[11]In addition, former vice-president of the FED, Alan Blinder (1998), has pointed out that policymakers employ their instruments in such a way that only "small" variations in the economic variables take place and for this type of changes any convex objective function is approximately quadratic.

The solution yields the optimal response of the monetary authorities, i.e., their reaction function:

$$\pi = \frac{\alpha^2 \pi^e}{\beta + \alpha^2} + \frac{\alpha k}{\beta + \alpha^2} + \frac{\alpha \varepsilon}{\beta + \alpha^2} - \frac{\xi(b+d)}{2(\beta + \alpha^2)}. \tag{8}$$

This behavior is anticipated by the private sector who takes rational expectations on inflation, prior to having observed the realization of the shock, but bearing in mind the pair of incentive schemes offered to the central banker. Therefore, the expected rate of inflation is obtained by taking expectations in (8) and solving for π^e, which yields:

$$\pi^e = \frac{\alpha k}{\beta} - \frac{\xi(b+d)}{2\beta}. \tag{9}$$

Plugging this value for the expected inflation into equation (8) and solving for π, we obtain:

$$\pi = \frac{\alpha k}{\beta} + \frac{\alpha \varepsilon}{\beta + \alpha^2} - \frac{\xi(b+d)}{2\beta}. \tag{10}$$

Remark 1: *The size of the inflation bias depends on the penalization rates b and d. Moreover, this bias is eliminated if and only if:*

$$b + d = \frac{2\alpha k}{\xi}. \tag{11}$$

Proof:

Substituting equation (11) into (10) yields the following expression for the inflation level:

$$\pi = \frac{\alpha}{\alpha^2 + \lambda}\varepsilon. \tag{12}$$

whose expected value is zero. ∎

Now, moving up to the first stage of the game, we characterize the government's and the interest group's best responses. They take account of each other's behavior and the solutions to the (following) stages just described. In order to do so, first, we need to express the expected utilities of the government, the interest group and the central banker in terms of the variables which define both contracts, namely, A, b, C and d. With this aim, first we substitute (1) into (5), (6) and (7). Then, we plug the values for π^e and π (appearing in equations (9) and (10)) into the resulting three expressions for U_{CB}, U_G and U_{IG}. After doing so, taking expectations yields:

$$E(U_{CB}) = \xi(A + C) + \frac{\xi^2}{4\beta}b^2 + \frac{\xi^2}{4\beta}d^2 + \frac{\xi^2}{2\beta}bd - K_0 \tag{13}$$

$$E(U_G) = -\phi A + \frac{(\phi + \xi)\alpha k}{\beta}b - \frac{(\xi + 2\phi)\xi}{4\beta}b^2 + \frac{\alpha k \xi}{\beta}d -$$
$$\frac{\xi^2}{4\beta}d^2 - \frac{(\phi + \xi)\xi}{2\beta}bd - K_0 \tag{14}$$

$$E(U_{IG}) = -\psi C + \frac{\alpha k \xi}{\beta}b - \frac{\xi^2}{4\beta}b^2 + \frac{(\psi + \xi)\alpha k}{\beta}d - \frac{\xi(2\psi + \xi)}{4\beta}d^2 -$$

$$\frac{\xi(\psi+\xi)}{2\beta}bd - K_1 \tag{15}$$

where $K_0 = \frac{(\beta+\alpha^2)k^2}{\beta} + \frac{\beta\sigma_\varepsilon^2}{\alpha^2+\beta}$ and $K_1 = \frac{\alpha^2 k^2}{\beta} + (y_{IG} - \bar{y})^2 + \frac{\beta\sigma_\varepsilon^2}{\alpha^2+\beta}$..

We now show that in the context considered in this subsection, where the interest group and the government share the same weight to inflation but the former's output objective is greater than the latter's, if both principals design competing Walsh contracts a deflation bias arises.

We prove this statement in several steps. When the government choose the value of the strategic variables A and b, (i. e., the ones that shape the contract that it offers to the central bank), it takes into account: (i) the requirement that the central bank accept the resulting contract; and (ii) the values achieved by the strategic variables chosen by the interest group (i. e., the values of C and d which define the contract which it designs). By the same token, when the interest group selects the values of the strategic variables that characterize the incentive scheme that it proposes to the central bank (i.e., C and d), it bears in mind: (i) that the agent must not reject the contract; and (ii) the values of A and b, which determine the contract designed by the government.

Item (ii) implies that we will now focus on the Nash equilibrium of the game defined by the pay-off functions of the government and the interest group appearing in (14) and (15). As for item (ii), it refers to the participation constraint which states that the expected utility obtained by the central banker when signing both contracts must be greater or equal to a given reservation utility level, Z. Therefore, the set of contracts that can be offered and accepted is reduced to those satisfying such a constraint. Formally, the government faces the following problem:

$$\max_{\{A,b\}} \quad E(U_G)$$
$$s.t. \quad E(U_{CB}) \geq Z,$$

which results in the following Lagrangian function:

$$\pounds = E(U_G) + \mu E(U_{CB}).$$

Therefore, the Kuhn-Tucker first order conditions of this problem are:

$$\frac{\partial \pounds}{\partial A} = \frac{\partial \pounds}{\partial b} = 0,$$
$$\frac{\partial \pounds}{\partial \mu} \geq 0 \quad \text{and} \quad \left(\frac{\partial \pounds}{\partial \mu} = 0 \quad if \quad \mu > 0; \quad \frac{\partial \pounds}{\partial \mu} > 0 \quad if \quad \mu = 0\right).$$

Result 1: *The indifference curves of the government and the central bank are tangent at the equilibrium point*

Proof:
The first two conditions can be restated as follows:

$$\frac{\partial \pounds}{\partial A} = \frac{\partial E(U_G)}{\partial A} + \mu \frac{\partial E(U_{CB})}{\partial A} = 0, \tag{16}$$
$$\frac{\partial \pounds}{\partial b} = \frac{\partial E(U_G)}{\partial b} + \mu \frac{\partial E(U_{CB})}{\partial b} = 0. \tag{17}$$

Solving (16) and (17) for the Lagrangian multiplier, μ, and equating the values appearing in the resulting two expressions yields:

$$\mu = -\frac{\frac{\partial E(U_G)}{\partial A}}{\frac{\partial E(U_{CB})}{\partial A}} = -\frac{\frac{\partial E(U_G)}{\partial b}}{\frac{\partial E(U_{CB})}{\partial b}}. \tag{18}$$

Now, rearranging, we obtain this tangency (or efficiency) condition of the indifference curves of the government and the central banker. Namely, the equality of the marginal rates of substitution of both players:

$$\left.\frac{\partial A}{\partial b}\right|_{E(U_G)} = \frac{\frac{\partial E(U^G)}{\partial A}}{\frac{\partial E(U^G)}{\partial b}} = \frac{\frac{\partial E(U^{CB})}{\partial A}}{\frac{\partial E(U^{CB})}{\partial b}} = \left.\frac{\partial A}{\partial b}\right|_{E(U_{CB})} \tag{19}$$

These marginal rates of substitutions for the government and the central bank are, respectively:

$$\left.\frac{\partial A}{\partial b}\right|_{E(U_G)} = \frac{\alpha k\,(\phi + \xi)}{\beta \phi} - \frac{\xi\,(\xi + 2\phi)}{2\phi\beta}b - \frac{\xi\,(\xi + \phi)}{2\phi\beta}d, \tag{20}$$

$$\left.\frac{\partial A}{\partial b}\right|_{E(U_{CB})} = -\frac{\xi\,(b + d)}{2\beta}. \tag{21}$$

Equating (20) and (21), as condition (19) requires, and solving for b one finds the reaction function of the government:

$$b = \frac{2\alpha k}{\xi} - \frac{\xi}{\xi + \phi}d \tag{22}$$

Notice that the value of b depends on the one taken by d.

Result 2: *The participation constraint holds with equality.*

Proof:

According expression (18), the value of the Lagrangian multiplier is:

$$\mu = \frac{\phi}{\xi} > 0.$$

Notice that the value of this multiplier is strictly positive, which implies that the second Kuhn-Tucker condition is satisfied when $\frac{\partial \pounds}{\partial \mu} = 0$. In other words, the participation constraint is binding.

On the other hand, the interest group faces a problem which is similar in structure to the one solved by the government, namely, it maximizes its utility subject to the constraint that the agent accepts the contract:

$$\max_{\{C,d\}} \quad E\,(U_{IG})$$
$$s.t. \quad E(U_{CB}) \geq Z,$$

Making use of the Kuhn-Tucker first order conditions, in a similar way to the one applied to solve the government's problem, yields the optimal penalization embedded in the output contract selected by the interest group, i. e., its reaction function:

$$d = \frac{2\alpha k}{\xi} - \frac{\xi}{\xi + \psi} b. \tag{23}$$

Now, solving simultaneously both principals reaction curves (appearing in (22) and (23)) yields:

$$b = \frac{2\alpha k \phi (\xi + \psi)}{\xi (\psi \xi + \phi \xi + \phi \psi)}, \tag{24}$$

$$d = \frac{2\alpha k \psi (\xi + \phi)}{\xi (\psi \xi + \phi \xi + \phi \psi)}. \tag{25}$$

Finally, substituting these values into (10) we obtain an inflation rate equal to:

$$\pi = -\frac{\alpha k \phi \psi}{(\psi \xi + \phi \xi + \phi \psi) \beta} + \frac{\alpha \varepsilon}{\beta + \alpha^2}. \tag{26}$$

The first term on the right-hand side of (26) is the expected inflation rate. Notice that this term is negative, which proves that in the setting analyzed a deflation bias arises.

An important conclusion from the previous analysis emerges. We have studied an scenario in which, contrary to the one considered by Walsh (1995a), the ability to offer the central bank a linear inflation contract is not exclusive to the government but also applies to an interest group, which has a higher output objective. We have shown that the presence of such a second principal changes the result obtained by Walsh (1995a), namely, average inflation is no longer equal to zero. In fact, the resulting contract competition brings about a deflation bias, even though both principals dislike this outcome.

We now explain why, when the transfer is costly to both the government and the interest group, a deflation bias arises. To understand the intuition behind this result, imagine that we start from a situation where there is no inflation bias and the participation constraint holds with equality. In this scenario, we show that, for instance, the government would have an incentive to increase the penalization on inflation (b) by a "small" amount, creating deflation. Why? Let us denote by ΔT_G and ΔT_{IG} the increases in the transfer paid by, respectively, the government and the interest group following the increase in b. This greater b would increase the monetary authorities' expected utility by $\Delta T_G + \Delta T_{IG}$ (because they would be rewarded for creating deflation). Therefore, the government could take advantage and extract the total "surplus" in expected utility obtained by the central bank (in excess of the reservation level). It would do so by decreasing the fixed part of its contract in $\Delta T_G + \Delta T_{IG}$, obtaining a net expected utility gain of ΔT_{IG}.

To sum up, the government, by increasing b would be made better-off. Notice that to make our explanation simpler, we have purposely ignored the effects that this increase in b has on the stabilization of output and inflation, i e., the first parts of the utility functions (appearing in (2) and (3)). The reason is that, in the terms of the envelop theorem, these are only "second-order effects" (since we departed from an optimal stabilization of inflation and output, i.e., with no inflation bias). That is, they are "negligible" in comparison with the other (first-order) effects referred to in our explanation. By an analogous reasoning, the interest group would also have an incentive to deviate in the same direction (creating deflation) from this ideal scenario with no deflation nor inflation bias.

It is worth noting that the assumption that the transfer is costly to the government and the interest group is crucial for reaching our conclusion that a deflation bias arises (notice that the bias disappears when, in (26), we set $\phi = \psi = 0$). When each principal care about the transfer paid to the central bank, there exist incentives for it to try to save these costs. How? By manipulating its contract with the aim of shifting its share of the total transfer to its counterpart. In doing so, both principals impose a negative externality to one another which results in an suboptimally low level of inflation.

Now, we study how this bias is related to the some parameters of the economy. Taking derivatives of the deflation bias, i.e., in the absolute value of the inflation bias (appearing in (26)) one finds:

$$\frac{\partial |\pi^e|}{\partial \phi} = \alpha k \psi^2 \frac{\xi}{(\psi\xi + \xi\phi + \phi\psi)^2 \beta} > 0, \tag{27}$$

$$\frac{\partial |\pi^e|}{\partial \psi} = \alpha k \phi^2 \frac{\xi}{(\psi\xi + \xi\phi + \phi\psi)^2 \beta} > 0, \tag{28}$$

$$\frac{\partial |\pi^e|}{\partial \xi} = -\frac{k\alpha\phi\psi^2 + k\alpha\phi^2\psi}{\beta (\phi\xi + \phi\psi + \xi\psi)^2} < 0, \tag{29}$$

$$\frac{\partial |\pi^e|}{\partial \beta} = -\frac{(\phi + \psi) k\alpha\phi\psi}{\beta (\phi\xi + \phi\psi + \xi\psi)^2} < 0. \tag{30}$$

As (27) and (28) shows, the deflation bias increases when the transfer paid to the central bank is more costly to the principals. On the other hand, (29) and (30) indicate that this deflation bias is reduced when there is an increase in, respectively, the central bank's valuation of the transfer and the players' concern over inflation stabilization. The intuition for these variations in the deflation bias is similar to the one just referred to understand why such bias arises.

3.2 Different Weights to Inflation

In this section we explore a setting where the interest group's output objective coincides with the government's but the former' relative weight to inflation stabilization is greater, i.e., in (2), (3) and (4) we have that $y_{IG} = y_G$ and $\lambda > \beta$.

It it widely accepted that the banks are especially vulnerable to the negative effects of price instability since their profits tend to decrease with inflation. This point has been well discussed by Posen (1995). Therefore it is no surprise that there may exist lobbies that try to influence the monetary authorities so that they put a high weight to inflation stabilization.

We analyze how the inflation bias is affected in this new scenario. In this case, we have that the utility functions of the government, the central bank and the interest group are, respectively:

$$U_G = -[\beta\pi^2 + (y - y_G)^2] - \phi(A - b\pi), \tag{31}$$

$$U_{CB} = -[\beta\pi^2 + (y - y_G)^2] + \xi[(A - b\pi) + (C - d\pi)], \tag{32}$$

$$U_{IG} = -[\lambda\pi^2 + (y - y_G)^2] - \psi(C - d\pi), \tag{33}$$

where $\lambda > \beta$. Again we look for a subgame perfect equilibrium. Therefore, we apply backward induction to the game outlined in Section 2, for the specific case analyzed in this subsection. We follow a similar procedure as the one used in the previous subsection.

In the last stage, once expectations on inflation have been formed and prior to having observed the realization of the shock (ε), the central banker chooses the value for π that solves (bearing in mind the incentive schemes designed by the government and the interest group):

$$\max_{\{\pi\}} \quad -(\beta\pi^2 + (y - y_G)^2) + \xi[(A - b\pi) + (C - d\pi)]$$

$$s.t. \qquad y = \overline{y} + \alpha(\pi - \pi^e) - \varepsilon.$$

The solution of this problem is:

$$\pi = \frac{\alpha^2\pi^e}{\beta + \alpha^2} + \frac{\alpha k}{\beta + \alpha^2} + \frac{\alpha\varepsilon}{\beta + \alpha^2} - \frac{\xi(b + d)}{2(\beta + \alpha^2)}. \tag{34}$$

Previously, the private sector takes rational expectations in (34) which results in:

$$\pi^e = \frac{\alpha k}{\beta} - \frac{\xi(b + d)}{2\beta}. \tag{35}$$

Substituting the value in (35) for the expected inflation into equation (34) and solving for π, we obtain:

$$\pi = \frac{\alpha k}{\beta} + \frac{\alpha\varepsilon}{\beta + \alpha^2} - \frac{\xi(b + d)}{2\beta}. \tag{36}$$

Now, in the first stage, the government and the interest group chose simultaneously the values of the variables that define the two contracts designed by them. In order to do so, we write the expected utilities for the government, the interest group and the central banker in terms of the strategic variables of the two principals, that is, A, b, C and d. With this aim, first we substitute (1) into (2), (31) − (33). Then, we plug the values of π^e and π (appearing in equations (35) and (36)) into the resulting three expressions for U_{CB}, U_G and U_{IG}. The expected values of these utility functions are:

$$E(U_{CB}) = \xi(A + C) + \frac{\xi^2}{4\beta}b^2 + \frac{\xi^2}{4\beta}d^2 + \frac{\xi^2}{2\beta}bd - K_0$$

$$E(U_G) = -\phi A + \frac{(\phi + \xi)\alpha k}{\beta}b - \frac{(\xi + 2\phi)\xi}{4\beta}b^2 + \frac{\alpha k\xi}{\beta}d - \frac{\xi^2}{4\beta}d^2 - \frac{(\phi + \xi)\xi}{2\beta}bd - K_0$$

$$E(U_{IG}) = -\psi C + \frac{\lambda\alpha k\xi}{\beta^2}b - \frac{\lambda\xi^2}{4\beta^2}b^2 + \frac{(\psi\beta + \lambda\xi)\alpha k}{\beta^2}d-$$

$$\frac{(2\psi\beta + \lambda\xi)\xi}{4\beta^2}d^2 - \frac{(\psi\beta + \lambda\xi)\xi}{2\beta^2}bd - K_2$$

where $K_2 = \frac{k^2(\alpha^2\lambda + \beta^2)}{\beta^2} + \frac{(\alpha^2\lambda + \beta^2)\sigma_\varepsilon^2}{(\alpha^2 + \beta)^2}$.

We now show that in this scenario where the interest group has a greater dislike for the deviations of inflation for the common desired levels, a deflation bias arises as well. However, we prove that this bias is smaller than the one occurring in the previous subsection.

Beginning by the last stage of the game, the problem to be solved by the governments is :

$$\max_{\{A,b\}} \quad -\phi A + \frac{(\phi+\xi)\alpha k}{\beta}b - \frac{(\xi+2\phi)\xi}{4\beta}b^2 + \frac{\alpha k\xi}{\beta}d - \frac{\xi^2}{4\beta}d^2 - \frac{(\phi+\xi)\xi}{2\beta}bd - K_0$$

$$s.t. \quad \xi(A+C) + \frac{\xi^2}{4\beta}b^2 + \frac{\xi^2}{4\beta}d^2 + \frac{\xi^2}{2\beta}bd - K_0 \geq Z,$$

From the Kuhn-Tucker first order conditions we conclude, again, that the indifference curves of the government and the central bank are tangent at the equilibrium point. Therefore, the equality of the marginal rates of substitution of both players yields the government's reaction function:

$$b = \frac{2\alpha k}{\xi} - \frac{\xi}{\phi + \xi}d. \tag{37}$$

On the other hand, the interest group is faced with the following problem:

$$\max_{\{C,d\}} \quad -\psi C + \frac{\lambda\alpha k\xi}{\beta^2}b - \frac{\lambda\xi^2}{4\beta^2}b^2 + \frac{(\psi\beta + \lambda\xi)\alpha k}{\beta^2}d - \frac{(2\psi\beta + \lambda\xi)\xi}{4\beta^2}d^2 - \frac{(\psi\beta + \lambda\xi)\xi}{2\beta^2}bd - K_2$$

$$s.t. \quad \xi(A+C) + \frac{\xi^2}{4\beta}b^2 + \frac{\xi^2}{4\beta}d^2 + \frac{\xi^2}{2\beta}bd - K_0 \geq Z.$$

From the first order conditions, we obtain the interest group's reaction function:

$$d = \frac{2\alpha k}{\xi} - \frac{\lambda\xi}{\psi\beta + \lambda\xi}b. \tag{38}$$

Therefore, both principals reaction functions intersect (solving (37) and (38)) when:

$$b = \frac{2\alpha\phi k(\psi\beta + \lambda\xi)}{\xi(\psi\beta\phi + \lambda\xi\phi + \psi\beta\xi)}, \tag{39}$$

$$d = \frac{2\alpha k\psi\beta(\phi + \xi)}{\xi(\psi\beta\phi + \lambda\xi\phi + \psi\beta\xi)}. \tag{40}$$

Now, substituting (39) and (40) into (36) one finds the value of inflation:

$$\pi = -\frac{\alpha k\psi\phi}{\psi\beta\phi + \lambda\xi\phi + \psi\beta\xi} + \frac{\alpha\varepsilon}{\beta + \alpha^2}, \tag{41}$$

whose first term is again negative, namely, a deflation bias also arises in this context. However, comparing the first term in (41).with the corresponding one in (26), we conclude that this bias is smaller than the one associated to the scenario studied in the previous subsection
.

In the setting studied in this subsection both principals also have incentives, as in the previous scenario, to engage in a competition for saving transfer costs. Therefore, it is no surprise that here the "side-effect" of this type of competition, i.e., a deflation bias, also occurs. However, in the present setting this bias will be smaller since the interest group has now a greater concern over this side-effect, and as a result will fuel this competition to a lesser extend.

4 Conclusions

Walsh (1995a) showed that the inflation bias to discretionary monetary policy can be eliminated if the government sets the central banker's remuneration contingent upon realized inflation. This pathbreaking paper and the subsequent literature on central bank contracts generally assumes that the monetary authorities are not benevolent in the sense that they are not only concerned about social welfare but also about pecuniary incentives. This assumption implicitly opens the possibility that other principals may offer the central banker additional contracts with the aim of exerting an influence on monetary policy.

This paper has studied how the inflation bias is affected when we extend the basic principal-agent framework to allow for the existence of a another principal, namely, a generically labelled "interest group" with preferences which are different from the government's. We have considered two scenarios where the transfer payments derived from the contracts are costly to both principals. In the first scenario, the interest group has an output objective that exceed the government's. In this context, we have shown that if both principals design competing Walsh contracts a deflation bias arises. The reason is that each principal tries to save the costs implied by the transfer, by manipulating their respective contract (i.e., by raising their respective penalization on inflation). In doing so, both the government and the interest group aim at shifting its share of the total cost of the incentive schedules to one another. In doing so, both principals impose a negative externality which results in a deflation bias. In the second scenario considered, the interest group has a greater dislike for the deviations of inflation from the common desired levels. In this setting, both principals are also engaged in a competition for saving transfer costs. However, since now the interest group is more concerned about deflation, this competition is less fierce. As a consequece a smaller deflation bias occurs.

References

Barro, R. and D. Gordon (1983a): "A positive theory of monetary policy in a natural rate model", *Journal of Political Economy*, **91**, 589-610.

Barro, R. and D. Gordon (1983b): "Rules, discretion and reputation in a model of monetary policy", *Journal of Monetary Policy*, **17**, 3-20.

Beetsma, R. and H. Jensen (1998): "Inflation targets and contracts with uncertain central banker preferences", *Journal of Money, Credit and Banking*, **30**, 384-403.

Bernanke, B. (2004): "What have we learned since October 1979?", Conference on Reflections on Monetary Policy 25 years after October 1979, Federal Reserve Bank of St. Louis, http://www.federalreserve.gov/boarddocs/speeches/2004/20041008/default.htm

Blinder, A. (1998): *Central banking in theory and practice*, MIT Press, Cambridge, MA.

Campoy, J.C. and J.C. Negrete (2006): "A decentralized and state-independent mechanism for internalizing international monetary policy spillovers", *Economic Letters*, Forthcoming.

Campoy, J.C. and J.C. Negrete (2006): "Common agency in central banking: the importance of considering the participation constraint", Mimeo.

Candel, F. and J.C. Campoy (2004): "Is the Walsh contract really optimal?", *Public Choice*, **120**, 29-39.

Chortareas, G. and S. Miller (2004): "Optimal central banker contracts and common agency", *Public Choice*, **121**, 131-155.

Dixit, A. and H.Jensen (2003): "Comon agency with rational expectations: theory and application to a monetary union', *The Economic Journal*, **113**, 539-549.

Dixit, A. and L. Lambertini (2003a): "Symbiosis of monetary and fiscal policies in a monetary union", *Journal of International Economics*, **60**, 235-247.

Dixit, A. and L. Lambertini (2003b): "Interactions of commitment and discretion in monetary and fiscal policies", *American Economic Review*, vol. 93, n. 5, 1522-1542.

Havrilesky, T. (1994): "The political economy of monetary policy", *European Journal of Political Economy*, **10**, 111-134.

Jensen, H. (2000): "Optimal monetary policy cooperation through state-independent contract with targets", *European Economic Review*, **44**, 517-539.

Kydland, F. and E. Prescott. (1977): "Rules rather than discretion: the inconsistency of optimal plans", *Journal of Political Economy*, **85**, 473-491.

Negrete, J. (2000): "Cooperative design for central banks versus cooperative implementation of monetary policy", *Review of International Economics*, **8**(2), 252-260.

Nordhaus, W. (1975): "The political business cycle", *Review of Economics Studies*, **42**, 169-190.

Persson, T. and G. Tabellini (1993): "Designing institutions for monetary stability", *Carnegie Rochester Series on Public Policy*, **39**, 33-84.

Persson, T. and G. Tabellini (1995): "Double-edged incentives: institutions and policy coordination" in Grossman and Rogoff (eds), *Handbook of International Economics*, vol 3, Amsterdam, North-Holland.

Persson, T. and G. Tabellini (2000): *Political economics. Explaining economic policy*, MIT Press, Cambridge, MA.

Posen, A. (1995): "Declarations are not enough: Financial sector sources of central bank independence", *NBER Macroeconomics Annual*, **252**-274. MIT

Rogoff, K. (1985): "The optimal degree of commitment to an intermediate monetary target", *Quarterly Journal of Economics*, **100**, 1169-1190.

Svensson, L. (1997): "Optimal inflation targets, conservative central bank, and linear inflation contracts", *American Economic Review*, **87**, 98-114.

Waller, C. (1995): "Performance contracts for central bankers", *Federal Reserve Bank of St. Louis. Economic Review*, September-October, 3-14.

Walsh, C. (1995a): "Optimal contracts for central bankers", *American Economic Review*, **85**, 150-167.

Walsh, C. (1995b): "Is New Zealand's Reserve Bank act of 1989 an optimal central bank contract"

Walsh, C. (2003). *Monetary theory and policy*. Cambridge, MA: MIT Press.

Walsh, C. (2002): "When should central bankers be fired?", *Economics of Governance*, **3**, 1-21.

Woodford, M. (2003): *Interest and prices: foundations of a theory of monetary policy*, Princeton University Press.

In: Inflation, Fiscal Policy and Central Banks
Editor: Leo N. Bartolotti, pp. 101-119

ISBN: 1-60021-122-4
© 2006 Nova Science Publishers, Inc.

Chapter 5

ESTIMATING INFLATION PERSISTENCE IN THE EURO-AREA[*]

George Hondroyiannis[**]

Bank of Greece, Economic Research Department
and Harokopio University, Athens, Greece

Abstract

The importance of inflation persistence has received considerable attention over the last two decades. This interest, especially in the recent years, is mainly due to the fact that the size of inflation persistence directly affects the conduct of monetary policy. The paper estimates inflation persistence in Euro-area employing quarterly data for the period 1971 to 2002. Four empirical procedures, the recursive OLS, the rolling OLS, the Kalman filter and the second-generation random coefficient procedures (RC), are employed to estimate inflation persistence using a univariate autoregressive (AR) modeling. The RC estimation procedure allows the profiles of the inflation persistence to be traced over time and relaxes several restrictions imposed in applied work. The empirical results from all the estimation procedures indicate that inflation persistence might have changed over this period. This empirical finding is very important since inflation persistence has immediate consequences for conducting monetary policy. Changes in the degree of inflation persistence overtime indicates different time horizons at which monetary policy successfully can preserve price stability, facilitate economic growth and achieve efficient use of resources.

Keywords: CPI inflation, persistence, structural change.

JEL Classification: E31, E37.

---

[*] The views expressed are solely of the author, and should not be interpreted as reflecting those of the Bank of Greece. I am grateful to Benoit Mojon for providing the data used in this study.

[**] Address for correspondence: George Hondroyiannis, Bank of Greece, Economic Research Department, 21 El. Venizelos, 102 50 Athens, Greece, Tel. (0030210) 320. 2429, Fax (0030210) 323. 3025, E-mail: ghondroyiannis@bankofgreece.gr

1 Introduction

Over the last two decades there has been a remarkable attention on the importance of the degree of inflation persistence. Inflation persistence refers to the tendency of inflation to converge towards the central bank's inflation target as a result of changes in this target or various other disturbances. Inflation persistence refers to the "time" it takes for inflation to react in the presence of a shock. Therefore we could view the degree of inflation persistence as the time horizon at which monetary policy successfully can preserve price stability, facilitate economic growth and achieve efficient use of resources.

It is important to understand the patterns of inflation persistence since the size of inflation persistence directly affects the conduct of monetary policy. For example, when the size of persistence is low this indicates that prices are stabilized in a shorter time period following a shock. On the contrary, when the size of persistence is high this implies that the appearance of any inflation shock will lead to longer inflation effects, impeding the effective conduct and transmission of monetary policy since longer period of time is needed to achieve the goals of policy.

However, the size of inflation persistence does not have the same implication in periods of high inflation as in periods of deflation or price stability. Persistence in high inflation periods has a negative implication, whereas in low inflation periods it may not. For example, high inflation persistence in inflationary periods implies that high inflation rates are accompanied by high inflation in the future, whereas in disinflation the inertia of inflationary expectations breaks down and inflation is steadily falling.

The definition of inflation persistence is not unanimous. Following Batini and Nelson (2001) and Batini (2002) three types of inflation persistence are distinguished. The first, the "extrinsic persistence" is due to the fluctuations of some determinants of inflation such as the output gap. The second, the "intrinsic persistence" is due to past inflation and finally, the "expectations-based persistence" is due to inflation expectations. Although in theory the distinction among the different types of inflation persistence is clear, empirically is very difficult to distinguish among the different types of inflation.

There are many empirical studies, dealing with the US economy and other industrial economies and applying different empirical methodologies that have studied inflation persistence. Most studies have found that post-war inflation in these countries exhibits very high persistence. Alogoskoufis and Smith (1991), looking at historical data for the US and the UK inflation, point out that the post-Bretton Woods regime of managed floating was associated with more persistent inflation. Bordo (1993) and Bordo and Schwartz (1999) find that inflation was more stable during the heyday of Bretton Woods. More recently, Brainard and Perry (2000), Taylor (2000), Kim, Nelson and Piger (2001) and Benati (2002) find evidence that USA inflation persistence has been lower during the Volcer-Greenspan era. Batini (2002) supports that the degree of inflation persistence in the US and the UK was rather low during the gold standard, peaked in the 1970s, and fell again in the 1990s. For other industrial and European countries, Batini (2002) and Levin and Piger (2004) find little or no evidence of an upward shift in inflation persistence in post-1980 data, while there was a substantial downward shift in the average value of inflation.[1] Finally, for the euro area Batini (2002) finds that there is a decrease in the degree of inflation persistence during the recent

---

[1] For an extensive review on inflation persistence see among others, Hondroyiannis and Lazaretou (2004).

period. Other empirical studies for the euro area have found mixed results. Empirical studies such as Altissimo, Mojon and Zaffaroni (2004), Gadzinski and Orlandi (2004), O'Reilly and Whelan (2004) and Robalo Marques (2004) find a high degree of persistence when they compute a simple estimate of the degree of inflation persistence over long time samples. Contrary, other studies such as Dossche and Everaert (2004), Gadzinski and Orlandi (2004) and Robalo Marques (2004) find a fairly low degree of inflation persistence when estimating inflation persistence over small samples or taking into account time-variations in the mean of inflation.

The present study focuses on the estimation of the degree of inflation persistence in the euro area. The paper studies the time profile of the degree of inflation persistence in the euro area applying different methodologies for the period 1971 to 2002 utilizing quarterly consumer price index data. A univariate autoregressive (AR) model for the inflation rate is estimated and the possibility of a structural break in the slope parameter and the intercept term of the AR equation are considered. For this purpose, we initially estimate inflation persistence over the total period without taking into consideration regime shifts. Next, we estimate inflation persistence taking into account structural changes during the estimation period.

Four alternative econometric procedures are employed to estimate the time varying coefficients of AR model and to trace the degree of inflation persistence over time. That is the recursive OLS, rolling OLS, Kalman filter (K) and a second generation random coefficients (RC).[2] The Kalman filter and the RC estimation procedures have the advantage that can capture the dependence structure of the series both in terms of the mean and variance. This type of modeling is employed to analyze time series when the data generating mechanism is subject to regime shifts. This type of behavior enables the estimated model to accurately capture nonlinearities and asymmetries, which are present in the inflation modeling. Inflation behavior, in many occasions, includes sharp increases and decreases. Other statistical models fail to estimate consistent and efficient parameters since they are not able to detect regime shifts and to correct the estimated model at periods when the regime changes. In addition, RC estimation has the advantage that relaxes several restrictions routinely imposed in applied work such as a specific functional form, often imposed in the empirical literature.[3] Thus, the evolution of the degree of inflation persistence can be modelled during a period of structural breaks or monetary policy regimes.

The remainder of the paper is organized as follows. Section 2 presents the empirical methodology. Section 3 discusses the empirical results from the different estimation methods. Section 4 concludes.

2   Empirical Methodology

The purpose of the empirical analysis is to estimate the evolution of the degree of inflation persistence in the euro area. Willis (2003, p.7) defines inflation persistence as the 'speed with which inflation returns to baseline after a shock'. This definition implies that the degree of inflation persistence shows the speed with which inflation responds to a shock. When the

---

[2] Hondroyiannis and Lazaretou (2004) employed similar methodology to estimate inflation persistence in Greece.
[3] For a detailed analysis on second generation RC estimates, see Swamy and Tavlas (1995, 2001).

value is high, inflation responds quickly to a shock. On the contrary, when the value is small, the speed of adjustment is low, the response of inflation to a shock is slow and the overall variability of inflation is small. Following the methodology proposed by Batini and Nelson (2001), Batini (2002) and Hondroyiannis and Lazaretou (2004), measures of inflation persistence are referred to positive serial correlation in inflation series.

2.1   Classical Estimation Analysis

The degree of inflation persistence is estimated employing different methodologies. Initially, the degree of inflation persistence is estimated employing a univariate process for inflation across different time periods, following the classical analysis, based on the approach of Batini (2002) and Levin and Piger (2004).[4] In the empirical analysis quarterly data of consumer price index (CPI) for the euro area is used for the period 1971Q1-2002Q4. A main aspect of the empirical analysis is to allow for structural breaks since failure to account for structural breaks would provide high estimates of the degree of inflation persistence.

In order to estimate the degree of inflation persistence a simple AR(k) process for the inflation series is considered

$$\Delta p_t = \text{constant} + \sum_{j=1}^{k} \alpha_j \Delta p_{t-j} + u_t$$

(1)

where Δp_t is annualized quarterly inflation, i.e. $\Delta p_t = (p_t - p_{t-1})*4$, p_t is the logarithm of the CPI, α_j is the autoregressive coefficient and u_t is a serially uncorrelated, but possibly heteroskedastic, random error term.

As in Andrews and Chen (1994), a measure of the degree of inflation persistence is the sum of the estimated lagged-terms autoregressive coefficients, i.e. $\rho \equiv \sum \alpha_j$, where ρ indicates the parameter of persistence. To measure persistence in terms of the sum of AR(k) coefficients, equation (1) is formulated as follows,

$$\Delta p_t = \text{constant} + \rho \cdot \Delta p_{t-1} + \sum_{j=1}^{k-1} \beta_j \Delta \Delta p_{t-j} + u_t$$

(2)

where ρ is the persistence parameter, while β_j parameters are transformations of AR coefficients in equation (1), $\beta_{k-1} = -\alpha_k$. The inflation process has a unit root if ρ takes a value close to unity. The parameter ρ provides a reduced-form measure of inflation persistence, namely it directly measures the degree with which the inflation process responds to shocks.

Estimating equation (2), a measure of inflation persistence is obtained, while the regression on a constant produces estimates of the sample mean of inflation and its standard deviation. Before estimating equation (2) it is necessary to choose the appropriate number of lag order. The AR(k) lag order is chosen based on both Akaike Information Criterion and Schwarz Criterion.

---

[4] Hondroyiannis and Lazaretou (2004) employed the same methodology for Greece.

In addition, we test for multiple breaks in the average inflation and multiple breaks in the slope (persistence) using the test developed by Bai and Perron (1998, 2003). Bai and Peron (1998) suggested a method based on sequential testing of the null hypothesis of l breaks against the alternative of l+1 breaks employing the sup $F_T(l+1/l)$ type test. In addition, Bai and Perron (2003) showed that the performance of this procedure could be improved by estimating the double maximum tests, namely UD max $F_T(M,q)$ and WD max $F_T(M,q)$, where M is the maximum number of breaks and p is the number of parameters allowed to structural change, in order to detect at least one break point.

Further to the detection of multiple breaks we investigate how stable the estimated parameters are. Therefore, equation 2 is estimated without dummy variables employing recursive and rolling OLS. This is a first effort to investigate the time profile of the estimated coefficients and present the evolution of the degree of inflation persistence.

2.2 Kalman Filter Estimates

An alternative methodology to estimate the time profile of the degree of inflation persistence is the state space modeling. The advantage of this method in the estimation of a dynamic system is that it allows unobserved variables to be incorporated and estimated along with the observed model. In particular, a linear single equation model with time varying parameters is estimated. The linear model for a variable Y_t takes the following general form

$$Y_t = C_t + B_t X_t + u_t$$

where B_t is a vector of unobserved state variables which are generated from the following process

$$B_{t+1} = D_t + T_t B_t + v_t$$

and C_t, $X_{t,}$, D_t and T_t are conformable vectors and matrices and u_t and v_t are error terms with zero mean. The first equation is called the "signal" equation while the second the "state" equation. Equation (2) is estimated employing the Kalman filter, which is a recursive algorithm for sequentially updating the one step ahead estimate of the state mean and variance given new information. In the empirical analysis the Y_t variable is the inflation rate and the unobserved vector B_t is the degree of inflation persistence.

2.3 Random Coefficients Estimation Method

Finally, another alternative approach to measuring the degree of inflation persistence is the RC methodology.[5] Consider the simple AR(k) process of the previous section, i.e. equation (2), which we reproduce for convenience here,

---

[5] For other recent applications of RC methodology on inflation persistence see Hondroyiannis and Lazaretou (2004) and on different topics, see Hondroyiannis, Swamy and Tavlas (2000, 2001a, b) and Brissimis, Hondroyiannis, Swamy and Tavlas (2003).

$$\Delta p_t = \beta_0 + \rho \Delta p_{t-1} + \sum_{j=1}^{k} \beta_j \Delta\Delta p_{t-j} + u_t \tag{2}$$

where Δp_t is the annualized inflation rate ($\Delta p_t = (p_t - p_{t-1})*4$), p_t is the logarithm of the CPI) and $\Delta\Delta p_{t-j}$ is the second difference of inflation, while β_j parameters are transformations of AR coefficients in equation (1) and u_t is a serially uncorrelated but possibly heteroskedastic random error term. Two lags are used in the estimation as in the OLS estimation. The degree of persistence is equal to the value of the estimated ρ coefficient.

Standard estimation procedures often impose a number of restrictions when applied to equations such as equation (2) above, including the following: (i) β_0, ρ, β_1, and β_2 are constant; (ii) excluded explanatory variables are proxied by an error term and, therefore, these excluded variables are assumed to have means equal to zero and to be mean independent of the included explanatory variables;(iii) the true functional form is known (whether linear or nonlinear); and, (iv) the variables are not subject to measurement error.

Swamy and Tavlas (1995, 2001) and Chang, Swamy, Hallaham and Tavlas (2000) define that, first, any variable or value that is not mis-measured is true (definition I) and, second, any economic relationship with the correct functional form, without any omitted explanatory variable and without mis-measured variables is true (definition II). Using these definitions, we can specify a class of functions which is wide enough to cover the true inflation persistence function. To rewrite this class in a form that has the same explanatory variables as equation (2), we assume that explanatory variables that are in the true inflation persistence function but excluded from equation (2) are related (linearly or nonlinearly) to the explanatory variables included in equation (2). This assumption is reasonable, given that economic variables are rarely, if ever, uncorrelated and may not be linearly related to each other. To account for measurement errors, we assume that each variable in equation (2) is the sum of the underlying true value and the appropriate measurement error. These assumptions imply that equation (2) does not correspond to the true inflation persistence function unless it is changed to:

$$\Delta p_t = \gamma_{ot} + \gamma_{1t} \Delta p_{t-1} + \gamma_{2t} \Delta\Delta p_{t-1} + \gamma_{3t} \Delta\Delta p_{t-2}, \quad t=1,2,..,T, \tag{3}$$

where the real-world interpretations of the coefficients follow from the derivation of equation (3): γ_{0t} is the sum of three parts: (a) the intercept of the inflation persistence equation; (b) the joint effect on the true value of Δp_t of the portions of excluded variables remaining after the effects of the true values of the included explanatory variables have been removed; and (c) the measurement error in Δp_t. The coefficient γ_{1t} (γ_{2t} or γ_{3t}), which is the estimated persistence, is also the sum of three parts: (a) a bias-free effect of the true value of Δp_{t-1} ($\Delta\Delta p_{t-1}$ or $\Delta\Delta p_{t-2}$) on the true value of Δp_t; (b) a term capturing omitted-variables bias; and (c) a mis-measurement effect due to mis-measuring Δp_{t-1} ($\Delta\Delta p_{t-1}$ or $\Delta\Delta p_{t-2}$) (see Chang, Swamy, Hallaham and Tavlas 2000). The bias-free effects provide economic explanations. An implication of these interpretations is that the explanatory variables of equation (3) are correlated with their coefficients. With these correlations, none of the explanatory variables is exogenous. The effects of such dynamic factors as technical change in the economic activity and excluded lagged explanatory variables are captured in the omitted-variables bias component of each of the coefficients of equation (3). Consequently, equation (3) is a dynamic specification.

One question that needs to be answered before estimating equation (3) is that of parameterization: which features of equation (3) ought to be treated as constant parameters? Inconsistencies arise if this parameterization is not consistent with the real-world interpretations of γ's. To achieve consistency, the γ's are estimated using coefficient drivers. A formal definition of coefficient drivers is provided in Chang, Swamy, Hallaham and Tavlas (2000) and Swamy and Tavlas (2001). Intuitively, these may be viewed as variables that are not included in the equation used to estimate inflation persistence, but help deal with the correlations between the γ's and the included explanatory variables (Δp_{t-1}, $\Delta\Delta p_{t-1}$, $\Delta\Delta p_{t-2}$).

Assumption I. The coefficients of equation (3) are linear functions of λ variables, called coefficient drivers, including a constant term with added error terms which may be contemporaneously and serially correlated. The error terms are mean independent of the coefficient drivers.

Assumption II. The explanatory variables of equation (3) are independent of their coefficients' error terms, given any values of the coefficient drivers.

Assumption II captures the idea that the explanatory variables of equation (3) can be independent of their coefficients conditional on the given values of coefficient drivers even though they are not unconditionally independent of their coefficients. This property provides a useful procedure for consistently estimating the bias-free effects contained in the coefficients of equation (3).

Under Assumptions I and II, equation (3) can be written as

$$\Delta p_t = \pi_{00} z_{0t} + \sum_{j=1}^{\lambda-1} \pi_{0j} z_{jt} + \pi_{10}\Delta p_{t-1} z_{0t} + \sum_{j=1}^{\lambda-1} \pi_{1j} z_{jt}\Delta p_{t-1} + \pi_{20}\Delta\Delta p_{t-1} z_{0t} + \sum_{j=1}^{\lambda-1} \pi_{2j} z_{jt}\Delta\Delta p_{t-1} +$$
$$\pi_{30}\Delta\Delta p_{t-2} z_{0t} + \sum_{j=1}^{\lambda-1} \pi_{3j} z_{jt}\Delta\Delta p_{t-2} + \varepsilon_{0t} + \varepsilon_{1t}\Delta p_{t-1} + \varepsilon_{2t}\Delta\Delta p_{t-1} + \varepsilon_{3t}\Delta p_{t-2} \quad (4)$$

where the z's denote "coefficient drivers" and the ε's denote the error terms of the coefficients of equation (3).[6] In our empirical work we set λ=4, z_{0t}=1 for all t, z_{1t} is the annualized GDP deflator, z_{2t} is the short-term interest rate and z_{3t} is the unemployment rate.[7,8] This means that we use four coefficient drivers to estimate the γ's. We are attempting to capture the bias-free effect contained in γ_{1t} by using a linear function $(\pi_{10} + \pi_{11} z_{1t})$ of the annualized rate of GDP deflator. The biased and mis-measurement effects are captured by using a function $(\pi_{12} z_{2t} + \pi_{13} z_{3t} + \varepsilon_{1t})$ of the short term interest rate, unemployment rate

---

[6] Adding coefficient drivers successively should reduce the RMSE of the estimated regressions.

[7] Economic theory provides many categories of variables that may, indirectly or directly, influence the inflation process. In particular, interest rates reflect monetary conditions in the economy. Unemployment reflects the labor market conditions. It is often argued that labor markets in Europe are rigid. High firing costs, unemployment benefits and strong unions contribute to high unemployment and slow labor adjustment. Cross country evidence shows a positive relationship between unemployment and inflation persistence. Output is considered as a measure of demand pressure and thus affects inflation expectations.

[8] All data are obtained from Eurostat.

and ε_{1t}. The measures of bias-free effects contained in γ_{2t} and γ_{3t} are $\pi_{20} + \pi_{21}z_{1t}$ and $\pi_{30} + \pi_{31}z_{1t}$, respectively, and those of omitted-variable and mis-measurement effects contained in γ_{2t} and γ_{3t} are $\pi_{22}z_{2t} + \pi_{23}z_{3t} + \varepsilon_{2t}$ and $\pi_{32}z_{2t} + \pi_{33}z_{3t} + \varepsilon_{3t}$, respectively. The components of the coefficients of equation (3) can take different values in different phases of the business cycle. Inflation persistence is estimated as the value of γ_{1t} to estimate the total effect (biased effect) and the estimated value of $(\pi_{10} + \pi_{11}z_{1t\,2t})$, to estimate the bias-free effect. Inflation persistence may be lower in periods of low inflation compared to periods of high inflation. Consequently, changes in the values of the included explanatory variables that occur during the peak of a business cycle may exhibit very different effects on persistence than the same changes that occur during the trough of a business cycle. If so, more accurate results can be obtained by taking changing conditions into account.

Note that equation (4) has four error terms, three of which are the products of ε's and the included explanatory variables of equation (1). The sum of these four terms is both heteroskedastic and serially correlated. Under Assumptions I and II, the right-hand side of equation (4) with the last four terms suppressed gives the conditional expectation of the left-hand side variable as a nonlinear function of the conditioning variables. This conditional expectation is different from the right-hand side of equation (1) with u_t suppressed. This result shows that the addition of a single error term to an equation and the exclusion of the interaction terms on the right-hand side equation (4) introduce inconsistencies in the usual situations where measurement errors and omitted-variable biases are present and the true functional forms are unknown. A computer program developed by Chang, Swamy, Hallaham and Tavlas (2000) is used to estimate equation (4).

3   Empirical Results

3.1   Classical Estimation Empirical Results

Initially, equation 2 is estimated for the whole period 1971Q1 to 2002Q4. Before estimation the appropriate number of lags is estimated. Given the quarterly frequency of data the maximum lag length k is equal to five. Based on both Akaike Information Criterion and Schwarz Criterion, a lag of 2 is chosen for the inflation series. Table 1 presents the estimates on the degree of inflation persistence.

We test for the case of multiple breaks in the average inflation and multiple breaks in the slope (persistence) using the test developed by Bai and Perron (1998, 2003). The empirical analysis, based on the statistics developed by Bai and Perron, suggests the existence of two break points for the average inflation. The first is located in 1984Q1 and the second in 1995Q1. Therefore, equation 2 is estimated employing two dummy variables. The first dummy variable takes the value 1 for the period 1984Q2-1995Q1 and the second dummy takes the value one for the period 1995Q2-2002Q4. The empirical results, from the OLS estimation, indicate that the estimated inflation persistence for the total period is 0.94. Contrary, when the two dummies are included in the regression equation to account for changes in the mean the persistence parameter is reduced to 0.58.

Table 1. OLS Estimates of Inflation Persistence in Euro Area
(Sample Period 1971Q1-2002Q4)

Variables	Model 1	Model 2	Model 3	Model 4	Model 5
Constant	0.059***	0.003	0.042***	0.010***	0.04***
	(17.64)	(1.02)	(4.67)	(2.78)	(4.65)
Δp_{t-1}		0.940***	0.580***	0.703***	0.445***
		(20.97)	(6.47)	(8.45)	(4.29)
D1			-0.025***		-0.018**
			(-4.32)		(-2.92)
D2			-0.034***		-0.030***
			(-4.39)		(-3.90)
$D3*\Delta p_{t-1}$				0.203***	0.164**
				(3.33)	(2.44)
Adj-R^2	0.00	0.78	0.81	0.79	0.81
Se	0.038	0.018	0.017	0.017	0.016
DW	0.29	2.14	2.09	2.16	2.11
LM(2)		1.64	3.62	4.11	2.77
ARCH(1)		2.80	1.16	2.97	2.17
ARCH(2)		1.64	0.58	1.63	1.10

Notes: The lag length structure of $\sum_{j=1}^{k} \beta_j \Delta\Delta p_{t-j}$ term is determined using the Akaike and Schwarz criteria. Two lags are employed for all the estimated regressions except model 1. ***, ** indicate significance at 1% and 5% respectively.

Next we test for multiple breaks in the slope. One break is detected in 1982Q2. The OLS equation is re-estimated employing one dummy, D3 for the slope. The dummy variable takes the value one for the period 1971Q1-1982Q2 and zero otherwise. The results of OLS estimates indicate a change in the persistence parameter from 0.90 in the first period (1971Q1-1982Q2) to 0.70 in the second period (1982Q3-2002Q4). Finally, all the dummies, that is the two dummies that detect changes in the mean and the dummy that detects changes in the slope, are incorporated into the OLS estimation. The OLS estimates indicate that the degree of persistence declines from 0.61 in the first period (1971Q1-1982Q2) to 0.44 in the second period (1982Q3-2002Q4).

To investigate how stable the estimated parameters are, equation 2 is estimated without dummy variables employing recursive and rolling OLS. For the rolling OLS estimation, two alternative window sizes of 40 and 48 are estimated. Figures 1, 2 and 3 present the estimates for the constant and the degree of inflation persistence employing recursive and rolling OLS. The estimates of recursive OLS show that the degree of persistence increased during the last period. Contrary, the estimates of rolling OLS for both window sizes show a decline of the degree of inflation persistence.

Figure 1
Recursive OLS Estimates

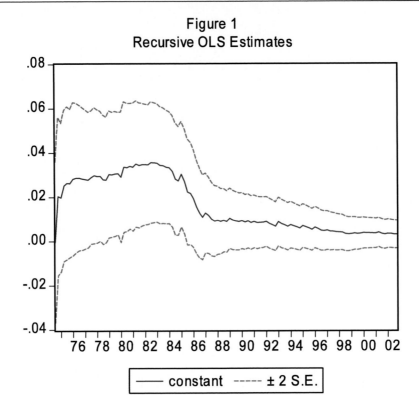

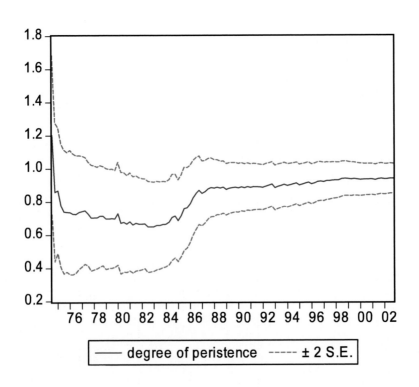

Figure 2 Rolling OLS Estimates of Inflation Persistence
(Window size 40)

Rolling Estimates of the Constant

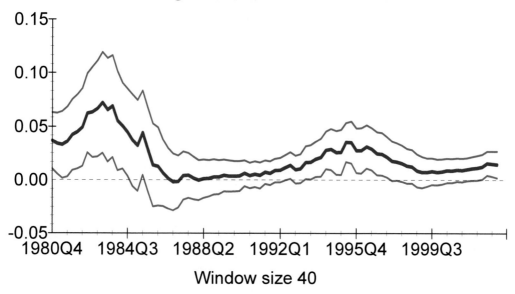

Window size 40

Rolling Estimates of the Degree of Persistence

Window size 40

3.2 Kalman Filter Empirical Results

Equation 2 is estimated using the Kalman filter estimation technique. The exact specification employed in the empirical estimation of Kalman filter is described by the following equations

Figure 3 Rolling OLS Estimates of Inflation Persistence
(Window size 48)

Rolling Estimates of the Constant

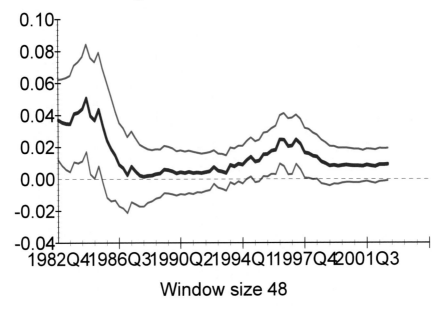

Window size 48

Rolling Estimates of the Degree of Persistence

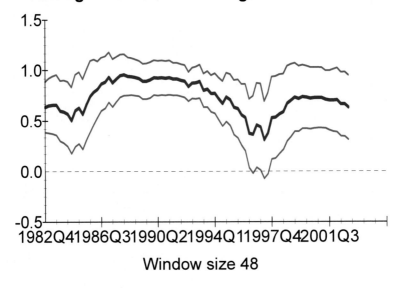

Window size 48

Signal equation

$$\Delta p_t = SV1 + SV2\Delta p_{t-1} + \sum \beta_j \Delta\Delta p_{t-j} + u_t$$

State equations

$$SV1 = SV1(-1)$$

$$SV2 = SV2(-1)$$

where SV1 and SV2 are the time varying coefficients. The first represents the constant and the second is the degree of inflation persistence. Figure 4 presents the evolution of the two time varying coefficients. The empirical results show a decline of the degree of inflation persistence until 1986. After 1986 the degree of inflation persistence increases in the euro area at a level of 0.67.

3.3   RC Estimation Empirical Results

The RC model is initially estimated with one coefficient driver, the constant term, and the estimated RMSE[9] is equal to 0.0136. Next the RC model is estimated employing two coefficient drivers, the constant and the annualized GDP deflator, and the estimated RMSE is equal 0.0123.When a third coefficient driver is added, that is the short term interest rate, the estimated RMSE is equal to 0.0083. Finally, the RC model is estimated employing four coefficient drivers, the constant, the annualized GDP deflator, the short-term interest rate and the unemployment rate and the estimated RMSE is equal to 0.0078. Figures 5 and 6 present the results from RC estimation with four coefficient drivers. Figure 5 presents the unbiased and bias-free inflation persistence (left scale) the actual inflation and the average inflation conditional on two breaks (right scale). Figure 6 presents the bias-free estimated coefficient for the constant (left scale), the actual inflation, the average inflation conditional on two breaks and the estimated long-run inflation (right scale).

The estimated bias-free average inflation persistence is 0.56, which is lower compared to OLS estimate. The average value of inflation persistence was 0.45 during the period 1971Q1-1984Q1, 0.61 for the period 1984Q1-1995Q1and 0.68 for the period 1995Q2-2002Q4. The RC results show a rise in the degree of inflation persistence, from 0.41 in the beginning of the period to 0.68 in the end of the period. This last estimate is close to the Kalman filter estimation method. Overall the empirical results indicate that as the mean value of inflation dropped from 9.7% in the first period to 1.8% in the end of the period, the degree of inflation persistence increased from 0.45 in 1971 Q1 to 0.68 in 2002 Q4 (bias-free effect). This estimate is similar to the estimate from the Kalman filter methodology.

---

[9] The estimation period for all RC models is 1971 Q1-2000 Q4 and the forecast period is 2001 Q1-2002 Q4. The estimation period for Figures 5 and 6 is 1971 Q1-2002 Q4.

Figure 4 Kalman Filter Estimates of Inflation Persistence

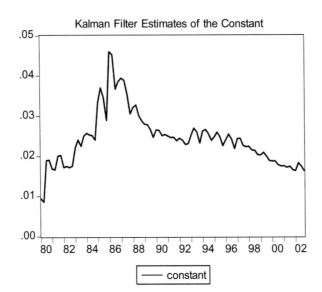

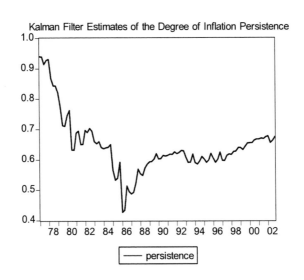

ROLS and recursive OLS provide much higher estimates, which are due to omitted-variable and measurement-error biases. ROLS estimation for different size windows is a way of testing for stability if the structure is changing. However, ROLS estimation does not give consistent estimates of the changing parameters. Unlike RC estimation, an underlying assumption of rolling and recursive estimation is that the coefficients are constant. Also, recursive estimation does not write off the past. Rolling estimation writes off the past slowly as the estimation period changes. If a regime change has occurred, it averages the old regime with the new regime with changing weights; the weight of the new regime becomes larger as more and more observations are added. Using recursive estimation, the best estimate of a model is that produced by the entire sample. In contrast, RC estimation picks up a new regime quickly. By consistently estimating changing coefficients, it attempts to estimate how the true coefficient is changing at each point in time. Therefore, the RC estimates are the true degree of persistence implying the true response of inflation to a shock at each point in time.

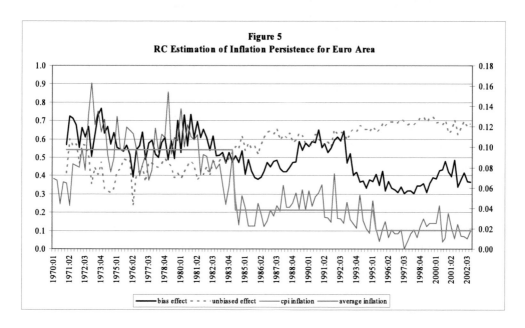

Figure 5
RC Estimation of Inflation Persistence for Euro Area

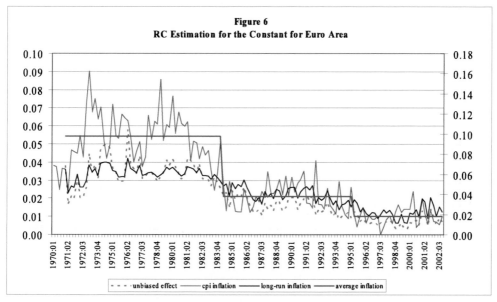

Figure 6
RC Estimation for the Constant for Euro Area

Finally, Table 2 summarizes the results from all the methodologies employed in the empirical an analysis. The first column of the table presents the actual inflation over the corresponding period. Next, for each methodology, the estimated long-un inflation and the estimated persistence parameter are presented. Both OLS and RC procedures estimate long-run inflation very close to the actual.

Table 2. Summary of the Empirical Estimates of Inflation Persistence in the Euro Area

Period	Actual Average Inflation	OLS estimation		Kalman filter estimation		RC estimation	
		Long-run inflation	Inflation Persistence	Long-run inflation	Inflation Persistence	Long-run inflation	Inflation Persistence
1971Q1-2002Q4	0.0581	0.0534	0.940			0.0444	0.574
1971Q1-1984Q1	0.0975	0.099	0.580			0.0609	0.445
1984Q2-1995Q1	0.0384	0.0392	0.580	0.0686	0.581	0.0400	0.605
1995Q2-2002Q4	0.0181	0.0184	0.580	0.0563	0.637	0.0223	0.683
1971Q1-1982Q2	0.103	0.106	0.900			0.0615	0.438
1982Q3-2002Q4	0.036	0.0337	0.700	0.0637	0.609	0.0348	0.625

Notes: The estimation period for all OLS and RC models is 1971 Q1-2000 Q4 and the forecast period is 2001 Q1-2002 Q4. The RMSE for OLS without dummy variables is 0.0164, with the two dummy variables for the constant is 0.0103, when the dummy for the slope is employed, RMSE is equal to 0.0190 and finally when the three dummies are included (two for the constant and one for the slope) RMSE is equal to 0.0109. The RMSE for the RC model with the four coefficient drivers is 0.0078. Kalman filter estimation starts after 1980 Q1.

4   Conclusion

Recent theoretical and empirical works have studied the fundamental importance of inflation persistence since the size of inflation persistence has important implications in terms of economic efficiency and wealth distribution for the economy. The knowledge of the degree of inflation persistence allows the policy makers to form the appropriate monetary policy to maintain price stability. In this paper various methodologies are employed to estimate the evolution of the degree of inflation persistence in the euro area. The paper empirically estimates the degree of inflation persistence employing recursive and rolling OLS, Kalman filter estimation and RC estimation. The RC estimation method relaxes key restrictions typically made in empirical work so that the estimated coefficients provide the closest possible approximations to the correct underlying model, taking into account asymmetries and nonlinearities that appear in inflation and allows an assessment of how the degree of inflation persistence changes over time.

From the empirical analysis significant conclusions can be drawn about the evolution of the degree of inflation persistence in the euro area. First, it appears the inflation persistence is not constant over the estimated period and is time varying. Second, the empirical results suggest that the degree of inflation persistence has fallen in the more recent period. Third, taking into account changes in monetary policy regime either by restricting the sample or by estimating the evolution of the degree of inflation persistence the empirical findings imply that the degree of inflation persistence may have fallen over the last decade.

The empirical results are consistence with other empirical studies that show that inflation persistence has fallen in the recent regime of low and stable inflation. These empirical results might imply that inflation can be stabilized in shorter time following a shock. A lower degree of persistence implies that the policy maker must respond relatively less aggressively to inflationary shocks. However, the presence of a large degree of uncertainty about the inflation persistence should be taken under consideration when conducting monetary policy. A possible increase of the inflation rate above the level which is consistent with price stability may increase inflation persistence, imposing an additional constraint to the European Central Bank to keep inflation low and avoid further increase. Therefore, the policy makers should respond cautiously to inflation disturbances and assign more weight to long-run price stability which unavoidably leads to a reduction in inflation persistence.

References

Alogoskoufis, G. and Smith, R. (1991), 'The Phillips Curve, the Persistence of Inflation and the Lucas Critique: Evidence from Exchange Rate Regime, *American Economic Review*, Vol. 81, pp. 1254-1275.

Altissimo, F., Mojon, B. and Zaffaroni P. (2004), 'Fast Micro and Slow macro: Can Aggregation Explain the Persistence of Inflation', *Mimeo, ECB*.

Andrews, D. and Chen, W. K. (1994), 'Approximately Median-Unbiased Estimation of Autoregressive Models', *Journal of Business and Economic Statistics*, Vol. 12, pp. 187-204.

Bai, J. and Perron, E. (1998), 'Estimating and Testing Linear Models with Multiple Structural Changes', *Econometrica*, Vol. 66, pp. 47-78.

Bai, J. and Perron, E. (2003), 'Computation and Analysis of Multiple Structural Change Models', *Journal of Applied Econometrics*, Vol. 18, pp. 1-22.

Batini, N. (2002), 'Euro Area Inflation Persistence', *ECB, Working Paper*, No. **201**, December.

Batini, N. and Nelson, E. (2001), 'The Lag from Monetary Policy Actions to Inflation: Friedman Revisited', *International Finance*, Vol. 4, No. 3, pp. 381-400.

Benati, L. (2002), 'Investigating Inflation Persistence across Monetary Regimes', *Bank of England, mimeo.*

Bordo, M. D. (1993), 'The Bretton Woods International Monetary System: An Historical Overview', in M. D. Bordo and Eichengreen, B. (eds.), *A Retrospective on the Bretton Woods System*, Chicago University Press, pp. 3-108.

Bordo, M. D. and Schwartz, A. J. (1999), 'Under What Circumstances, Past and Present, Have International Rescues of Countries in Financial Distress Been Successful?', *Journal of International Money and Finance*, Vol. 18, pp. 683-708.

Brainard, W. and Perry, G. (2000), 'Making Policy in a Changing World', in Perry G. and Tobin, J. eds, Economic Events, Ideas and Policies: The 1960s and after, Brookings Institution, Washington DC.

Brissimis, S. N., Hondroyiannis, G., Swamy, P.A.V.B. and Tavlas, G. S. (2003), 'Empirical Modelling of Money Demand in Periods of Structural Change: The Case of Greece', *Oxford Bulletin of Economics and Statistics*, Vol. 65, No. 5, pp. 605-628.

Chang, I.L., Swamy, P.A.V.B., Hallaham, C. and Tavlas, G. S. (2000), 'A Computational Approach to Finding Causal Economic Laws', *Computational Economics*, Vol. 16, pp. 105-36.

Dossche, M. and Everaert, G. (2004) 'Measuring Inflation Persistence: A Structural Time Series Approach', *Mimeo, National Bank of Belgium.*

Gadzinski, G. and Orlandi F. (2004), 'Inflation Persistence for the EU Countries, the Euro areaand the US', *ECB Working Paper*, No. **414**.

Hondroyiannis, G. and Lazaretou S. (2004), 'Inflation Persistence during Periods of Structural Change: An Assessment Using Greek Data', *ECB Working Paper*, No. 370.

Hondroyiannis, G., Swamy, P.A.V.B. and Tavlas, G. S. (2000), 'Is the Japanese Economy in a Liquidity Trap?', *Economics Letters*, Vol. 66, pp. 17-23.

Hondroyiannis, G., Swamy, P.A.V.B. and Tavlas, G. S. (2001a), 'The Time-Varying Performance of the Long-Run Demand for Money in the United States', *Economic Inquiry,* Vol. 39, No. 1, pp. 111-123.

Hondroyiannis, G., Swamy, P.A.V.B. and Tavlas, G. S. (2001b), 'Modelling the Long-run Demand for Money in the UK: A Random Coefficient Analysis', *Economic Modelling*, Vol. 18, No.3, pp. 475-501.

Kim, C., Nelson, C. and Piger J. M. (2001), 'The Less-Volatile U.S. Economy: A Bayesian Investigation of Timing Breadth and Potential Explanations', *mimeo Federal Reserve Bank of St. Louis.*

Levin, A. T. and Piger, J. M. (2004), 'Is Inflation Persistence Intrinsic in Industrial Economies?', *ECB Working paper* No. **334**.

O'Reilly, G. and Whelan K. (2004), 'Has Euro-area Inflation Persistence Changed over Time?', *ECB Working paper* No. **335**.

Robalo Marques, C. (2004), 'Inflation Persistence: Facts or Artefacts?' *ECB Working Paper No. 371.*

Swamy, P.A.V.B. and Tavlas, G. S. (1995), 'Random Coefficient Models: Theory and Applications', *Journal of Economic Surveys*, Vol. 9, pp. 165-96.

Swamy, P.A.V.B. and Tavlas, G. S. (2001), 'Random Coefficient Models' in Baltagi, B. H. (ed.), *Companion to Theoretical Econometrics*, Basil Blackwell, Oxford, pp. 410-28.

Taylor, J. B. (2000), 'Low Inflation, Pass-Through and the Pricing Powers of Firms', *European Economic Review*, Vol. 44, pp. 1389-1408.

Willis, J. L. (2003), 'Implications of Structural Changes in the US Economy for Pricing Behavior and Inflation Dynamics'*, Economic Review, Federal Reserve of Kansas City*, First Quarter, pp. 5-24.

In: Inflation, Fiscal Policy and Central Banks
Editor: Leo N. Bartolotti, pp. 121-131

ISBN: 1-60021-122-4

Chapter 6

HOW PRODUCTIVE IS GOVERNMENT EMPLOYMENT? EVIDENCE FROM A SAMPLE OF OECD COUNTRIES

Georgios Karras[*]

University of Illinois at Chicago, February 2004

Abstract

This paper updates the research in Karras (2000) estimating the productivity of government and private employment for a panel of 22 OECD economies over the 1961-2001 period, effectively adding the decade of the 1990s to the time frame of the earlier study.The paper finds that (i) the output elasticity of private employment is six to seven times higher than government employment's; (ii) the difference between the marginal products of private and government employment is not statistically significant, so that government employment can be characterized as neither overprovided nor underprovided; and (iii) in most of the countries examined, government workers continue to be overpaid in the sense that the government/private wage ratio exceeds the corresponding ratio of marginal products.

JEL classification: E24, E62.

Keywords: Employment, Government Employment, Productivity, Wages.

1 Introduction

This paper updates the research in Karras (2000), investigating the productivity of government employment in a sample of twenty-two OECD countries during the period 1961-2001, effectively extending the period of analysis by a decade (the 1990s).Estimating the productivity of government employment is important not only because we would like to compare it to the productivity of private employment, but also because it will allow us to

---

[*] Professor of Economics; Mailing Address: Department of Economics, University of Illinois at Chicago, 601 S. Morgan St., Chicago, IL 60607-7121; e-mail: gkarras@uic.edu.

examine the extent to which wage differentials between the government and private sectors reflect differences in their labor productivities.

While a substantial amount of empirical research has been devoted to estimating the productivity effects of government *capital*, the productivity of government *employment* has been the topic of a much smaller number of studies.[1]Recent developments, however, have increased the urgency of this line of research.Budgetary pressures, labor market reforms, privatization, and other policies have resulted in a certain amount of government downsizing which may be expected to persist, and which has serious implications for the labor market in terms of both prices and quantities.The critical issue for policy makers is the determination of the optimal participation of the government in the labor market.Is government employment overprovided?How high should government wages be?In order to address these questions we must have a clear idea of how productive government employment is, particularly in relation to private employment's productivity. This is the subject of the present paper.

Using annual data from the period 1961-2001 for 22 OECD countries during the 1961-1992 period, the paper estimates that the output elasticities of private and government employment are statistically significantly different from each other, private employment's elasticity being 6 to 7 times higher than government employment's.At the same time, the difference between the marginal products of private and government employment is statistically insignificant.This suggests that government employment can be characterized as neither overprovided nor underprovided, and thus, shifting employment from one sector to the other is not likely to produce substantial output gains.Finally, in the majority of the countries examined, government workers appear to be overpaid in the sense that the government/private wage ratio exceeds the highest estimated value of the corresponding ratio of marginal products.

The rest of the paper is organized as follows.The empirical methodology is outlined in section 2, while section 3 discusses the data sources and definitions.The empirical results are presented and discussed in section 4.Section 5 examines whether the ratio of private to government wages corresponds to the ratio of marginal products, on a country-by-country basis.Section 6 concludes.

2   Empirical Methodology

The methodology implements a modification of the approach of Karras (2000).Assume that the production function is given by

$$Y_{i,t} = A_{i,t} F\left(N_{i,t}^P, N_{i,t}^G, K_{i,t}\right),\qquad(1)$$

where i indexes over countries and t over time, Y is real output, A is total factor productivity, N^P is private employment, N^G is government employment, and K is the capital stock at the

---

[1] This literature on the effects of government *capital* is well known.Contributions by Aschauer (1989), Evans and Karras (1994a), Holtz-Eakin (1994), and others, have focused on U.S. aggregate and state data.Berndt and Hanson (1992), Evans and Karras (1994b), Girard, Gruber, and Hurst (1995), de Haan, Sturm, and Sikken (1996), among others, have investigated data from Europe and other OECD countries.Gramlich (1994) and Sturm, Kuper, and de Haan (1996) survey this literature.For the effects of government *employment*, in addition to Karras (2000), see Demekas and Kontolemis (2000), and Algan, Cahuc, and Zylberberg (2002) who also survey the related literature.

beginning of the period.It is assumed that F is time-invariant and twice continuously differentiable with $F_j > 0$, and $F_{jj} < 0$, for $j = 1,2,3$.Barro and Sala-i-Martin (1995) discuss some of the properties of production functions such as this.

Differentiating equation (1) with respect to time and dividing by Y, we obtain

$$\left(\frac{\dot{Y}}{Y}\right)_{i,t} = a^P \left(\frac{\dot{N}^P}{N^P}\right)_{i,t} + a^G \left(\frac{\dot{N}^G}{N^G}\right)_{i,t} + MPK \left(\frac{\dot{K}}{Y}\right)_{i,t} + u_{i,t}, \qquad (2)$$

where a dot indicates a time derivative, and $u_{i,t} = \left(\dot{A}/A\right)_{i,t}$ is multifactor productivity growth.[2]The parameters to be estimated are $a^P = \left(\partial F/\partial N^P\right)\left(N^P/Y\right)$ and $a^G = \left(\partial F/\partial N^G\right)\left(N^G/Y\right)$, the elasticities of output with respect to private and government employment, respectively; and $MPK = \partial F/\partial K$, the marginal product of capital.Empirical estimation of equation (2) will also permit an evaluation of the marginal products of private and government employment, MPN^P and MPN^G, respectively.This in turn will allow us to compare them, and examine whether private and government workers are paid in proportion to their marginal productivities.

Of course, an important caveat to keep in mind is that, in the national accounts, the "output" of the public sector is measured by its costs (including wage payments).While in a certain sense, therefore, a government worker produces what he or she costs, this does not mean that his or her marginal product is his or her wage because this would ignore any effects on the output of the private sector.Ideally, one would like to estimate separate production functions for the private and public sectors, but current data availability prohibits it.

3   The Data

All data are from the OECD Statistical Compendium on CD-ROM.Output is measured by Real GDP, and total investment by Real Gross Fixed Capital Formation.Both series are expressed in constant prices and are obtained from the National Accounts, Volume I database.Total and government employment are obtained from the Economic Outlook database, and private employment is calculated as the difference between the total and government series.Compensation per employee (private sector) is used for the private wage, and the government wage is calculated by dividing the wage component of government consumption by government employment.These series are also from Economic Outlook.

Since 1960, government employment in the OECD has varied significantly both across countries and over time.The first data column of Table 1 reports government employment as a fraction of total employment for 22 OECD countries, averaged over the 1961-2001 period.The average share of government employment has ranged from 7.87% in Turkey to 27.26% in Sweden.In addition to Turkey, the share of government employment takes

---

[2] See Karras (1996, 1997, 2000) for similar applications.Lack of capital stock data for many of the countries in the sample for sufficiently long time periods precludes estimation of specific functional forms like CES, translog, or the cost function approach of Morrison and Schwartz (1992), and Berndt and Hansson (1992).

relatively low values in Japan (8.27%), Greece (9.51%), and Spain (10.28%).Similar to Sweden, the other two Scandinavian countries also have a relatively high government employment ratio (Denmark 24.38%, Norway 23.86), but so do the UK (21.05%), France (21%), and Canada (21.11%).

Table 1. Summary Statistics and Estimated Marginal Product Ratios: 1961-2001.

	Sample Statistic		Estimated MPN^G/MPN^P	
	N^G/N	W^G/W^P	(FE)	(RE)
1. Australia	15.07	1.26	0.83	0.92
2. Austria	11.60	1.47	1.17	1.29
3. Belgium	16.48	1.03	0.76	0.83
4. Canada	21.11	1.04	0.54	0.59
5. Denmark	24.38	1.10	0.51	0.57
6. Finland	18.81	1.10	0.71	0.78
7. France	21.00	0.91	0.56	0.61
8. Germany	12.83	1.18	1.01	1.12
9. Greece	9.51	1.83	1.52	1.67
10. Iceland	15.65	1.11	0.83	0.91
11. Ireland	12.44	1.32	1.06	1.17
12. Italy	14.93	1.26	0.86	0.95
13. Japan	8.27	1.24	1.60	1.77
14. Netherlands	12.46	1.67	1.02	1.13
15. New Zealand	15.99	1.30	0.76	0.84
16. Norway	23.86	0.86	0.50	0.55
17. Spain	10.28	1.54	1.56	1.72
18. Sweden	27.26	0.96	0.43	0.48
19. Switzerland	11.96	NA	1.10	1.22
20. Turkey	7.87	NA	1.70	1.87
21. U.K.	21.05	0.78	0.56	0.61
22. U.S.	15.42	1.09	0.79	0.87

Notes: N^G is government employment; N is total employment; W^G and W^P are government and private wage, respectively; MPN^G and MPN^P are estimated marginal products of government and private employment, respectively.Variables are averaged over the 1961-2001 period.FE refers to the model with fixed effects, and RE to the model with random effects.Variables are averaged over the 1961-2001 period.

Figure 1 adds a time dimension to these numbers.For most of these 22 countries (such as Austria, Denmark, Finland, France, Germany, Greece, Iceland, Italy, Norway, Sweden, and the U.K.), the fraction of employment absorbed by government increased almost monotonically during the 1960s, 1970s, and the early 1980s.However, even in some of the countries with the steepest increase, such as the Scandinavian countries, the trend has been mitigated and often reversed since the mid-1980s (note particularly Germany and Ireland, but also Denmark, Finland, the Netherlands, and Sweden).Whether the result of conscious policy choice or the outcome of historical or economic circumstance, this marked variability of government employment both across economies and over time should facilitate an empirical identification of its role for economic growth.

GOVT EMPLOYMENT AS % OF TOTAL EMPLOYMENT

1961-2001

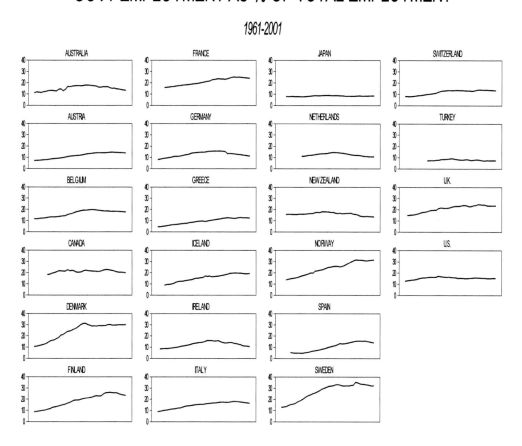

Figure 1. Government Employment as a percent of Total Employment, 1961-2001

4   Empirical Results and Discussion

Table 2 reports several estimated versions of equation (2), together with F-statistics for the null hypotheses that the output elasticities or the marginal products of private and government employment are equal. The actual method of estimation depends on the modeling of $\dot{A}/A$, the growth rate of multifactor productivity. The simplest approach would be to model it as

$$\left(\frac{\dot{A}}{A}\right)_{i,t} = c + B(L)oil_t + u_{i,t},$$

(3)

where c is a constant, $B(L)$ is a polynomial in the lag operator L, *oil* is the growth rate of the price of oil, included in order to capture the effects of energy prices on multifactor productivity, and $u_{i,t}$ an error term.

Table 2. Regression Results: Estimation of Equation (2)

| | OLS | | | GLS | |
| | | Fixed Effects | | Random Effectss | |
	(1)	(2)	(3)	(4)	(5)
$lk\,a^P$	.458**	.461**	.474**	.460**	.468**
	(.035)	(.036)	(.035)	(.035)	(.035)
a^G	.061	.061	.069*	.064	.073*
	(.034)	(.035)	(.033)	(.034)	(.033)
MPK	.155**	.203**	.205*	.177**	.180**
	(.026)	(.034)	(.032)	(.029)	(.028)
(oil_t)	-.003	-.003	-.003*	-.003	-.003*
	(.002)	(.002)	(.002)	(.002)	(.002)
(oil_{t-1})	-.008**	-.008**	-.007**	-.008**	-.007**
	(.002)	(.002)	(.002)	(.002)	(.002)
ρ	.315**	.269**			.285**
	(.034)	(.035)			(.035)
ρ_i			$-.22 < \rho_i < .69$		$-.21 < \rho_i < .68$
R^2	.360	.340	.380	.347	.385
DW	2.05	2.02	1.97	2.03	1.99
F-Tests					
$a^P = a^G$	59.75**	57.51**	64.29**	59.01**	63.43**
$MPN^P = MPN^G$	0.23	0.22	0.12	0.17	0.03

Notes:The estimated fixed and random effects are not reported here and are not included in the calculation of the R^2 s.Estimated standard errors in parentheses.**:significant at 1%, *:significant at 5%.

Assuming $u_{i,t}$ is uncorrelated across countries, equation (2) can be consistently estimated by Ordinary Least Squares (OLS), as reported in the first column of Table 2.To account for the persistence exhibited by the output growth rate, the error term is modeled as $u_{i,t} = \rho u_{i,t-1} + e_{i,t}$, where ρ is the autoregressive parameter and e is assumed to be white noise.[3]All estimated coefficients have the right sign, and all but a^G and the contemporaneous oil parameter are statistically significant at the 5% level (both a^G and contemporaneous oil are actually significant at the 10% level).In addition, the estimated values for the private inputs are quite plausible: the estimated elasticity of output with respect to private employment is $a^P = 0.458$, and the estimated marginal product of capital is $MPK = 0.155$.The elasticity of output with respect to government employment is estimated at $a^G = 0.061$, suggesting that a 10% decrease in N^G, holding all other inputs constant, would reduce output by 0.61%.Interestingly, while the null hypothesis that $a^P = a^G$ is soundly rejected ($F = 59.75$, in favor of $a^P > a^G$), the null of $MPN^P = MPN^G$ cannot be rejected at any reasonable significance level ($F = 0.23$).Thus, there is no evidence that the marginal productivities of private and government employment differ statistically.[4]

If $u_{i,t}$ is not uncorrelated across countries, its variance-covariance matrix will not be diagonal, and OLS will not be appropriate (see Judge et al., 1985; Arellano, 2003).To address this possibility, one can allow for country-specific effects by modeling technological growth as

$$\left(\frac{\dot{A}}{A}\right)_{i,t} = w_i + B(L)oil_t + u_{i,t}, \tag{4}$$

where the w_is can be treated as fixed or random effects.[5]Then, equation (2) can be estimated by Generalized Least Squares (GLS).Columns 2 and 4 of Table 2 report the results for fixed and random effects, respectively, again modeling the error term as AR(1): $u_{i,t} = \rho u_{i,t-1} + e_{i,t}$.The results are very robust across the two specifications and, qualitatively, very similar to those obtained by OLS.Note that again $a^P = a^G$ can be safely rejected ($F = 57.51$ for fixed effects and $F = 59.01$ for random effects), whereas MPN^P and MPN^G are not statistically different ($F = 0.22$ for fixed effects and $F = 0.17$ for random effects).Do the fixed effects belong in the equation?The answer is Yes, as the F-statistic for

---

[3] Higher-order processes were also tried for the autocorrelation adjustment, but AR(1) seemed to be sufficient.

[4] For the purposes of this test, the *MPN*s are estimated at sample means, as $MPN^j = a^j\left(\overline{Y}/\overline{N}^j\right)$ for $j = P$, G.Thus, given the estimated a^P and a^G elasticities and the observed N^G/N ratios, it is not surprising that the estimated *MPN*s are almost equal.In particular, $MPN^G/MPN^P = \left(a^G/a^P\right)/\left(\overline{N}^G/\overline{N}^P\right)$, which is approximately 1, because (from column (1) of Table 2) $a^G/a^P = .061/.458 ..133$, and (from Table 1) $\overline{N}^G/\overline{N}^P .0.156$.

[5] Technological growth may also contain non-oil related time-specific effects, so we generalized further by modeling it as $\left(\frac{\dot{A}}{A}\right)_{i,t} = w_i + v_t + u_{i,t}$, and using again GLS for (2).The results are not appreciably different and so are not reported to preserve space.All results are available on request.

the null hypothesis that the estimated w_is (as fixed effects) are jointly zero is 1.85 (significance level: 0.012).

Next, the assumption that the autoregressive parameter is the same for all countries is relaxed, specifying $u_{i,t} = \rho_i u_{i,t-1} + e_{i,t}$, so that a different ρ is estimated for each country. These results are found in columns 3 and 5 of Table 2 for the fixed and random effects, respectively. It is clear that allowing the ρ s to differ across countries strengthens the results with respect to government employment. Not only are the estimated a^Gs somewhat higher, they are also more decisively statistically significant. This is not so surprising, once it is noted that the estimated ρ s have quite a substantial range (from –0.22 to 0.69 for the fixed effects, and from –0.21 to 0.68 under random effects). It follows that estimating a common ρ for all countries imposes a false restriction on the data.

Interestingly, however, allowing the ρ s to vary across countries does not alter the statistical comparison of the output effects of the two types of employment. Once more, the elasticity of output with respect to private employment is statistically significantly higher than the elasticity with respect to government employment ($F = 64.30$ for fixed effects and $F = 63.43$ for random effects), whereas the two marginal products are not statistically different ($F = 0.12$ for fixed effects and $F = 0.03$ for random effects).

5   Are Government Workers Overpaid?

We are now ready to ask whether the government-private wage structure is consistent with the corresponding marginal products. If private and government workers are paid their marginal products, the ratio of their wages, W^G/W^P, should equal the ratio of their marginal products, MPN^G/MPN^P, in each country. In essence, therefore, we now ask whether government workers are overpaid ($W^G/W^P > MPN^G/MPN^P$), underpaid ($W^G/W^P < MPN^G/MPN^P$), or "competitively" paid ($W^G/W^P = MPN^G/MPN^P$), relative to the private sector.

In practice, government/private wage ratios have been moderately less variable than the fraction of employment absorbed by the government. The second data column of Table 1 gives the government/private wage ratio for twenty of the sample's countries averaged again over the 1961-2001 period.[6] This wage ratio has ranged from 0.78 in the U.K. to 1.83 in Greece. The ratio has been greater than one in all but four of the countries -- the four exceptions being France, Norway, Sweden, and the UK, where the average government wage has been lower than the private wage.

These averages, however, may mask the ratio's variability over time, which for some of the countries is considerable. The solid lines of Figure 2 plot the W^G/W^P ratios over time for each country except Switzerland and Turkey (see footnote 6). It is interesting to note that, with two exceptions, government/private wage ratios have either hovered around one (as in Canada, France, and the U.S.), or have gradually approached unity from above (as in Austria,

---

[6] Data availability on government wages for Switzerland and Turkey was very limited to be of use in this study.

Finland, Italy, and Spain).The two exceptions are Greece and the Netherlands, where the government/private wage ratios have not only been relatively high, but they have actually been diverging from unity.Unity, of course, is the *a priori* "equilibrium" value for the MPN^G/MPN^P and W^G/W^P ratios: if $MPN^G \neq MPN^P$ (and assuming the skills of the representative private and government workers to be comparable), output in a frictionless economy can be increased simply by shifting labor from one sector to the other.

MARGINAL-PRODUCT AND WAGE RATIOS: GOVT/PRIVATE

1961-2001

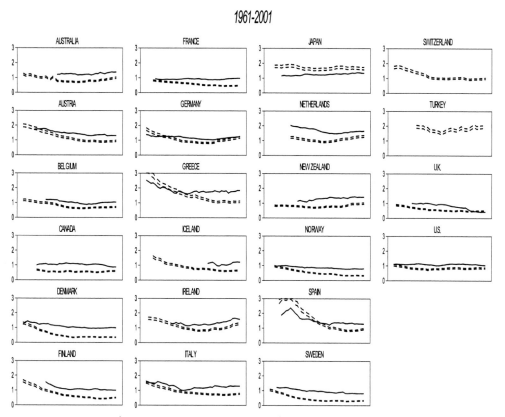

Notes. Solid lines: W^G/W^P. Dashed lines: MPN^G/MPN^P (upper line from model with fixed effects, lower line from model with random effects).

Figure 2. Wage and Marginal-Product Ratios, 1961-2001

Do the observed wage patterns correspond to the productivities implied by the estimated model?For each of the 22 countries, Figure 2 superimposes the W^G/W^P ratios on plots of two computed ratios of government-to-private marginal products of labor,

MPN^G/MPN^P .[7]The upper MPN^G/MPN^P ratio is based on the model with fixed effects (column (3) of Table 2), and the lower one on the model with random effects (column (5) of Table 2).

Figure 2 shows that there is only one country, Japan, for which the wage ratio has been constantly below the band of the two marginal product ratios, and only four countries (Germany, Greece, Spain, and the UK) for which the same has been true for at least a part of the 1961-2001 period.For all the rest (as well as for Germany, Greece, and Spain since at least the early 1980s), the W^G/W^P ratio is habitually above the MPN^G/MPN^P band's upper bound, suggesting that government workers are overpaid (in the sense that $W^G/W^P >$ MPN^G/MPN^P).

Similar conclusions can be reached from the last two columns of Table 1, which report the MPN^G/MPN^P ratios by country, averaged over 1961-2001.With the exception of Japan and Spain, countries have had average government/private wage ratios that exceed the highest estimated ratio of government/private marginal products of labor.While it is possible that these trends are due to the effects of government employment policy, labor market rigidities, or different productivity gains between the tradable (mostly within the private sector) and nontradable sectors, further research is clearly needed in order to identify the empirical importance and policy implications of these results.

6   Conclusions

This study investigated the productivity of government and private employment for a sample of twenty-two OECD countries during the 1961-2001 period, and compared the ratio of the estimated marginal products to the government/private wage ratio.Doing so, the paper has updated the results of an earlier study by Karras (2000), effectively extending the time period to include the decade of the 1990s.

The empirical results support a number of conclusions, which are qualitatively similar to, though quantitatively somewhat different from, those of Karras (2000).In particular:

(i) The elasticities of output with respect to private and government employment, a^P and a^G, respectively, are statistically significantly different from each other.In fact, a^P (very tightly estimated around 0.46) is estimated to be six to seven times greater than a^G (ranging from 0.061 to 0.073), depending on the econometric specification used.

(ii) At the same time, the hypothesis that the marginal products of private and government employment, MPN^P and MPN^G respectively, are equal cannot be rejected at any reasonable significance level.This suggests that government employment is neither

---

[7] For country i at time t, the marginal products of government and private employment are computed using
$$MPN_{i,t}^j = a^j \left(Y_{i,t} / N_{i,t}^j \right), \text{for } j = G, P.$$

overprovided nor underprovided.In other words, shifting employment from one sector to the other is not likely to produce substantial output gains.

(iii) Finally, in the majority of the countries examined, government workers still appear to be overpaid, as the ratio of government to private wages exceeds the highest estimated value of the corresponding ratio of marginal products.

These results are robust to all the specifications examined.

References

Algan, Yann, Pierre Cahuc, and Andre Zylberberg. "Public Employment: Does it Increase Unemployment?" *Economic Policy*, April 2002, 9-65.

Arellano, Manuel. *Panel Data Econometrics*, 2003, Oxford University Press.

Aschauer, David Alan. "Is Public Expenditure Productive?" *Journal of Monetary Economics*, **23**, 1989, 177-200.

Barro, Robert J. and Xavier Sala-i-Martin. *Economic Growth*, x edition, ????, MIT Press????.

Berndt, Ernst R. and Bengt Hansson. "Measuring the Contribution of Public Infrastructure Capital in Sweden." *Scandinavian Journal of Economics*, **94**, 1992, S151-S168.

Demekas, Dimitri G. and Zenon G. Kontolemis. "Government Employment, Wages, and Labour Market Performance." *Oxford Bulletin of Economics and Statistics*, **62**, 2000, 391-414.

Evans, Paul and Georgios Karras. "Are Government Activities Productive? Evidence from a Panel of U.S. States." *Review of Economics and Statistics*, **76**, 1994a, 1-11.

Evans, Paul and Georgios Karras. "Is Government Capital Productive? Evidence from a Panel of Seven Countries." *Journal of Macroeconomics*, **16**, 1994b, 271-279.

Girard, Jacques, Harald Gruber, and Chris Hurst. "Increasing Public Investment in Europe: Some Practical Considerations." *European Economic Review*, **39**, 1995, 731-738.

Gramlich, Edward M. "Infrastructure Investment: A Review Essay." *Journal of Economic Literature*, **32**, 1176-1196.

Haan, Jakob de, J.E.Sturm, and B.J.Sikken. "Government Capital Formation: Explaining the Decline." *Weltwirtschaftliches Archiv*, **132**, 1996, 55-74.

Holtz-Eakin, Douglas. "Public-Sector Capital and the Productivity Puzzle." *Review of Economics and Statistics*, **76**, 1994, 12-37.

Judge, G.G., W.E. Griffiths, R.C. Hill, H. Lutkepohl, and Tsoung-Chao Lee. *The Theory and Practice of Econometrics*, 1985, John Wiley and Sons.

Karras, Georgios. "Private and Government Employment in the OECD: Productivities and Wages." *Economic Notes*, **29**, 2000, 267-279.

Karras, Georgios. "The Optimal Government Size: Further International Evidence on the Productivity of Government Services." *Economic Inquiry*, **XXXIV**, 1996, 193-203.

Karras, Georgios. "On the Optimal Government Size in Europe: Theory and Empirical Evidence." *The Manchester School of Economic and Social Studies*, **65**, 1997, 280-294.

Sturm, Jan-Egbert, Gerard H. Kuper, and Jakob de Haan. "Modelling Government Investment and Economic Growth on a Macro Level: A Review." CCSO Series 29, [forthcoming in S.Brakman, H.van Ees, and S.K.Kuipers (eds.) *Market Behaviour and Macroeconomic Modelling*, MacMillan.]

In: Inflation, Fiscal Policy and Central Banks
Editor: Leo N. Bartolotti, pp. 133-151

ISBN: 1-60021-122-4
© 2006 Nova Science Publishers, Inc.

Chapter 7

LOBBYING OVER FISCAL POLICY

Gil S. Epstein[*]

Department of Economics, Bar-Ilan University, Ramat Gan, 52900 Israel, CReAM,
London and IZA, Bonn

Abstract

Lobbying is costly and differs between groups as a function of the groups needs and possibility to obtain resources from government. In this chapter we start by reviewing the different reasons for the existence for lobbying over fiscal policy. We consider how the needs of each of the groups affect its lobbying activities and therefore, how these lobbying activities affect the resources allocated to each group under fiscal policy. Lobbying also affect the burden of taxation imposed on each of the groups to finance fiscal policy. Moreover, we also determine the optimal taxation levied to finance the fiscal policy. Using element from game theory and Nash equilibrium shows that if both groups have the same utility from each dollar obtained from fiscal policy, then both groups will invest the same amount of resources in trying to obtain a larger proportion of the budget. The group with the larger needs, in equilibrium, will obtain the largest proportion of the budget and a higher probability of affecting fiscal policy. In the case where the politicians prefer the wealthier group, this group, in equilibrium, will have a higher expected utility than the other group. It is shown that is not always beneficial to increase the wealth of a certain group. Increasing the wealth of one of the groups may put this group in a worse position as it may decrease the probability of obtaining the funds from the government and decreasing the effectiveness this group has on affecting fiscal policy of the government. Therefore, groups that obtain funds from the government may not use them with accordance to what the government had wished for as this may decrease the probability of obtaining further funds in the future. Finally we show how the variance of the needs of the groups, i.e., the magnitude of the difference between the needs of the groups, affects the taxation levied on the different groups.

1 Introduction

It is often assumed that government and bureaucrats have full information about the needs of the different groups in the economy and that it determines fiscal policy so that social welfare

---

[*] E-mail address: epsteig@mail.biu.ac.il

is maximized. This, however, is not always the case. While the intentions of the politicians may be pure, they may not have all the information needed in order to make the correct decisions. In order to obtain current and accurate information, the politicians and the bureaucrats meet and talk to different groups that have specific interests in different parts of the proposed fiscal policy. By doing so, the politicians are enabling the interest groups to transfer information that is not always precise or true. The politicians know this for a fact. However they are not always able to separate the facts from the lobbing efforts. The politicians obtain such information from the different interest groups that will be affected by the fiscal policy. In such a way, the politicians can examine the different items of information it receives and try, to the best of their knowledge, to separate important material from lobbying efforts. It may be however, that the politicians' intentions are not always pure. The politicians may want the interest groups to compete against each other, investing effort in trying to convince them that the policies are or aren't necessary. The reason for this is that the politicians not only obtain utility from enhancing social welfare but also from the lobbying efforts of the different interest groups. In general, it can be said that lobbying efforts affect fiscal policy. In this paper we will focus on this element of fiscal policy.

Lobbying and its effect on policy is not new. Dharmapala (2003) presents a formal model of legislative decisionmaking, using a common agency formulation to represent interest group lobbying of legislators. This framework is used to analyze the effects of decentralizing appropriations authority. The conditions under which decentralization leads to higher spending are characterized. It is argued that the conventional view that divestiture caused higher levels of spending only holds if decentralization created barriers to lobbying and political bargaining across different committees. Tabellini and Persson (1999) survey the recent literature that has tried to answer how fiscal policy varies greatly across time and countries. Adopting a unified approach in portraying public policy as the equilibrium outcome of an explicitly specified political process, the material is divided into three parts. Part I focuses on median-voter equilibria that apply to policy issues where disagreement between voters is likely to be one-dimensional, thus studying general redistributive programs typical of the modern welfare state. Part II studies special interest politics. Here the policy problem is multidimensional so the focus is on specific political mechanisms: legislative bargaining, lobbying, and electoral competition, as well as the possible interactions between these different forms of political activity. Finally, Part III deals with a set of questions that can be brought under the label of comparative politics, dealing with policy choice under alternative political constitutions, modeling some stylized features of congressional and parliamentary political systems and focusing on their implications for rent extraction by politicians, redistribution and public goods provision. On the other hand Ghate, (2001) constructs a one-sector growth model to examine the impact of political lobbying on the formation of fiscal policy. The model predicts that lobbying can induce endogenous regime switches, development traps, and a sub-optimal allocation of government expenditures between productive and unproductive ends, leading to long run income losses in the economy. Finally, Mohtadi and Roe (1998) consider the possibility that the benefits of lobbying may spill over to other members of society and is incorporated into an endogenous growth framework to show that an increase in lobbying may improve welfare and growth even when motivated by self-interest.

Our approach differs from the ones presented above. We consider the effect of lobbying on fiscal policy where fiscal policy can be seen, in general, as a redistribution of resources.

On the one hand, the government imposes taxation on certain groups to finance its budget constraints and on the other hand, redistributes these resources. When redistributing the funds, the politicians take into account two main elements: 1. the actual needs of the different groups, i.e., all other things equal - the needy will receive, on average, more funds, and 2. the lobbying effort of the interest groups will affect the politicians' decisions on how to redistribute its budget. These two elements will be incorporated into the contest success function (CSF), which will determine the proportion of the resources each of the interest groups will obtain from the budget. For each level of the government's budget, an optimal redistribution will be obtained giving the equilibrium lobbing efforts of the interest groups and their needs. However, taxes must be levied on the different interest groups in order to finance this budget. This paper will not only determine the equilibrium effect of lobbying on the redistribution but also on the equilibrium optimal taxation imposed on the different groups in the population in order to finance the governments' policy. In section 2.1 we present an overview of the mechanism used to analyze the lobbying effect on fiscal policy, in section 2.2 we consider the lobbying effort and outcome when there exists a fixed budget and relate these results to the different benefits obtained. Moreover, in this section we describe the information mechanism that transfers lobbying effort into the outcome. In section 2.3 we analyze the effect of Heterogeneous benefits of the different groups and how it affects fiscal policy. Finally, given the equilibrium lobbying efforts, we analyze the optimal taxation on each of the groups.

2   The Model

2.1   An Overview

We consider two risk neutral interest groups that lobby over fiscal policy. Each of the groups wants to affect the allocation of resources by the central government. The way in which each group affects the determination of fiscal policy and the allocation of public goods is through lobbying activities. Lobbying activates can also be see as transfers of funds to the politicians that make the decisions. Such transfers could be donations and campaign contributions and in the more extreme case these transfers may also be forms of bribes used to influence the ruling politicians' decisions. In other words, the resources allocated to such activities by the interest groups may be transfers to the politicians or wasteful resources in the form of lobbying activities.[1] In order to focus our distinction we will consider the case where the interest groups lobby the politicians without specifying if the resources are transfers or wasteful resources (for such a distinction see Epstein and Nitzan, 2003).

Each group invests recourses in order to affect the politicians' decisions in determining fiscal policy and the allocation of resources by the politicians at a level of x_i ($i = 1,2$). The proportion of resources allocated to group i is denoted by Pr_i and is a function of the resources invested by both groups. The proportion of recourses allocated to each group can

---

[1] Lobbying activities which are not the direct transfers of resources to the politicians may also be seen as transfers as the politician may obtain a positive utility from such lobbying activities. For example, demonstrations in favor or against a politician can be see as a positive transfer or resources from the interest groups to the politicians as the demonstrations are "few" publicity for a politician even if the demonstrations are against a politician.

also be seen as a contest success function (CSF) under which the two groups are competing over a given prize. Each wins this contest with a probability of Pr_i .The expected prize level is the part of the prize allocated to each of the groups. Moreover the proportion of the resources is also a function of the real needs of each of the groups, or of the subjective objectives of the government and its politicians. For example, one of the main objectives of the government, or at least its stated political platform during elections, is/was that the government's budget would is divided in order to decreases the poverty in the country, then the politicians would prefer that the group representing the low income individuals would, all the rest given, receive a higher proportion of the budget. On the other had, as the higher income individuals will be financing this redistribution, the higher level individuals will exert resources to prevent this allocation and minimize the amount of recourses this groups receives in order to reduce the amount of taxes imposed on them to finance such activities. Let us consider a different example: Consider a government that during its political election campaign set out as a goal to set forward the country and explore out of space. In the US case this would be to transfer resources to NASA to develop the out of space availability. As government's budget is given, transferring resources to such activities will affect resources devoted to internal policy and the production of public goods. On the one hand we will see groups interested in the development of the space frontier and thus requiring that funds will be allocated to such activities and on the other had there will be those that think that the money and resources should be invested in the provision of public goods. Both interest groups will compete against each other over the two topics and the allocation of the resources that are a direct result of the fiscal policy of the government. If the government's stated policy is the development of the space frontier, then given that both groups invest the same amount of resources in the contest over division of the budget, the government will put a higher weight on the space related topics and the proportion of funds devoted to the out of space activities will be greater than the resources devoted to the provision of public goods (assuming of course that these to issues are the only issues finances in fiscal policy).Therefore, the interest groups that are against such policies as out of space activities will have to invest larger amounts of resources to increase the proportion of the budget going to the provision of internal public goods.

In this chapter we will consider three different cases: In the first case we consider the struggle over fiscal policy where the budget to be divided is fixed and both groups compete to gain a larger portion of the budget. This first case will be the benchmark for the rest of the results obtained in this chapter. Moreover we will assume that each group has the same utility from each dollar spent by the government. This of course may not be the case – we will develop this further on in the chapter. In the second part we will consider the case where the utility each groups gains from the budget differs and depends on its needs. For example, if a public good that is supplied affects the lower income group more than the higher income group then the lower income group will have a higher utility from this public good than the higher income individuals. We will assume here that the proportion of the budget obtained is also a function of the needs or the government's objective. In the third case will discuss the optimal taxation levied on the different groups to finance the allocation of resources determined by the politicians and fiscal policy.

2.2 Fixed Budget and Benefits

In this section of the chapter we consider the case where each group has the same benefit from each dollar spent by the government. A government's fiscal policy is to divide its budget between the two different groups. The expected utility of the two risk neutral groups is given as follows:

$$E(u_1) = A_1 + \text{Pr}_1 W - x_1 \tag{1}$$

and

$$E(u_2) = A_2 + \text{Pr}_2 W - x_2 \tag{2}$$

where A_1 and A_2 are the given wealth levels of the two different groups. The proportion of the budget that will be allocated to each of the groups will equal to Pr_1 and Pr_2 respectively for group 1 and group 2. The total budget to be divided between the two groups equals to W and the exerted effort / resources invested in this struggle is denoted by x_1 and x_2. [2]

Each group determines the level of effort / resources to be extracted in this contest such that the expected utility from the division of the budget is maximized. It is assumed that as the level of investment of group number one increases (an increase in x_1), the proportion it receives from the budget will increase. While as group number two increases it effort in the contest (an increase in x_2), the proportion that group number one will receive will decrease. Therefore it is assumed that the proportions (contest success function – CSF) of the budget each groups receives will have the following properties,

$$\frac{\partial \text{Pr}_i(x_i, x_j)}{\partial x_i} > 0 \quad and \quad \frac{\partial \text{Pr}_i(x_i, x_j)}{\partial x_j} < 0 \text{ for all } i,j = 1, 2 \text{ and } i \neq j \tag{3}$$

It is assumed that effort has a decreasing marginal effect on the proportion of budget obtained by each of the groups, thus,

$$\frac{\partial^2 \text{Pr}_i(x_i, x_j)}{\partial x_i^2} < 0 \quad \text{for all } i = 1, 2 \tag{4}$$

The first order condition that determines the optimal amount of resources invested by the two different groups in this struggle over the fiscal policy is given by the following:

---

[2] An alternative approach would be that each of the groups proposes the optimal fiscal policy to be adopted by the government. In this case the expected benefit of the groups would differ as a function of the proposed policy of the groups and , in equilibrium, the optimal proposals will be determined. For a discussion on such a presentation of a political contest see Epstein and Nitzan, 2004.

$$\frac{\partial E(u_1)}{\partial x_1} = \frac{\partial \mathrm{Pr}_1}{\partial x_1} W - 1 = 0 \qquad (5)$$

and for the second group,

$$\frac{\partial E(u_2)}{\partial x_2} = \frac{\partial \mathrm{Pr}_2}{\partial x_2} W - 1 = 0 \qquad (6)$$

Under the assumptions made in (4) it is clear that the second order condition for maximization will hold: $\dfrac{\partial^2 E(u_1)}{\partial x_1^{\,2}} = \dfrac{\partial^2 \mathrm{Pr}_1}{\partial x_1^{\,2}} W < 0$ and $\dfrac{\partial^2 E(u_2)}{\partial x_2^{\,2}} = \dfrac{\partial^2 \mathrm{Pr}_2}{\partial x_2^{\,2}} W < 0$.

The optimal amount of resources invested in the contest, x_1^* and x_2^* are therefore the resources that satisfy (5) and (6).Note of course that as all the budget is divided between both groups it most hold that the sum of the proportions equals to one unit: $Pr_1 + Pr_2 = 1$.

2.2.1   The Information Structure

The question we wish to focus here is: why would the politicians determining the budget distribution wish to have such a contest between both interest groups. We present here two different explanations. In the first case we show that it is optimal for the politicians to create a contest in order to obtain resources / rents from the interest groups. Under the alternative explanation, we present the case where under such a contest the politicians determining the fiscal policy obtain important information from such a contest and choose optimally it actions.

The arguments presented below are presented in general terms in order to enable us to use them in all the different three cases presented in this chapter.

a. Politicians obtaining resources and rents

The government and politicians could decide to select the fiscal policy that results in the realization of the highest benefit to the economy or to their self. Welfare is assumed to be equal to the sum of the expected utilities of the groups; therefore, in order to obtain a situation where the politicians maximize total social welfare would happen if the government would divide the resources such that the group that needed them the most will obtain the highest amount of resources. We should remember that in our story there are only two groups, therefore, only one will obtain the resources. Let us define the utility of group H by n_H (H for the group with the utility). Note that in the first case presented above both groups have the same utility W from the fiscal policy. However, latter on we will assume different utility from the same fiscal policy. The group with the lower utility from fiscal policy is denoted group L. An alternative option for the government is to choose randomly between the two different policies that it faces. Clearly, if the utility the government derives from the selection of a policy is positively related to the aggregate expected utility of the interest groups, then it would never randomize, that is, it would select the policy that generates the highest utility. The probabilities of realization of the two policies in the complete-information public-policy contest are given by the contest success function (CSF). This function specifies the relationship between the interest groups' investment in the so called influence, lobbying or rent-seeking activities, x_1 and x_2 , and the probability/proportion of the budget, Pr_1 and Pr_2, of realization of the two policies. The expected utility of interest group i, as presented above, is given by $E(u_i)$ and the effort invested by each interest group is denoted by x_i. (latter on in this chapter we examine the relationship between the CSF, $E(u_i)$ and x_i).

As commonly assumed in the recent political economy literature, Grossman and Helpman (1996, 2001), Persson and Tabellini (2000), Epstein and Nitzan (2003, 2006) let the government's objective function be a weighted average of the expected social welfare $(E(u_L) + E(u_H))$ and lobbying efforts:

$$G(.) = \alpha g(E(u_L) + E(u_H)) + (1 - \alpha)f(x_L + x_H) \qquad (7)$$

Where $g(.)$ and $f(.)$ are increasing function in social welfare, $E(u_L) + E(u_H)$, and lobbying effort of the interest groups, $x_L + x_H$, respectively. The parameters α and $(1-\alpha)$ are the weights assigned to the expected social welfare and the contestants' lobbying resources. If the government decides not to generate a contest and choose the fiscal policy that results in the higher welfare for the group with the highest available welfare from this contest n_H, then the value of the government's objective function is equal to αn_H. It is therefore sensible for the government to create a contest between the two groups if and only if the expected value of its objective function increases as a result of the existence of the contest. That is,

$$\alpha g(E(w_L) + E(w_H)) + (1 - \alpha)f(x_L + x_H) > \alpha \, g(n_H) \qquad (8)$$

In Epstein and Nitzan (2006) it is shown that in the linear case, when $g(E(w_L) + E(w_H)) = E(w_L) + E(w_H)$ and $f(x_L + x_H) = x_L + x_H$, if the weight, α assigned to the lobbying resources, (x_1 and x_2) is greater than that assigned to the expected welfare, $E(w_L) + E(w_H)$, a contest based on a contest success function (CSF) / proportion obtained from the budget, such as the commonly assumed all-pay auction (see for example Hillman and Riley, 1989) or Tullock's (1980) lottery logit functions can be preferable to no contest that is, random government behavior is therefore rational. In the case of the Tullock's lottery function, the proportion of the budget obtained by group i equals to $x_i / (x_i + x_i)$. Moreover, in the case where both groups have the same stakes: $n_L = n_H$, then it is shown by Epstein and Nitzan (2006) that there will always be optimal for the politician to create a contest between both interest groups.

Note than in this section both groups obtain the same utility from the budget therefore both will have the same stakes and thus it will always be optimal for the politicians to create a contest between the politicians. As stated above, further on in this chapter we will consider the case where the stakes of the contestants are not identical, as both groups will obtain different utilities from the fiscal policy. However in the general case Epstein and Nitzan (2006) have also generated conditions that will ensure that it will be optimal for the politicians to create a political contest between the two groups.

b. Bounded rationality

Let us now consider an alternative explanation to the creation of a contest between both groups. Consider politicians that have to choose how to divide the budget between the two or more groups (of course it may not actually be a division of resources directly to the interest groups rather it may be to the causes for which the groups fight for).Neoclassical economic theory assumes that the government or politicians have a utility that allows them to rank these alternatives, and after ranking the alternatives the politicians will choose the highest ranked. Psychologists (e.g. Luce (1959), Tversky (1969) and (1972)) criticized this deterministic approach, arguing that the outcome should be viewed as probabilistic process. Their approach is to view utility as deterministic but the choice process to be probabilistic. The politicians and thus the government do not necessarily choose the alternative that yields the highest utility /welfare and instead has a probability of choosing each of the various possible alternatives. Luce (1959) (see also Sheshinski, 2000)) shows that when choice probabilities satisfy a certain axiom (the choice axiom), a scale, termed utility, can be defined over alternatives such that the choice probabilities can be derived from scales, utilities, of alternatives.

The contest present below, may not be designed by the politician rather it may well be that the groups believe that such a contest exists. In the literature, it has been shown that interest groups invest time and effort to affect the politicians' decision making process in determining the fiscal policy. Thus, even though from the politicians' point of view the contest may not exists it may well exist in the eyes of the groups that believe that this contest determines the proportion of the budget they obtain from the government. And the interest groups invest accordingly in such a contest.

Let us now consider a specific contest success function (probability of winning the contest or/and the proportion of the budget that will be obtained by each of the groups under fiscal policy) which will determine the proportion each of the groups will obtain in the contest of the fiscal policy. The function presented below satisfies both type of explanations for generating a contest that where presented above -the optimal contest and the bounded rationality conditions.

Luce's (Multinomial) Logit Model

Luce's (Multinomial) *Logit Model* postulates that the probability that an individual chooses some alternative $a \in S$, Pr_a, is given by

$$\text{Pr}_a = \frac{e^{q_a u(a)}}{\sum_{b \in s} e^{q_b u(b)}} \tag{9}$$

Where the parameter q_a represents the preferences of the government (discrimination, or in our context, the ability to lobby the government or politicians).If $q_b = 0$ for all b then each group has equal probability or will receive the same proportion of the fiscal budget. The uncertainty is emphasized in the case where the government or politicians do not have full information regarding the real needs of the groups. In this setting $u(a)$ represents the value attributed by the government to the value added to social welfare from helping this group . As stated above, the groups invest effort and recourses in lobbing seeking activities that causes the politicians not to know actually their (and their opponents) actual added welfare. The utility that is attributed by the politicians to group i is given by $u(d_i, x_i)$. Where x_i represents the lobbing effort invested by group i and d_i represents the real needs of this group such that as d_i decreases, group i is less well off and thus its needs are greater. We will assume that the government wishes to help this groups that need to be helped and therefore will give them a higher probability of obtaining a higher proportion of the budget.

In order to simplify the calculations and to be able to reach a closed form let the utility be the logarithmic function such that $u(d_i, x_i) = Ln\left(x_i / d_i\right)$. Thus, the utility increases with the investment in lobbying seeking activity of the groups, x_i. As the group's investment level increases it better disguise itself as a group that needs more resources from the government and convinces the politicians that they really needs these resources. The value d_i, represent the well being of group i. As this group is better off, it will need fewer resources from the government. However, this can also be seen as a weight sent by the politicians on the politicians own preferences. If their prefer group i over group j they will give group i a lower d than that for group j and therefore group i will obtain a higher weight in the probability or proportion of resources obtained from the government.

We thus obtain a contest-success function, that interest group i's probability of success or proportion obtained from the budget in competing against group j is given by:

$$\Pr_i(x_i, x_j) = \frac{\dfrac{x_i}{d_i}}{\dfrac{x_i}{d_i} + \dfrac{x_j}{d_j}} \quad \forall i \neq j \ and \ i, j = 1, 2 \tag{10}$$

where $e^{q_i} = \dfrac{1}{d_i}$ represents the lobbying seeking ability of the interest group.

This contest success function is a variant of the non-discriminating rule of Tullock (1980) (see also Hirshleifer, 1989 and Hillman and Riley, 1989). The probability of winning the contest or the proportion of the budget obtained by group i is therefore determined by the following variables:

a. The level of investment and resources invested in lobbying seeking activities in the contest of both interest groups, x_1 and x_2,

b. The lobbying seeking abilities of the groups, d_1 and d_2. These abilities can be as a result of the groups real needed (for example, as the group is less well off, they have more needs than the other group and as a result the politicians will give them a higher weight in the decision regarding the division of the budget resources) or the preferences it could also represent of the politicians (if the politicians prefer one group over another, for different various reasons, then this enables the group to be more efficient in their lobbying effort)

These two characteristics of the function can be presented in the following way:

$$\frac{\partial \Pr_i(x_i, x_j)}{\partial x_i} > 0, \quad \frac{\partial \Pr_i(x_i, x_j)}{\partial x_j} < 0, \quad \frac{\partial \Pr_i(x_i, x_j)}{\partial d_i} < 0, \quad \text{and} \quad \frac{\partial \Pr ob_i(x_i, x_j)}{\partial d_j} > 0.$$

Optimal lobbying effort

Let us now calculate the optimal lobbying effort exerted by the group in the struggle over fiscal policy. Given (5), (6) and (10) the optimal amount of resources invested in the lobbying contest over the fiscal policy satisfies:

$$\frac{\partial E(u_1)}{\partial x_1} = \frac{\frac{1}{d_1}\frac{x_2}{d_2}}{\left(\frac{x_i}{d_i} + \frac{x_j}{d_j}\right)^2} W - 1 = 0 \tag{11}$$

and for the second group,

$$\frac{\partial E(u_2)}{\partial x_2} = \frac{\frac{1}{d_2}\frac{x_1}{d_1}}{\left(\frac{x_i}{d_i} + \frac{x_j}{d_j}\right)^2} W - 1 = 0 \tag{12}$$

Solving (11) together with (12) we obtain the Nash equilibrium lobbying effort invested in the struggle over fiscal policy and is given by:

$$x_1^* = \frac{d_1 d_2}{(d_1 + d_2)^2} W \quad and \quad x_2^* = \frac{d_1 d_2}{(d_1 + d_2)^2} W \tag{13}$$

As we can see from (13), even though the groups may differ from each other in their needs or in their relationship to the politicians, i.e. the preferences of the politicians, both interest groups will spend the same amount of recourses in order to try and convince the politicians to create a fiscal policy with accordance to their needed.

The total amount of resources invested in such a contest, i.e., the rent dissipation, will equal to:

$$X^* = x_1^* + x_2^* = 2\frac{d_1 d_2}{(d_1 + d_2)^2} W < W \tag{14}$$

Since $\dfrac{d_1 d_2}{\left(d_1 + d_2\right)^2}$ <1 it is clear that the rent dissipation will be less that the total fiscal budget. Namely, the groups will not spend out all the resources they may gain in this struggle over fiscal policy. In other words, there will not be full dissipation of the rent. Notice that in the case that both groups are identical and have identical needs, $d_1 = d_2$, the resources invested in the contest and the rent dissipation will equal:

$$\text{For } d_1 = d_2, \quad x_1^* = x_2^* = \frac{1}{4}W \quad and \quad X^* = x_1^* + x_2^* = \frac{1}{2}W \tag{15}$$

Even though the investment of resources in the contest will equal to each other, $x_1^* = x_2^*$, this doesn't mean the probability of wining will be identical. Inserting (13) in to (10) we obtain that the equilibrium probability of winning the contest of each of the groups equal:

$$\text{Pr}_i(x_i, x_j) = \frac{d_j}{d_i + d_j} \quad \forall i \neq j \text{ and } i, j = 1, 2 \tag{16}$$

Namely, the probability of winning is a function of the relative needs of the different groups. As group i has greater needs, d_i is smaller, then the probability of winning or the proportion of the budget group i receives will increases.

Using (16) together (13), (1) and (2) we obtain that the expected utility of each of the groups is given by:

$$E\left(u_i\right) = A_i + \frac{d_j^2}{\left(d_i + d_j\right)^2}W \quad \forall i \neq j \text{ and } i, j = 1, 2 \tag{17}$$

If the needs of group i are greater than that of group j, namely $d_i < d_j$ then the net benefit, i.e., the income minus cost of the lobbying over fiscal policy, will be grater for group i then

for group j: $\dfrac{d_j^2}{\left(d_i + d_j\right)^2}W < \dfrac{d_i^2}{\left(d_i + d_j\right)^2}W$.

Let us sum up the result presented above in the following:

If both groups have the same utility from each dollar obtained from fiscal policy then both groups will invest the same about of resources in trying to obtain a larger proportion of the budget. The group with the larger needs or in the case where the politicians have an interest in a specific group, this group will, in equilibrium, obtain a largest proportion of the budget and a higher probability of affecting fiscal policy or receiving money funds for will gain a larger proportion of the budget. In the case where the politicians prefer the wealthier group, the group that has a larger A, this group in equilibrium, will have a higher expected utility than the other group.

2.3   Heterogeneous Benefits from Fiscal Policy

In the pervious section we assumed that each group benefits identically from the each dollar spent by the government in fiscal policy. This is not always the case. Fiscal policy does not affect all the population is the same way. For example, if a group is badly off and need resources from the government then each dollar they reactive will be worth a lot more than a group that is well off. Therefore the resources received by the different groups will depend on how well off they are and how much they really need the resources allocated to them in the budget.

In order to focus our discussion we will assume that the utility a group receives from the amount of resources received via fiscal policy is a function of its wealth A_i. As this group is better off, it may need fewer resources from the government. However, this can also be seen as a weight assigned by the politicians on their own preferences. In our story, if their prefer group i over group j they will give group i a lower d than that for group j and therefore group i will obtain a higher weight in the probability or proportion of resources obtained from the government. We are assuming here that the government prefers to help the less well off groups in the population. In this case there is no difference by writing A or d as both represent the same thing. However, it may well be the case that the less well of can generate less utility from the budget obtained that the less well off. There may well be however a negative relationship between A or d. In other words, the one that needs more from the government may generate less utility from each dollar it receives.[3]

The expected utility of the two risk neutral groups is thus given by the following functions:

$$E(u_i) = A_i + \mathrm{Pr}_i\, W(A_i) - x_i \quad \forall i = 1,2 \tag{18}$$

It is assumed that as the level of wealth of group i decreases, A_i decreases, the benefit the group can receive from the fiscal policy may increase or decreases. In other words, those worse of can be helped easier or harder than those better off. The worse off may receive a higher or lower utility from each dollar they receive relative to the better of groups: $\dfrac{\partial W(A_i)}{\partial A_i} \overset{<}{>} 0 \ \forall i = 1,2$.

The proportion / contest success function of the budget that group i obtains in this contest is as presented in (10):

$$\mathrm{Pr}_i(x_i, x_j) = \frac{\dfrac{x_i}{d_i}}{\dfrac{x_i}{d_i} + \dfrac{x_j}{d_j}} \quad \forall i \neq j \ and \ i, j = 1,2 \tag{10}$$

---

[3] An example for this would be two interest groups which represent the capital owners and the workers union. In this case, even though the capital owners may better off, the government may well give them a higher weight in the probability function as the capital owners may have a stronger affect on fiscal policy as a result of their direct effect on the politician which may not be the case for the worker's union.

Using (18) and (10) together with (5) and (6) we can obtain the Nash equilibrium optimal levels of resources invested in the contest on the fiscal policy:

$$x_1^* = \frac{d_1 d_2 \, W(A_1)^2 \, W(A_2)}{(d_1 W(A_2) + d_2 W(A_1))^2} \quad and \quad x_2^* = \frac{d_1 d_2 \, W(A_1) W(A_2)^2}{(d_1 W(A_2) + d_2 W(A_1))^2} \tag{20}$$

In this more general case it is clear that the groups will not invest the same amount of resources in the contest. The question: who will invest more, depends on which of the levels of resources spent in the contest, x, is larger. The first group will invest more resources in the contest if: $\dfrac{d_1 d_2 \, W(A_1)^2 \, W(A_2)}{(d_1 W(A_2) + d_2 W(A_1))^2} > \dfrac{d_1 d_2 \, W(A_1) W(A_2)^2}{(d_1 W(A_2) + d_2 W(A_1))^2}$ namely, group number one will invest more resources if it has a higher benefit from the budget it receives than what the other group obtains from the same budget: $W(A_1) > W(A_2)$. Therefore, we conclude that *the group that has the highest benefit from receiving the funds from the government will spend the highest amount of resources to obtain it.*

Inserting (20) into (10) we obtain that the equilibrium probability of winning the contest of each of the groups equal:

$$\Pr_i(x_i, x_j) = \frac{W(A_i) d_j}{W(A_j) d_i + W(A_i) d_j} \quad \forall i \neq j \ and \ i, j = 1, 2 \tag{21}$$

Namely, the probability of winning is a function which is relative to the needs of the different groups. Let us now see how a change in the groups needs affects the probability of receiving more funds from the government. In order to answer this question let us look at d_i as a function of A_i: $d_i(A_i)$. The relationship may be negative or positive depending on what the relationship between the ability of the groups to obtain utility from the different resources they obtain from the government. Increasing the wealth of group i will change the probability of obtaining the resources from the government in the following way:

$$\frac{\partial \Pr_i(x_i, x_j)}{\partial A_i} = \frac{\dfrac{\partial W(A_i)}{\partial A_i} d_j \left(W(A_j) d_i + W(A_i) d_j \right) - W(A_i) d_j \left(W(A_j) \dfrac{\partial d_i}{\partial A_i} + \dfrac{\partial W(A_i)}{\partial A_i} d_j \right)}{\left(W(A_j) d_i + W(A_i) d_j \right)^2} \tag{21}$$

The sign of (21) equals the sign of

$$\frac{\partial W(A_i)}{\partial A_i} W(A_j) d_i d_j - W(A_i) W(A_j) d_j \frac{\partial d_i}{\partial A_i} \tag{22}$$

Rewriting (22) we obtain,

$$\frac{W(A_j)W(A_i)d_id_j}{A_i}\left(\frac{\partial W(A_i)}{\partial A_i}\frac{A_i}{W(A_i)}-\frac{\partial d_i}{\partial A_i}\frac{A_i}{d_i}\right) \qquad (23)$$

Let us denote by η_W the elasticity of the utility a group obtains from receiving the funds from fiscal policy, W, with respect to the wealth of the group, A:

$\eta_W = \dfrac{\partial W(A_i)}{\partial A_i}\dfrac{A_i}{W(A_i)}$ .Denote by η_d elasticity of the of the change in the weight assigned to this group by the politicians, d, as a result of a change in the level of wealth of the group A:

$\eta_d = \dfrac{\partial d_i}{\partial A_i}\dfrac{A_i}{d_i}$ .Therefore, the effect of an increase in the wealth of group i has an effect on the probability/proportion of the budget obtained by this group and it may be appositive of negative effect. This ambiguity is resolved by obtaining the sign of the following expression:

$$\eta_W - \eta_d \qquad (24)$$

This expression tells us that we have two effects that must be considered: increasing the wealth may increase or decrease the effectiveness of the marginal utility from obtaining resources from the government and at the same time it may well have an effect on the weight assigned by the government to that specific group. Let us consider the case where increasing the wealth decreases the weight assigned by the government to a specific group. The idea is that the government wishes to help the less well off groups. In this case the elasticity of the change in the level of wealth of the group, η_d, will be negative. On the other hand, increasing the wealth may increase or decrease the utility obtained by the interest group from the funds it received. If there is a negative relationship between the wealth and the utility obtained, then increasing the wealth of a group will decrease the amount resources invested in the contest. Therefore, if the less well off group becomes more well off then this group will invest less effort in the contest and have a lower probability of winning the a higher proportion of the budget. On the other hand, if the more wealth the group has the higher is its utility it can obtain from the rescores it obtains (for example because it is more efficient etc.) then the total effect of becoming wealthier is not clear. On one hand it increases the weight the government assigns to the group however the group has less to gain from winning. This will depend on which effect is stronger: which has a larger elasticity. If the wealth effect on the utility is stronger than the effect on the government assigned weight then the probability will increase, (24) will have a positive sign: $\eta_W - \eta_d > 0$ and if the utility effect is weaker than the probability will decrease, (24) will have a negative sign: $\eta_W - \eta_d < 0$.

It is not always beneficial to increase the wealth of a certain group. Increasing the wealth of one of the groups may put this group in a worse position as it may decrease the probability of obtaining the funds from the government and decreasing the effectiveness this group has on effecting fiscal policy of the government.

2.4   Optimal Taxation

In order to finance fiscal policy, the government must impose taxation on the groups. The total amount of tax that must be lived on the groups equals to W. However, as stated above, each group receives a different utility from the benefits it may obtain from the fiscal policy and is a function of its own wealth A. As we have only two groups, in equilibrium either each of the groups will not contribute to the tax pool and will not receive any benefits, or one group will be a net contributor and the other a net receiver. Namely, in equilibrium one will pay fewer taxes than benefits it receives from the government and the other will pay more taxes than its benefits. Still both groups will compete against each other to minimize the cost or maximize the benefits each can obtain. In this scenario we are assuming that the government is a leading player. The government knows how the groups will try to affect fiscal policy and the government takes this it into account in its decisions regarding the policy. A different scenario would be that the groups know how the government reacts to their actions and determines the optimal policy and distribution accordingly. This would mean that the groups are the leading players. We do not assume this and we assume the first explanation under which the government is a leading player, i.e., as in Epstein and Nitzan (2003) we are considering a Stackelberg-Nash equilibrium where the government is the leading player.

Denote by β the proportion of taxes lived on one of the groups, say group number 1, and $(1-\beta)$ will be the proportion lived on the second group. The expected utility of both groups will thus equal to:

$$E(u_1) = A_1 + \Pr_1 W(A_1) - x_1 - \beta W(A_1) \tag{25}$$

and for the second group,

$$E(u_2) = A_2 + \Pr_2 W(A_2) - x_2 - (1-\beta)W(A_2) \tag{26}$$

Note that since $Pr_1 + Pr_2 = 1$, (25) and (26) can be written in the following way:

$$E(u_1) = A_1 + (\Pr_1 - \beta)W(A_1) - x_1 \text{ and } E(u_2) = A_2 + (\beta - \Pr_1)W(A_2) - x_2 \tag{27}$$

As we can see from (27) the first order conditions stated in (5) and (6) hold and thus all the results obtained above hold.

Let us now consider the objective function of the government. To simplify matters we will assume that the object of the government is to maximize social welfare. We will thus look at a specific case of the objective function presented above in (7) where it is stated that the objective function of the government equals to $G(.) = \alpha g(E(u_1) + E(u_2)) + (1-\alpha)f(x_1 + x_2)$. We assume therefore that the government's objective function equals:

$$G(.) = \alpha \left(E(u_1)^{0.5} + E(u_2)^{0.5} \right) + (1-\alpha)(x_1 + x_2) \tag{28}$$

This function assumes decreasing returns to the social welfare from increasing one the expected utilities of the interest groups: $\dfrac{\partial G(.)}{\partial E(u_i)} > 0$ and $\dfrac{\partial^2 G(.)}{\partial E(u_i)^2} < 0$. The objective of the government is to maximize (28) by determining the optimal burden of taxes on the two different groups. Since a change in β has no effect on the lobbying effort of the interest groups[4], the first order conditions for determining β (and thus $1-\beta$) equals[5]:

$$\frac{\partial G(.)}{\partial \beta} = \alpha 0.5\left(E(u_1)^{-0.5}\frac{\partial E(u_1)}{\partial \beta} + E(u_2)^{-0.5}\frac{\partial E(u_2)}{\partial \beta}\right) = 0 \qquad (29)$$

Rewriting (29) together with (27) we obtain:

$$\frac{\partial G(.)}{\partial \beta} = \alpha 0.5\left(E(u_2)^{-0.5}W(A_2) - E(u_1)^{-0.5}W(A_1)\right) = 0 \qquad (30)$$

The first order condition stated in (30) is satisfied if and only if the following equation is satisfied:

$$\left(\frac{E(u_1)}{E(u_2)}\right)^{0.5} = \frac{W(A_1)}{W(A_2)} \qquad (31)$$

Denote the equilibrium proportion β that satisfies (31) by β^*.

The condition stated in (31) tells us that the burden of the taxation of the groups will in an oppose relationship to the wealth each of the groups can obtain.

Let us now consider the effect of a change in d_1 on the equilibrium proportion of the tax that group number has to pay, β^*. Let us remember that increasing the value of d, decrease the chances or the proportion of the funds that this group will receive from the fiscal policy set by the government. It can be verified that $\dfrac{\partial \beta^*}{\partial d_1} = -\dfrac{\dfrac{\partial^2 G(.)}{\partial \beta \partial d_1}}{\dfrac{\partial^2 G(.)}{\partial \beta^2}}$. As the second order

---

[4] This is a direct result of (20) and (27).

[5] The second order condition is satisfied: $\dfrac{\partial^2 G(.)}{\partial \beta^2} = -0.25\alpha\left(E(u_2)^{-1.5}W(A_2)^2 + E(u_1)^{-1.5}W(A_1)^2\right) < 0$

conditions are satisfied, $\dfrac{\partial^2 G(.)}{\partial \beta^2} < 0$, the sign of $\dfrac{\partial \beta^*}{\partial d_1}$ equals the sign of $\dfrac{\partial^2 G(.)}{\partial \beta \partial d_1}$. Let us

thus calculate the value of $\dfrac{\partial^2 G(.)}{\partial \beta \partial d_1}$.

$$\frac{\partial^2 G(.)}{\partial \beta \partial d_1} = -\alpha 0.25 \left(E(u_2)^{-1.5} \frac{\partial E(u_2)}{\partial d_1} W(A_2) - E(u_1)^{-1.5} \frac{\partial E(u_1)}{\partial d_1} W(A_1) \right) \quad (32)$$

Notice that $E(u_i)$ are the equilibrium levels of the expected utility of the different groups $E(u^*_i)$.

Let us now write the expected utilities of the different groups in equilibrium. From (27), (21) and (20) we obtain:

$$E(u_1^*) = A_1 + \frac{W(A_1)^3 d_2^2}{\left(W(A_2)\, d_1 + W(A_1)\, d_2\right)^2} - \beta W(A_1) \quad (33)$$

and for the second group,

$$E(u_2^*) = A_2 + \frac{W(A_2)^3 d_2^2}{\left(W(A_2)\, d_1 + W(A_1)\, d_2\right)^2} - (1-\beta)W(A_2) \quad (34)$$

Using (32) together with (33) and (34) we obtain,

$$\frac{\partial^2 G(.)}{\partial \beta \partial d_1} = \alpha\, 0.5 \left(E(u_1)^{-1.5} \frac{W(A_1)^4 W(A_2) d_2^2}{\left(W(A_1)\, d_2 + W(A_1)d_2\right)^3} - E(u_2)^{-1.5} \frac{W(A_1)\, W(A_2) d_2 d_1}{\left(W(A_1)\, d_2 + W(A_1)d_2\right)^3} \right) \quad (35)$$

Therefore the sign of (35) equals to the sign of

$$E(u_1)^{-1.5} W(A_1)^4 W(A_2) d_2^2 - E(u_2)^{-1.5} W(A_1)\, W(A_2) d_2 d_1 \quad (36)$$

Rewetting (36) together with the first order conditions generated in (31), namely using that the government determines its proportion of the burden of taxation optimally $\left(\left(\dfrac{E(u_1)}{E(u_2)} \right)^{0.5} = \dfrac{W(A_1)}{W(A_2)} \right)$ we obtain that (36) becomes

$$W(A_1)W(A_2)^4 d_2^2 - W(A_1)\, W(A_2)^4 d_2 d_1 \quad (37)$$

We may conclude

$$\frac{\partial \beta^*}{\partial d_1} \begin{array}{c} > \\ < \end{array} 0 \quad \text{if and only if } d_2 \begin{array}{c} > \\ < \end{array} d_1 \tag{38}$$

Let us explain the result presented in (38):

a.   *This conditions states that if group number one is better off than group number two* $d_2 > d_1$ *(the politician's prefer group number on to group number two), then increasing d_1 will make this group less preferred by the politicians and thus will increase its burden of taxation. In other words, making group number and number two closer to each other in terms of their needs will increase the burden on group number one and decreases the tax burden on group number 2.*

b.   *However, if group number two is the preferred group, $d_2 < d_1$, and group number one becomes even less preferred, an increase in d_1, then this group will have a smaller burden of taxation. Namely, the government will on one had will decrease the proportion of funds it will receive however on the other hand will decrease its taxation burden. In other words, if both groups become less alike, then group number ones burden of taxation will decrease while the burden of taxation that group number 2 will pay will increase.*

3   Concluding Remarks

In this paper we investigated the relationship between lobbying effort and fiscal policy. By enabling the groups to lobby government and the politicians, we are enabling the interest groups to transfer information that is not always precise or true. It is assumed however that on average the groups that need the funds have a higher probability of receiving them. However, it is not clear that this will be the case as each of the groups can use its resources to lobby the politicians and affect their decisions.

We considered two risk neutral interest groups that lobby over fiscal policy. Each of the groups wants to affect the allocation of resources by the central government. The way in which each group affects the determination of fiscal policy and the allocation of public goods is through lobbying activities. Lobbying activities can also be seen as transfers of funds to the politicians that make the decisions. Such transfers could be donations and campaign contributions and in the more extreme case these transfers may also be forms of bribes used to influence the ruling politicians' decisions. Each group invests recourses in order to affect the politicians' decisions in determining fiscal policy. The proportion of recourses allocated to each group can also be seen as a contest success function (CSF) under which the two groups are competing over a given prize.

We show that if both groups have the same utility from each dollar obtained from fiscal policy then both groups will invest the same amount of resources in trying to obtain a larger proportion of the budget. The group with the larger needs or in the case where the politicians have an interest in a specific group, this group will, in equilibrium, obtain the largest proportion of the budget and a higher probability of affecting fiscal policy or receiving money funds which will gain a larger proportion of the budget. In the case where the politicians prefer the wealthier group, this group in equilibrium, will have a higher expected utility than the other group. It is also shown that it is not always beneficial to increase the wealth of a certain group. Increasing the wealth of one of the groups may put this group in a worse position as it may decrease the probability of obtaining the funds from the government and decreasing the effectiveness this group has on affecting fiscal policy of the government. Finally we investigated the optimal taxation policy and show that the taxation is a function of the variances of the needs of the different groups.

References

Dharmapala, D., Budgetary policy with unified decentralized appropriation authority, 2003*Public Choice,* **115**(3-4): 347-67.

Epstein G.S. and S. Nitzan, 2004 "Strategic Restraint in Contests", *European Economic Review* **48**,201-210

Epstein G.S. and S. Nitzan, 2003, "Political culture and monopoly price determination", *Social Choice and Welfare,* **21**, 1-19

Epstein G.S. and S. Nitzan, 2002a, "Public-policy contests, politicization and welfare", *Journal of public Economic Theory*, **4**(4), 661-677.

Epstein G.S. and S. Nitzan, 2006, "The Politics of Randomness" *Social Choice and Welfare*. Forthcoming.

Ghate, C., (2001) Lobbying, the Composition of Government Expenditures, and the Politics of Fiscal Policy, *Australian Economic Papers.* **40**(2): 133-45.

Grossman, G. and E. Helpman, 2001, *Special Interest Politics*, Cambridge: M.I.T. Press.

Grossman, G. and E. Helpman, 1996, "Electoral competition and special interest politics", *Review of Economic Studies*, **63**, 265-286.

Hillman, A.L. and Riley, J.G., "Politically Contestable Rents and Transfers", *Economics and Politics,* **1**, 1989, 17-39.

Hirshleifer, J., 1989, "Conflict and Rent Seeking Success functions: Ratio vs Difference Model of Relative Success" *Public Choice*, pp. 101-112.

Luce, R.D., 1959, *Individual Choice Behavior: A Theoretical Analysis* (Wiley).

Mohtadi, H. and Roe, T. (1998), Growth, Lobbying and Public Goods, *European Journal of Political Economy*, **14**(3): 453-73

Persson, T. and G. Tabellini, 2000, *Political Economics: Explaining Economic Policy*,Cambridge: M.I.T. Press.

Sheshinski, E., 2002, "Bounded Rationality and Social Optimal Limits on Choice: An Example", Hebrew University Jerusalem.

Tabellini, G. and Persson, T. (1999), Political Economics and Public Finance CEPR Discussion Paper: 2235

Tullock, G., "Efficient Rent-Seeking", In Buchanan, J.M., Tollison, R.D. and Tullock, G., 1980, *Toward a Theory of the Rent-Seeking Society*. College Station, TX: Texas A. and M. University Press. 1980, 97-112.

Tversky, A., 1969, "Intransitivity and Preferences" *Psychological Review*, **76**, pp. 31-48.

Tversky, A., 1972, "Elimination by Aspects: A Theory of Choice" *Psychological Review*, **79**, pp. 281-299.

In: Inflation, Fiscal Policy and Central Banks
Editor: Leo N. Bartolotti, pp. 153-159

Chapter 8

INFLATION AND GROWTH: AN EMPIRICAL STUDY FOR THE COMPARISON OF THE LEVEL AND THE VARIABILITY EFFECTS[‡]

K. Peren Arin[1][*] *and Tolga Omay*[2][**]
[1]Massey University, New Zealand
[2]Cankaya University, Turkey

Abstract

This paper analyzes the interaction between the inflation and growth within the Mankiw-Romer-Weil (1992) framework. Our results indicate that the inflation level has a significant negative effect on output in advanced capitalist economies, whereas inflation variability has a negative and significant effect on output in the long-run for all sub-samples. Our results also show that the variability effects are larger in terms of significance.

Keywords: Inflation, Economic Growth

1 Introduction

One of the most interesting research areas in the macroeconomics is the relationship between inflation and Growth. However, there is no single theory for inflation and economic growth in the literature, and the empirical evidence is scant and mixed.[1]

Two different views, namely structuralist and monetarist, dominate economic literature with respect to the relationship between inflation rate and economic growth. The monetarists

---

[‡] We would like to thank Chris Papageorgiou, Faik Koray, Ayca Altintig and the 2001 Southwestern Economic Association Meeting participants for their valuable suggestions. The usual disclaimer applies.

[*] Corresponding Author. Department of Commerce, Massey University, Auckland New Zealand, and Centre for Applied Macroeconomic Analysis (CAMA), Canberra, Australia. E-mail: k.p.arin@massey.ac.nz

[**] Department of Economics, Cankaya University, Ankara Turkey.

[1] Temple (2000) reviews the "stories- short and tall" that economists tell about the growth effects of inflation.

assert that price stability is a prerequisite for economic growth, claiming that inflation causes some distortions, and through these distortions, retards growth.In the structuralist view, on the other hand, wage adjustments lag behind price adjustments, changing the income distribution in favour of capitalists. Making the Kaldorian assumption that the capitalists have a higher propensity to save, this income redistribution will increase total savings, total investment, and consequently economic growth.Meanwhile, some economists remain sceptical, arguing that a nominal variable can not affect a real one.

Inflation may be considered a measure of relative price between present and future. Uncertainty about inflation creates inefficiency for allocation decisions of the current period. Uncertainty about inflation is often measured by the inflation variability. Unfortunately, to the authors' knowledge, no previous studies have attempted to compare the level and variability effects of inflation.

This paper aims to test the validity of the above stated hypotheses, by introducing three different inflation variables, to the Mankiw-Romer-Weil (1992) framework. By doing so, we aim to compare the level and variability effects of inflation on output growth.The following section reviews the related literature. Section 3 discusses the data and methodology used. Section 4 presents the empirical results. Section 5 concludes.

2 Previous Literature

Several channels have been suggested through which inflation variability can affect output. Friedman (1977) argues that increased inflation volatility makes it difficult to extract signals about relative prices from absolute prices; therefore creates economic inefficiency, which depresses future economic activity. He then conjectures that higher rates of inflation are generally associated with higher inflation variability. Engle (1983) claims that unpredictability of future inflation is the major component of welfare losses associated with inflation. When inflation is unpredictable, risk-averse economic agents will incur losses even if all prices and quantities are perfectly flexible as they cannot contract for unforeseen events.

The claim that the high and volatile inflation would affect growth negatively is supported by some empirical studies, and rejected by the others. If we begin with a single-country time series analysis, Grimes (1991) try to explain the effects of current and lagged inflation on output growth for 21 countries, and finds a significant and negative effect of inflation on growth for thirteen of them. Similarly, Stanners (1993) found only a weak (but negative) correlation between inflation and growth using time-series data for nine industrialized countries. However, the results of these studies may be unbiased First of all, in almost all countries there is a positive short-run relationship between growth and inflation, with the direction of causation running from higher growth to higher inflation. In addition, single-country time-series observations that exhibit a negative correlation may be picking up the results of the central banks' reactions: a period of high inflation (or inflationary pressures) is likely to provoke a tightening of monetary policy, which in turn and (in the short run) growth to decline. Some time-series studies have also assessed the importance of inflation variability. McTaggart (1992) contends that inflation variability had a positive effect on the growth rate, but Jansen (1989) argues that inflation has a significant negative relationship with output growth

Some studies attempted to test the effect of inflation on growth by using cross-country data. One of the earliest cross-sectional studies was by Kormendi and Meguire (1985). Using data for 47 countries over the 1950–77 period and a wide set of explanatory variables— each averaged over six-year periods—they found that inflation has a significant negative correlation with output growth, due to the negative association between inflation and investment. Grier and Tullock (1989) use pooled time series (five-year averages) and cross-sectional data between 1951 and 1980 for 113 countries and argue that a single empirical model could not explain differences in growth among these countries and therefore present different results for different country groups. For OECD countries, they find strong negative correlations between growth and the share of government spending in national income, and between growth and the variability of inflation, but no significant relation between growth and inflation. Elsewhere, the only significant relation between inflation and growth was a negative association in the African countries; and inflation variability had a significant negative relation with growth in the Asian countries. De Gregorio (1992, 1993) uses cross-sectional data for 12 Latin American countries to test the implications of an endogenous growth model in which the level and efficiency of investment are related negatively to the rate of inflation. He concludes that both inflation and its variance were negatively correlated with growth; the effect appeared to arise mainly because of a reduction in the efficiency of investment. Barro (1996) concludes that the unexpected inflation would affect growth negatively by decreasing the performance of households and firms. by using a sample of 100 countries for the 1960-1990 period. Finally, there are also a number of panel data studies, including Bruno and Easterly (1998) and Gylfason and Herbertsson (1996) which report a negative effect of inflation on economic growth. To our knowledge, none of these studies attempted to compare the level and variability effects of inflation.

3   Data and Methodology

The Neo-classical growth model proposed by Mankiw, Romer and Weil (1992) remains to be one of the most influential (therefore, most commonly used) models in analyzing the differences in levels of economic performance.The model suggests the accumulation of physical and human capital as the main source of differences in output levels. However, the model suggests the differences in saving rates as the only explanation for the differences in levels of physical and human capital accumulation. As stated above, one can argue that inflation, being a measure of relative price between present and future can also affect physical capital accumulation. In addition, uncertainty about inflation, measured by inflation variability, creates inefficiency for allocation decisions of the current period—therefore retards physical/human capital accumulation.

This study augments the neoclassical growth model proposed by Mankiw Romer Weil (1992), by using their original data, but introducing three different measures of inflation to the model: total inflation, average inflation, and inflation variability. Total inflation is the total percentage change in the price level (CPI) from the first year to the last year, , average inflation is the average percentage change in the annual price level during the sample period, and inflation variability is the standard deviation of the annual change in the price level for the sample period. All empirical models are estimated by using OLS.

4 Empirical Results

Table 1: Dependent variable: Log GDP per working age person in 1985

Sample:OECD	Regression 1.1	Regression 1.2	Regression 1.3	Regression 1.4
Constant	3.780686 (7.130)***	6.663897 (10.507)***	5.798625 (10.027)***	5.289195 (4.458)***
Ln(I/GDP)	0.621698 (2.471)***	0.270011 (0.130)	0.201236 (0.897)	0.856639 (2.219)**
Ln(school)	0.034017 (0.214)	0.350113 (2.504)***	0.221152 (1.609)*	0.114586 (0.239)
Ln(n+g+d)	-1.201374 (-4.271)***	-1.391434 (-6.994)***	-1.306004 (-5.503)***	-1.931092 (-4.774)***
Average Inflation	-	-0.021431 (-0.311)	-	-
Inflation variability	-	-	-0.001204 (-5.339)***	-
Total Inflation	-	-	-	-0.000528 (-3.985)***

R^2 : 0.3664 R^2 : 0.6973 R^2 : 0.6482 R^2 : 0.6482
$\overline{R}^2$: 0.3325 $\overline{R}^2$: 0.6715 $\overline{R}^2$: 0.6091 $\overline{R}^2$: 0.3325**

The values in the parentheses are t statistics
*: significant at 10%
**: significant at 5%
***: significant at 1%

The econometric results for the OECD countries are presented in Table 1. For OECD countries, inflation and the inflation variability have significant negative effects on output in the long-run. It is obvious that for the advanced capitalist economies, price stability is a pre-requisite for economic growth.

Table 2: Dependent variable: Log GDP per working age person in 1985

Sample: Intermediate	Regression 1.1	Regression 1.2	Regression 1.3	Regression 1.4
Constant	6.350345 (9.309)***	8.173361 (14.728)***	8.500437 (9.010)***	8.209541 (12.063)***
Ln(I/GDP)	0584849 (2.471)***	-0.123863 (-0.615)	-1.077290 (-2.312)**	-0.680526 (-2.431)***
Ln(school)	0.459652 (1.863)**	1.050604 (5.443)***	0.056889 (0.209)	1.514596 (4.321)***
Ln(n+g+d)	-0.999859 (-3.513)***	-1.101840 (-5.496)***	0.971299 (-1.857)**	-0.876060 (-4.046)***
Average Inflation	-	-0.074896 (-1.501)*	-	
Inflation variability	-	-	-0.816429 (-4.328)***	-
Total Inflation	-	-	-	-0.000312 (-1.499)*

$$R^2 : 0.3664 \qquad R^2 : 0.6973 \qquad R^2 : 0.6482 \qquad R^2 : 0.6482$$
$$\overline{R}^2 : 0.3325 \qquad \overline{R}^2 : 0.6715 \qquad \overline{R}^2 : 0.6091 \qquad \overline{R}^2 : 0.3325$$

The values in the parentheses are t statistics
*:   significant at 10%
**:   significant at 5%
***: significant at 1%

The estimation results for the intermediate sample are presented in Table 2. The less significant results for inflation may be due to the fact that output is below the potential output in these countries, and low levels of inflation may have some positive effects on growth.

Dependent variable: Log GDP per working age person in 1985

Sample: Non-oil	Regression 1.1	Regression 1.2	Regression 1.3	Regression 1.4
Constant	4.800196 (14.213)***	4.528793 (9.388)***	4.858776 (14.032)***	4.794478 (14.401)***
Ln(I/GDP)	1.127994 (7.865)***	1.175217 (7.550)***	1.115460 (7.716)***	1.046467 (7.099)***
Ln(school)	0.494755 (6.046)***	0.467996 (5.275)***	0.482967 (5.797)***	0.52069 (6.367)***
Ln(n+g+d)	-0.320808 (-1.684)**	-0.233675 (-1.060)	-0.307147 (-1.603)*	-0.198190 (-1.001)
Average Inflation	-	-0.029301 (0.789)	-	
Inflation variability	-	-	0.0064 (1.948)**	-
Total Inflation	-	-	-	-2.371418 (-0.798)
	R^2 : 0.6904 $\overline{R}^2$: 0.6805	R^2 : 0.6925 $\overline{R}^2$: 0.6792	R^2 : 0.7025 $\overline{R}^2$: 0.6897	R^2 : 0.8419 $\overline{R}^2$: 0.8350

The values in the parentheses are t statistics
*:   significant at 10%
**:   significant at 5%
***: significant at 1%

The regression results for the non-oil sample are presented in table 3. Although the total inflation and average inflation variables become insignificant, the inflation variability variable remains significant. This suggests that the negative effects of growth mostly come from inflation variability.

5   Conclusion

Although theoretical models suggest that there must be a significant negative effect of inflation on growth, it is hard to detect this influence in empirical studies. The best explanation for this observation comes from the Rational Expectations hypothesis. According to Rational Expectations theory, anticipated variables do not have any effect on the real variables, like output growth. However, separating anticipated inflation from the unanticipated one necessitates further research.

Our results show that price stability is very important for economic growth, especially for advanced capitalist economies. The results also reveal the fact that the negative effects of inflation come mostly from inflation variability.

References

Barro, R. J. (1996), 'Inflation and growth', *Federal Reserve Bank of St. Louis Review*, **78**(3), 153-169.

Bruno, M. and Easterly, W. (1998), 'Inflation crises and long-run growth', *Journal of Monetary Economics*, **41**(1), February, 3-26.

De Gregorio, J. (1992), 'The effects of inflation on economic growth', *European Economic Review*, **36**, 417-24.

De Gregorio, J. (1993), 'Inflation, taxation and long-run growth', *Journal of Monetary Economics*, **31**, 271-98.

Engle, R. F. (1983), 'Estimates of the variance of US inflation based on the ARCH model', *Journal of Money, Credit and Banking*, **15**, pages 286–301.

Friedman, M. (1977), 'Nobel lecture: inflation and unemployment', *Journal of Political Economy*, **85**, pages 451–72.

Grier, K. B. and Tullock, G. (1989), 'An Empirical analysis of cross-national economic growth', *Journal of Monetary Economics*, **24**, pages 259-279.

Grimes, A. (1991), 'The effects of inflation on growth: some international evidence' *Weltwirtschaftliches Archiv*, **127**, pages631-644.

Gylfason, T. and Herbertsson, T. T. (1996), 'Does inflation matter for growth?' *CEPR discussion paper* no. **1503**.

Jansen, D. W. (1989), 'Does inflation uncertainty affect output growth? Further evidence', *Federal Reserve Bank of St Louis Revie*w, July/August, pages 43–54.

Kormendi, R. C. and Meguire, P. G. (1985), 'Macroeconomic determinants of growth: cross-country evidence', *Journal of Monetary Economics,* **16**,pages 141–63.

Mankiw,G, Romer,D., and Weil, D. (1992), 'A contribution to the empirics of economic growth', *Quarterly Journal of Economics* **107**(2), , 407-437.

McTaggart, D. (1992), 'The cost of inflation in Australia', in *Inflation,Disinflation and Monetary Polic*y, Reserve Bank of Australia.

Temple, J. (2000), 'Inflation and growth: stories short and tall.' *Journal of Economic Surveys*, **14**(4), September, 395-426.

In: Inflation, Fiscal Policy and Central Banks
Editor: Leo N. Bartolotti, pp. 161-178

ISBN: 1-60021-122-4
© 2006 Nova Science Publishers, Inc.

Chapter 9

MONETARY POLICY IN THE TRANSITION TO A ZERO FEDERAL DEFICIT

Christopher F. Baum
Boston College
Meral Karasulu
International Monetary Fund[‡]

Abstract

In the mid–1990s, eradication of persistent U.S. federal deficits won broad bipartisan support. In the same time frame, political pressures mounted to strengthen the Federal Reserve's explicit concern with price stability. Proposals considered at that time implied a much narrower focus on the part of Fed policymakers, and could be interpreted as targeting the price level rather than a negligible rate of inflation. The deficit-reduction and price-stability policies should be analyzed in combination, as reductions in the real interest rate triggered by lower deficits will have an impact on optimal monetary policy with anti-inflation and stabilization objectives.

This chapter builds upon the analysis of Orphanides and Wilcox [2002] to evaluate optimal anti-inflation policy under a broader set of circumstances than considered in their work. We consider a monetary authority with two instruments: the funds rate (or rate of base money growth) and the discount rate, with the distinction that only movements of the latter are 'credible' alterations of the Fed's policy stance, reflecting reputational effects. The public forms expectations of inflation given realized inflation and the expected progress toward lower inflation, as evidenced by credible policy moves and the gradual eradication of the fiscal deficit.

The interaction between deficit reduction policy and the optimal monetary trajectory is analyzed, and the implications for the coordination of these strategies considered via stochastic simulations of the model. The impacts of a price level stabilization target on the Fed and a balanced-budget rule on the fiscal authorities are contrasted with their more flexible counterparts: an inflation target and restriction on deficit spending. Our results indicate that these more stringent political constraints on economic policy could have severe consequences on the ability of the monetary and fiscal authorities to mitigate adverse economic shocks.

[‡] This chapter should not be reported as representing the views of the IMF. The views expressed in this chapter are those of the authors and do not necessarily represent those of the IMF or IMF policy.

1 Introduction

From the late 1980s, a considerable literature has been developing on central banks' appropriate stance toward inflation. As inflation in many industrialized countries has been brought under control–in many cases reduced to low single-digit levels–attention has been focused on the policy actions that might be used to preserve that degree of control and effectively cope with any inflationary pressures. The roles of inflationary expectations and institutional arrangements which perpetuate a given rate of inflation, low or high, have been highlighted in this literature. In the United States and several other OECD economies, legal constraints on the central bank's policy objectives and behavior have been considered, and in some cases put into practice. In some instances, these constraints have been phrased in terms of the aggregate price level, rather than the rate of price inflation. For instance, the Economic Growth and Price Stability Act of 1995, introduced by Rep. Saxton in September 1995 (but not acted upon by the 104th Congress), called upon the Federal Reserve to establish an explicit numerical definition of "price stability" and maintain monetary policy to effectively promote long-term price stability. Such a mandate would seem to require that price increases would have to be met with deflationary policy to satisfy the constraint. More commonly, low or negligible inflation has been identified as an explicit and sole target of monetary policy.

In this chapter, we broaden this debate to take into account the interactions between Federal Reserve anti-inflation policy (either discretionary or mandated) and the simultaneous efforts on the part of the fiscal authorities to drive the Federal deficit to zero within a defined period. This emphasis on fiscal stability has also been phrased in terms of legislative mandates, but the repeated failure of the Congress to pass such legislation should not be viewed as a lack of resolve to deal with the issue of deficit spending. In the late 1990s, there appeared to be broad bipartisan support in both Congress and the Administration to enact a feasible plan to balance the budget over a realistic time frame. We consider monetary policy actions in this context, and consider, as other authors have suggested, that anti-inflation policy must take these fiscal measures into account.

We construct a stylized model of the monetary-fiscal interaction which takes several elements of this process into account: inflationary expectations, the credibility of monetary policy, and the dynamic interactions between progress toward budget balance, the underlying movements of the economy's real interest rate, and monetary responses. Although the model is preliminary, it manages to capture many of the implications of these interactions when applied as a nonlinear constraint to a fairly complex stochastic optimal policy problem. This problem takes as given the progress toward the fiscal goal of budget balance within five to ten years from the perspective of the late 1990s and generates closed-loop feedback rules for the manipulation of two monetary policy instruments, the funds rate and the discount rate, over a 40-quarter horizon.

The plan of the chapter is as follows. Section 2 reviews a selection of relevant literature, while the following section presents the econometric model and illustrates its properties. In Section 4, the optimal policy experiment is presented, and implications drawn for the interactions between the fiscal target path and monetary policy responses. Section 5 concludes and provides a sketch of further research.

2 Review of the Literature

The recent literature on the conduct of monetary policy is vast, and we can only acknowledge the major influences on our work in this chapter. The view of monetary policy as a process with identified goals and inherent constraints, rather than a sequence of discretionary actions, underlies the papers in several conference volumes. The Boston Fed's "Goals, Guidelines and Constraints Facing Monetary Policymakers" [1994], the Kansas City Fed's symposia "Budget Deficits and Debt: Issues and Options" [1995], "Achieving Price Stability" [1996] and the Bank of Japan's "Financial Stability in a Changing Environment" [1995] all contain papers highlighting the importance of the design of monetary policy and its interaction with the real economy. John Taylor's article in the Boston volume specifically addresses the interactions between the "implicit" real interest rate specified by monetary policymakers and the economy's equilibrium real interest rate. As the latter is altered by policy changes in the real economy (as we discuss in this chapter) Taylor demonstrates that the steady-state inflation rate will change, and by more than the equilibrium real rate, requiring a response from monetary policymakers.

William Poole's paper in the same volume is concerned with the choice facing monetary policymakers in using interest rates or monetary aggregates as their instrument. He finds reason for concern for the de facto abandonment of the aggregates as the instrument of policy, arguing that heavy reliance on the funds rate has rendered the financial markets hypersensitive to minor shifts (real or perceived) in the Fed's policy stance. Poole relates that "...the overwhelming majority of large changes in bond yields arise in response to actions by the monetary authorities and to releases of routine economic data." [1994, p. 106] This generates, in his view, a situation where "...the Fed cannot use the behavior of interest rates to provide useful information on how it should adjust the federal funds rate. The bond market today tells the Fed what the market thinks the Fed is going to do." [1994, p. 108] While realization of this dependence may do much to inflate the egos of Fed governors, it also creates a situation where, as Poole puts it, "...it is easy for the Fed to make a mistake because the bond market will not provide a strong contrary signal." [1994, p. 108] Thus, monetary policy actions must be taken with a clear understanding of how market participants' expectations will respond to those signals.

In a paper given at the 1995 Kansas City Fed conference, John Taylor specifically considers the interactions between the practice of monetary policy and an environment with greater fiscal discipline. He considers how monetary policymakers' objectives may have to be adjusted during the transition to a lower deficit, and how monetary policymaking might be constrained by the imposition of limits on budget deficits. A crucial distinction, shared by a number of researchers, arises between reducing the structural deficit to zero and prohibiting a deficit at any point in the cycle. Taylor suggests that "...ideal fiscal reform would preserve the cyclical variation in the actual deficit while forcing the structural deficit to be zero..." [1995, p. 163] but acknowledges that many of the rules being considered in Congress would actually constrain the total deficit. This severe constraint would force a change in monetary policy, as the "automatic stabilizers" of fiscal policy would be removed by a prohibition on deficit spending. He concludes that fiscal discipline need not have a sizable effect on the credibility of monetary policy, but would have significant benefits for the real economy in the form of higher productivity growth and higher real incomes.

In the Kansas City Fed's symposium on "Achieving Price Stability," Mervyn King considers how central banks should achieve price stability, drawing on his experience at the Bank of England. He considers the distinction between a central bank's *ex ante* inflation target and its discretionary response to shocks, and suggests that "...in general, it is not optimal to move immediately to a regime of price stability unless that regime can be made fully credible by institutional or other changes." [1996, pp. 57–58] His rationale for that conclusion is based on the hypothesis that there are costs of disinflation, increasing more than proportionally in the rate of disinflation, related to private agents' ability to determine whether a regime change has actually taken place. (This argument is very closely related to that put forth by Kozicki and Tinsley [1998] in their moving-endpoint models). King argues that "...expectations are likely to be influenced by the commitment to price stability among the public at large" [1996, p. 58] and suggests that central bank behavior can only influence that commitment. Private agents must learn about the new economic environment, and the central bank must learn about agents' revised behavior. In King's view, "pure rational expectations models are not a good basis on which to base policy because they ignore the process of learning." [1996, p. 79] From his viewpoint, a successful model of monetary policy must take the learning process into account.

In another paper in the same volume, Lars Svensson argues that an explicit inflation target is the best way to maintain low and stable inflation. In this paper and in several others, he puts forth the concept of the inflation forecast as an intermediate target, which in his view avoids the problems of lags, demand and supply shocks, and model uncertainty. Svensson considers the relative merits of "target rules" vs. "instrument rules," preferring the former on the grounds of feasibility and transparency. He also speaks directly to the issue of price level targeting vs. inflation targeting, pointing out an interesting consequence of an insistence on the former: a reduction in variance of the price level (i.e. price stability) will actually imply greater short-term variability of the inflation rate and output. As he argues, "...in order to stabilize the price level under price level targeting, higher-than-average inflation must be followed by lower-than-average inflation. This should result in higher inflation variability than inflation targeting, since base level drift is accepted in the latter case and higher-than-average inflation need only be succeeded by average inflation. Via nominal rigidities, the higher inflation variability should then result in higher output variability." [1996, p. 217]

A different aspect of the interactions between monetary policy and other sectors of the economy is given by participants in the Bank of Japan's conference on financial stability, in which the potentially conflicting objectives of the central bank are highlighted. On the one hand, any central bank has macroeconomic objectives, be they a statutory responsibility for low inflation, a stable price level, or maximum growth and employment consistent with objectives of stable prices. At the same time, central banks serve as regulators in the financial sector, and the policy responses required to counter threats to financial sector stability may run counter to their appropriate macro-policy stance. Charles Goodhart points out that a more prudent regulatory stance–for instance, insisting on market value accounting, which if applied in the 1980s would have rendered many banks and S&Ls technically insolvent far more rapidly than did regulatory standards of the time–is bound to conflict with macroeconomic objectives; in his words, "most measures aimed at encouraging more prudent bank behavior are liable to be procyclical in the short run, whereas...Central Bank actions to support banks through crises are likely to be anti-cyclical...Regulatory measures, e.g. capital ratios...tend to bite during (asset price) depressions, and are more commonly non-binding during (bubble) booms." [1995, p. 478] Goodhart also argues that one of the common remedies proposed for banking safety, "narrow bank" schemes, would make cyclical fluctuations more extreme through dis- (and re-) intermediation effects over the business cycle.

Writing in the same volume, Bennett McCallum considers the tension between "lender-of-last-resort" functions of the central bank and the call to focus monetary policy on a "macro-oriented rule" (e.g. those advocated by McCallum, Meltzer, or Taylor) such as a mandate for price stability or low inflation. He considers that interest rate smoothing, usually treated as a goal of short-term open market policy, may actually be able to reconcile both objectives, as it "would automatically trigger open-market purchases whenever a sharp increase in the demand for high-powered money happened to occur. But such week-to-week smoothing could perhaps be compatible with use of this interest rate as an instrument for hitting slightly lower–frequency (e.g., quarterly average) intermediate targets conforming to a monetary policy rule designed to yield desirable macroeconomic performance." [1995, p. 415] Thus, this strand of literature considers the importance of recognizing these dual objectives in any central bank's mandate, and taking into account the central bank's important role in promoting stability of the financial system when contemplating a single-minded macro objective.

Finally, we must acknowledge the very sizable contribution of a paper by Orphanides and Wilcox [2002] to our development of a model of these policy issues. In this paper, they introduce the "opportunistic approach" to disinflation: the concept that the Fed may actively combat inflation only when it threatens to increase, and otherwise should wait for external circumstances (e.g., recessions) that will bring the inflation rate down. This approach leads to a switching strategy, in which the Fed acts to stabilize output when inflation is low, but moves to fight inflation when it is high. The definitions of "low" and "high" are state-dependent in their model, so that there is no fixed rule defining the policy response to current conditions. Orphanides and Wilcox provide an appealing argument for this mixed strategy: that is, for the central bank's concern for output and employment. They suggest that the policymakers incur a "first-order loss from output deviations even when output is close to potential, and yet only a second-order loss from inflation deviations when inflation is close to its target." [2003, p. 65] They provide what is characterized as a highly speculative rationale for this ordering, in that "The deleterious effects of inflation are mainly allocative in nature..." while "...employment is an all-or-nothing proposition...", providing "a basis for treating deviations of output from potential as imposing first-order costs on the policy maker." [2003, p. 66]

They extend their model to consider more realistic aspects of aggregate demand and supply, but their model is cast in a single-period framework. We take a number of elements of their model as a starting point in developing the model presented in the next section, in which we use a multi-period framework in order to consider the dynamic interactions of monetary policy with fiscal discipline.

3   A Model of Monetary and Fiscal Interactions

In this section, the framework we have developed to evaluate the dynamic interactions between anti-inflation monetary policy and a deficit reduction strategy is presented. The model necessarily abstracts from many elements of a complete and interdependent treatment of expectations formation and policy design, but has been constructed to focus on key elements of this process in the context of historical evidence. The model consists of three estimated behavioral equations and a number of identities linking two monetary instruments to the targets of policy. Progress toward the fiscal objective is taken as exogenous; in future work we will relax this recursive structure, and allow for uncertainty in the attainment of fiscal goals. Unlike Orphanides and Wilcox' original work [2002], which is purely analytical, and their followup paper [Aksoy et al., 2003], which performs stochastic simulations in an historical setting, we utilize the model in a closed-loop optimal policy exercise, in which explicit penalties are applied to deviations from target values, and optimal feedback rules derived for the policy instruments.

The policy environment modelled here is one in which Federal Reserve actions can control short–term nominal interest rates, but cannot control real rates. As one of the major innovations of this model, we consider two instruments of monetary policy–the Federal funds rate and the discount rate–which are both assumed to have effects on the financial sector, but differ in their signalling capability. We make use of well-known stylized facts about the discount rate: that it has been altered infrequently, in small increments, and almost never subjected to a reversal [e.g., Baum and Karasulu, 1998]. These empirical regularities, coupled with the description of the discount rate by researchers inside and outside the Fed as an instrument with sizable "announcement effects," lead us to a description of policy in which a discount rate change is viewed as a credible signal of the stance of policy, precisely because such a signal is infrequently and cautiously emitted. The funds rate, on the other hand, is viewed as an instrument having direct effects on the financial sector, but which is far less credible as a signal of policy stance. Realistically, changes in the funds rate may reflect either the Fed's doing or their acquiescence to market forces–or even an allowed response to a threat to financial system stability. In the stylized environment of our model, we consider that changes in the funds rate are much less effective in influencing inflationary expectations than are discount rate changes.

In this setting, aggregate demand, as proxied by the GDP gap, responds (with some persistence) to movements in the real rate of interest relative to its long-run level; the current real rate is determined by the Fisher equation, incorporating the funds rate. The aggregate supply relation is inverted to generate the level of inflation consistent with the GDP gap and expected inflation. Inflation is modeled as a persistent phenomenon, implicitly reflecting contract terms and menu costs of price adjustment (along the lines of Fuhrer and Moore [1995]). Inflationary expectations are modeled with a partial adjustment scheme in which both past expectations and recently experienced inflation affect their revision. The deviation of the discount rate from the long-term real rate of interest is used to signal the Fed's willingness to credibly reduce inflation to that level.

On the fiscal side, we make use of the empirical regularity cited by Taylor, in which he cites "A close approximation of current fiscal policy in the United States is that the budget deficit (D) as a share of GDP rises by 0.5 times the percentage deviation (Y) of real GDP from potential GDP... That is, a fiscal policy rule which closely approximates the actual deficit is $D = -0.5Y + S$ where S is a constant." [1995, p. 162] S equals the structural deficit as a share of GDP; Taylor finds that it has been about 3.5 percent over the past decade. Using this regularity, we model fiscal discipline as a trajectory for S which reduces S from its 1995 level to near zero over a range of 20–40 quarters. We consider three trajectories for S, differing in the speed at which a zero structural deficit is attained, and in their pattern of reduction. In the current form of the model, we calculate the resulting accounting deficit (D) but it plays no further role in the model's workings. In an extension, we plan to take account of the feedback between continued deficits and financing costs, or "crowding out." We also do not take account in this version of the model of the likely obstacles to deficit reduction–political or external–that most sanguine observers of the process might expect to arise. Realistically, such roadblocks would both slow the transition path and create added uncertainty about its likely outcome.

The crucial link between deficit reduction and the financial sector is provided by an equation linking the change in the structural deficit to the change in the long-term real rate of interest. We do not model this as a response to the accounting deficit, as we want to express the long-run equilibrium rate of interest as independent of the business cycle. We make use of estimates presented by Taylor's simulation of his multi-country econometric model, in which a one per cent increase in the deficit/GDP ratio brings about a roughly 50 basis point increase in the long-term bond rate. [1993, pp. 202, 213–214] We use this estimated response coefficient to project the magnitude of the fall in the equilibrium real interest rate which will be generated by greater fiscal discipline. As Taylor suggests, there is fairly broad consensus that "lower budget deficits will lower real interest rates, increase investment, and thereby increase productivity growth and real incomes" [1995, p. 151]. As fiscal discipline reduces real interest rates, the monetary policy authorities must take this shifting anchor into account when setting their target for inflation.

We now present the estimated relationships and identities of our model, which were fit to quarterly data over the 1975-1995 period. The estimated equation for the GDP gap (defined as $Y = 100\log\left(GDP/GDP^p\right)$ where the $GDPP$ series was derived from CBO estimates) is a fourth-order autoregression in the gap augmented with the spread between the current real rate and its long run target. The coefficient estimates are presented in Table 1. The estimated coefficient on the spread has the expected negative sign. This equation is dynamically stable, with a maximum modulus of 0.943.

Table 1: Estimated Equation for the GDP Gap (Y), 1975:1–1995:4

Regressor	Coefficient	Standard Error	T–ratio
Y(t-1)	3.3635	0.0684	49.18
Y(t-2)	-4.5610	0.1953	-23.35
Y(t-3)	2.9594	0.1985	14.91
Y(t-4)	-0.7757	0.0716	-10.83
[r–r*]	-0.0063	0.0025	-2.53

Notes: estimation method is ordinary least squares with Hansen–White errors.

The estimated equations for realized and expected inflation form a block. Realized inflation–the inverted aggregate supply schedule–is modeled as a fourth-order autoregression augmented with the prior period's expected inflation series and the current GDP gap ratio. Expected inflation is modeled with a lag to account for delays in price-setting behavior. The coefficient estimates of the realized inflation equation are presented in Table 2. Expected inflation stimulates realized inflation, as does a higher value of the GDP gap variable (i.e. a smaller gap). The equation is dynamically stable, with a maximum modulus of 0.924.

Table 2: Estimated Equation for the Inflation Rate (π), 1975:1–1995:4

Regressor	Coefficient	Standard Error	T-ratio
$\pi(t-1)$	0.6261	0.1434	4.37
$\pi(t-2)$	-0.1833	0.2027	-0.90
$\pi(t-3)$	0.5515	0.1530	3.60
$\pi(t-4)$	-0.1182	0.1304	-0.91
$\pi^{\varepsilon}(\tau-1)$	0.1051	0.2723	0.39
$Y(t)$	0.1708	0.1117	1.53

Notes: estimation method is ordinary least squares with Hansen–White errors.

Expected inflation is modeled with a partial adjustment mechanism, in which a convex combination of lagged expected inflation and inflationary influences generates expectations. The influences considered include once- and twice-lagged actual inflation as well as the spread between the discount rate and the long-term real rate. As discussed above, the latter term is introduced to proxy for credible policy signals: a larger spread indicates that the Fed is willing to allow higher inflation to persist, while a narrowing of the spread would indicate an attack on inflation, in this framework perceived as credible. The coefficient estimates, obtained by nonlinear least squares, are presented in Table 3. A fairly high weight is placed upon current inflationary influences, and the effect of the spread is sizable and significant.

Table 3: Estimated Equation for the Expected Inflation Rate (π^{ε}), 1975:1–1995:4

$$\pi_t^e = \lambda \pi_{t-1}^e + (1-\lambda)\left(\eta_1 \pi_{t-1} + \eta_2 \pi_{t-2} + \eta_3\left(d_t - r_t^*\right)\right)$$

	Coefficient	Standard Error	T-ratio
λ	0.1801	0.2090	0.86
η_1	0.7136	0.1274	5.60
η_2	0.0403	0.1527	0.26
η_3	0.2183	0.0948	2.30

Notes: estimation method is nonlinear least squares with Hansen–White errors.

The expected inflation series used in these estimates was generated from a projection of realized inflation on eight lags of inflation, the GDP gap, the two policy instruments and a constant term. This series was then used to define the current real rate (R) as the difference between the Fed funds rate and expected inflation. The long term real rate, which enters the first two behavioral equations, was estimated as the sample mean of R over the period, equal to 2.21 percent.

To evaluate the reasonableness of the entire model, an *ex ante* dynamic simulation was performed for 1996:1–2005:4. Monetary policy instruments were held at their 1995:4 values while the structural deficit (S) was projected to decline linearly from its historical value of 3.65 percent of GDP to zero over the 40 quarter horizon. Resulting trajectories of the model's variables were sensible, with a modest loss of output (reaching just over two percent of GDP at the end of the horizon) and a steady reduction in realized and expected inflation. The single anomaly in this simulation was the accounting deficit, which fell only slowly through the period, never falling below one percent of GDP. Thus, the simulation does not reflect a true balanced budget rule, but rather an exercise in which the structural deficit is eradicated over the 10-year horizon. In summary, the model would appear to be reasonably well behaved, and capable of being used in an out-of-sample period to reflect the interactions of the real and financial sectors in the context of fiscal discipline and anti–inflation policy.

4   Optimal Monetary Policy Responses to Fiscal Discipline

The framework in which we pose an optimal policy problem is that developed by Chow [1975, 1981)] as an elaboration of the stochastic, dynamic linear-quadratic-Gaussian (LQG) optimal control framework. In a standard LQG exercise, the expectation of a multiperiod quadratic loss function is minimized, subject to the constraints posed by a linear econometric model, with stochastic elements arising from Gaussian errors. The solution is achieved by solution of the matrix Riccati equation, applying Bellman's principle of dynamic programming to generate optimal feedback rules for each period in the horizon. This framework is unduly restrictive in terms of both the loss function and the econometric model, as on the one hand we might often want to penalize deviations from targets in a non-quadratic (e.g., asymmetric) manner, and on the other hand we might have a model which is essentially nonlinear. Extensions to Chow's algorithm permit both of these generalizations by generating linearizations of a nonlinear model around each point on the target trajectory. A nonlinear model may contain complicated (and even nondifferentiable, or noncontinuous) functions of the underlying variables, which may then be targeted: allowing for non-quadratic elements in the loss function. With these generalizations of the LQG framework, we may consider a quite realistic setting for the interactions of policy instruments and goals.

The key elements of such an optimal policy problem are the relative weights applied to the components of the state vector. In the Chow framework, the dynamic system of arbitrary order in both endogenous (Y) and policy (X) variables is reduced to first order via the introduction of appropriate identities. In the case of our model, there are up to fourth-order lags on the Y variables, and as noted below, up to third-order lags on the X variables are referenced. Thus the state vector for this model consists of current through third-order lags on the Y variables (which, with identities and definitions, are 14 in number) and current through second-order lags on the two X variables. In a stochastic optimal policy exercise, the existence of more than two targeted elements of the state vector ensures that not all targets will be hit even in an expected sense. The expected multiperiod loss may be considered similar to a measure of mean square error (*MSE*), including both a "bias" term (indicating the magnitude in which the targets were not hit) and a "variance" term derived from the estimated variance-covariance matrix of the equations' error processes. Although in this framework the parameters are taken as given at their point estimates (i.e. there is no multiplicative uncertainty) the presence of additive uncertainty will generate expected loss even when "bias" is zero.

The loss function applied in this problem is an extension of that used by Orphanides and Wilcox [2002, p. 52] in their single-period model. They include three terms in their loss function $\ell_a = (\pi - \tilde{\pi})^2 + \gamma y^2 + \psi|y|$: the squared deviation of realized inflation from an inflation target, the squared GDP gap, and the absolute value of the GDP gap. The presence of the intermediate target for inflation, which they treat as merely a constant fraction of last period's inflation, and the weighting of both square and absolute value of the GDP gap give rise to their "opportunistic approach" to anti-inflation policy. They also demonstrate that the inflation term in their loss function is mathematically equivalent to targeting both the level of and changes in the rate of inflation: or in terms of the control literature, applying both proportional and derivative control.

In our policy problem, we are facing a multiperiod horizon, and have two instruments to work with. Our loss function takes additional factors into account, reflecting the more complex setting in which these instruments interact. The primary innovation in our multiple-instrument setting is the specification of loss associated with discount rate changes. As discussed above, we assume that changes in the discount rate are viewed as credible signals of policy stance by the public. The maintenance of this credibility relies upon the Fed's unwillingness to alter the instrument frequently and their desire to avoid reversals, or "whipsaw" actions. Although we cannot directly model the degree of credibility attached to a signal in the expectations formation process, we can take the maintenance of credibility into account in the loss function. The Fed, aware of the value of a credible signalling mechanism, should be unwilling to reduce this value through haphazard manipulations of the discount rate. Thus, we construct a "cost-of-change" variable (C) which takes into account both recent changes in the discount rate as well as the consistency of those changes: penalizing reversals more heavily than changes which merely reflect a trend, such as successive increases (decreases). The C function is defined as:

$$cc_t = \left| \log\left(d_t / d_{t-1} \right) \right| + 0.5 \left| \log\left(d_t / d_{t-2} \right) \right| + 0.333 \left| \log\left(d_t / d_{t-3} \right) \right|$$

$$rc1_t = \begin{cases} \left| \log\left(d_t / d_{t-1} \right) - \log\left(d_{t-1} / d_{t-2} \right) \right|, & (d_t - d_{t-1})(d_{t-1} - d_{t-2}) < 0 \\ 0, & (d_t - d_{t-1})(d_{t-1} - d_{t-2}) \geq 0 \end{cases}$$

$$rc2_t = \begin{cases} \left| 0.5 \log\left(d_t / d_{t-2} \right) - \log\left(d_{t-2} / d_{t-3} \right) \right|, & (d_t - d_{t-2})(d_{t-2} - d_{t-3}) < 0 \\ 0, & (d_t - d_{t-2})(d_{t-2} - d_{t-3}) \geq 0 \end{cases}$$

$$C_t = cc_t + rc1_t + rc2_t$$

The value of this cost-of-change variable is then targeted as an element of the loss function. To gain an understanding for the workings of the cost-of-change function, we plot its components (change cost and reversal cost) and their sum for the estimation period, 1975:1–1995:4, in Figure 1, and the total cost versus the discount rate in Figure 2. We may note that the Fed's actions, involving quite infrequent and consistent changes in the discount rate, correspond to a quite low cost throughout much of the historical period.

Figure 1
Cost of Change Function for the Discount Rate, 1975-1995

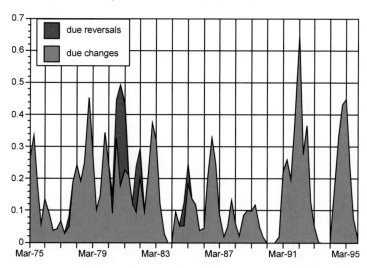

Two other elements derived from the policy instruments are targeted: the spread between the funds rate and the discount rate, and the spread between the current real rate and its long-run target. The rationale for the former relates to the mechanism by which the discount rate will provide incentives for member bank borrowing. The funds rate–discount rate spread is generally positive, reflecting that discount window borrowing is a privilege, and that "excessive" use of the discount windows will invite scrutiny. Therefore, banks with the need for reserves will turn to the Fed funds and repurchase agreement (RP) markets, paying a premium to conduct transactions free of this scrutiny. To model this empirical regularity, we target the funds rate–discount rate spread at 30 basis points, a value consistent with recent historical evidence. The latter spread–that between the current real rate and its long-run value–is targeted merely as a direct effect to speed convergence of the real rate to its long-run value.

Figure 2
Cost of Change Function and the Discount Rate, 1975-1995

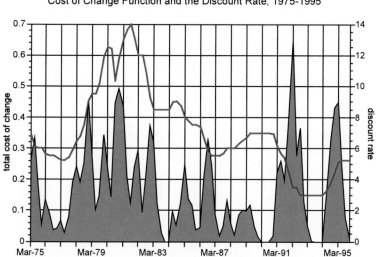

In the policy experiment, the heaviest weight of 1.0 is placed on the squared deviation of current inflation from its target value, reflecting the Fed's primary concern with the reduction of inflation. Following Orphanides and Wilcox, the intermediate target for inflation is taken to be 0.5 times last period's inflation, so that the long-run target for inflation is zero. Lower weights of 0.25 are applied to both the squared gap and the absolute value of the gap, with values chosen to generate some tension between anti-inflation and macroeconomic objectives. The cost-of-change function and the two spreads mentioned above are each targeted at 0.10, reflecting the second-order concern with instruments' values. It should be noted that, first, only relative weights matter, and second, that the magnitude of the variables affects the appropriate magnitude of the weights.

As stated above, we model the trajectory of fiscal discipline as deterministic, reflecting steady progress toward the goal of a zero structural deficit from the initial conditions of 3.65 percent of GDP. In the baseline experiment (denoted 40), the structural deficit is reduced linearly to zero over 40 quarters (the full horizon of the policy experiment). In the first alternative (denoted 20), the structural deficit is reduced to zero twice as fast–over the first 20 quarters of the experiment–and held at zero for the remaining period. In the second alternative (denoted CG), the structural deficit is reduced to 92% of its prior value in each period, with a terminal value close to zero. All other elements of the model are determined within the policy experiments.

The outcome of the policy experiment is a set of optimal feedback rules which express the appropriate settings for the two instruments as a function of the prior period's state vector. In this closed-loop optimal policy setting, the optimal policy is not expressed in terms of values for the instruments, but rather rules by which the instruments would be determined, contingent on economic conditions. The certainty-equivalent trajectory for each of the instruments may be derived by ignoring the stochastic elements of the problem and applying the feedback rules to each period's values for the state vector. These certainty-equivalent trajectories may then be examined to judge the qualitative nature of the optimal policy solution.

In Figure 3, results from the baseline experiment (in which the structural deficit is reduced to zero over 40 quarters) are presented for the GDP gap, the inflation rate, and the deficit/GDP ratio. Although the structural deficit is reduced linearly, the accounting deficit is subject to economic performance. For the first several years of the simulation, the output gap remains at about 0.5 percent of GDP, causing the accounting deficit to be larger than the structural deficit. The inflation rate declines abruptly at the beginning of the experiment, rebounds, and then falls steadily throughout the remaining period, nearing 0.5 percent in the later years. The inflation rate is juxtaposed with the two policy instruments in Figure 4. We see here that attainment of lower inflation brings about lower money-market rates, consistent as well with the reduction in the real rate. The decline in both the funds rate and the discount rate is steep at the outset, but fairly smooth due to the cost-of-change imposed on the discount rate.

Figure 3
GDP Gap, Inflation Rate, and Deficit/GDP Ratio, baseline experiment

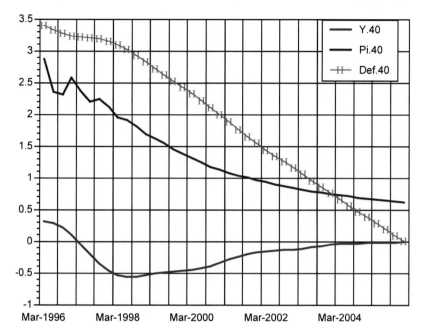

Figure 4
Inflation Rate, Fed Funds Rate, and Discount Rate, baseline experiment

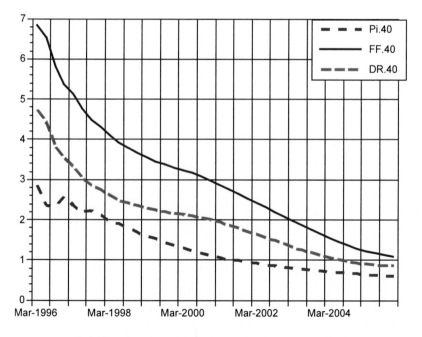

Figure 5 compares the expected trajectories of the GDP gap for the three deficit reduction strategies: the baseline (40-quarter) case, the 20-quarter alternative, and the constant reduction (CG) alternative. All three provide similar results at the outset, but the more rapid (Y.20) alternative demonstrates an improvement in the gap as soon as the structural deficit is eradicated in 2000. However, in the last two years, it actually underperforms the other scenarios. Equivalent findings for the current real interest rate are presented in Figure 6. The 40–quarter scenario yields the slowest decline in the rate over the period; the rapid balance (r.20) strategy brings about the lowest rates from the third year onward.

Figure 5
GDP gap for alternate deficit reduction strategies

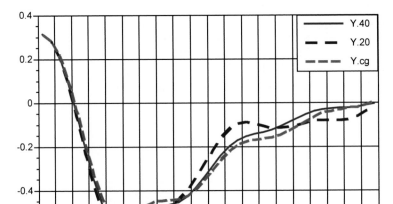

Figure 6
Real Interest Rate for alternate deficit reduction strategies

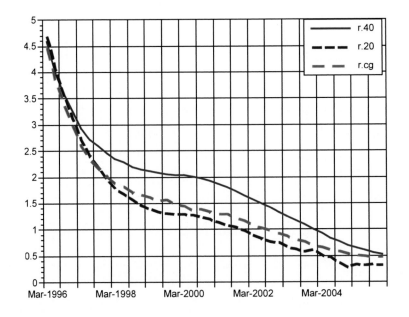

In Figure 7, the differing paths of the accounting deficit are presented. The CG alternative may be seen as an intermediate path, leading to the most rapid initial decline but higher accounting deficits from mid-1999 onward. These higher deficits are associated with higher real interest rates; in Figure 8, we may see the difference between the discount rates consistent with each strategy. The discount rate associated with the 40-quarter strategy (DR.40) is consistently higher than that associated with the other strategies, reflecting the necessity for the monetary authorities to coordinate their actions with the imposition of fiscal discipline. To contrast these discount rate paths with those experienced in the estimation period (presented in Figure 2), we illustrate the cost-of-change (C) and the expected trajectory for the discount rate (DR.40) for the baseline scenario in Figure 9. The weight placed upon cost-of-change renders reversals of the rate unlikely; the trajectory is quite smooth, leveling off in the middle years (leading to a lower cost of change) and then dipping downward in the later years.

Figure 7
Accounting Deficit/GDP for alternate deficit reduction strategies

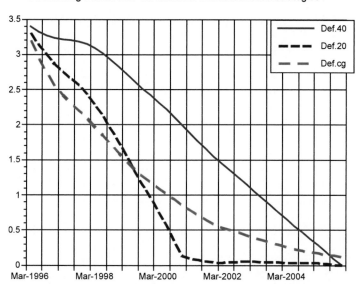

Although many additional insights might be gleaned from analysis of the optimal policy experiments and variations on those experiments, it should be evident that many elements of the interactions between fiscal discipline, expectations of policy actions, and the policies chosen by the Fed are captured in these results. Although the model presented here is simplistic and stylized, it demonstrates some of the key dynamic elements of the policy process.

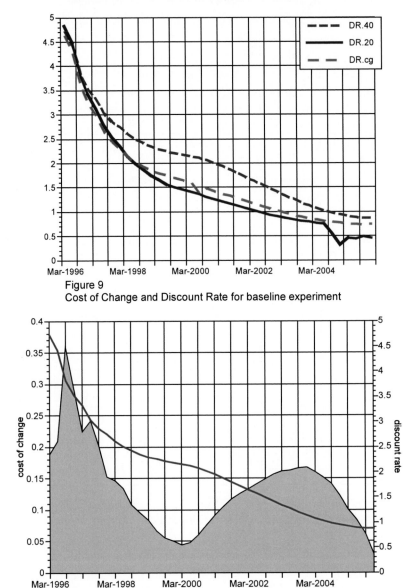

Figure 8
Discount Rate for alternate deficit reduction strategies

Figure 9
Cost of Change and Discount Rate for baseline experiment

5   Conclusions and Suggestions for Further Research

Should the Federal Reserve be instructed to stabilize prices (or the rate of price inflation?)
Much of the literature we have reviewed in this study concluded that the traditional stance of
our central bank, evincing concern for both price stability and macroeconomic performance,
has merit. In the context of a major fiscal initiative such as a steady course toward eradicating
the deficit, it may be all the more important that the Federal Reserve retain some flexibility to
counter unforeseen shocks, even if they might tend to temporarily weaken the anti–inflation
effort. At the same time, flexibility can degenerate into arbitrary, destabilizing policy actions.

In this chapter, we have stressed the importance of credibility of monetary policy through the introduction of a "credible signal" in the form of the discount rate. The historical manipulation of this policy instrument is consistent, we believe, with the underlying concept embedded in our cost-of-change function: that market participants value a credible signal, and the Fed acts so as to maintain that credibility in manipulating an instrument with a powerful "announcement effect." Although the model constructed here is in its early stages of development, we believe that it successfully demonstrates the dynamic interactions between fiscal and monetary strategies, and its employment in an optimal policy exercise goes beyond the usual simulation experiments.

In further development of this framework, we believe that the Orphanides and Wilcox "opportunistic" approach, which underlies much of the model presented in this chapter, and our own work on modelling discount policy may be fruitfully combined. The concept of threshold behavior, in which action is only taken when a threshold is reached, is attractive in the context of a policy instrument whose use incurs a sizable cost. It may be feasible to combine our *ad hoc* specification of a cost-of-change function in this chapter with an econometric approach to threshold modelling in order to generate a more realistic representation of monetary policymakers' actions.

References

Aksoy, Y., Orphanides, A., Small, D., Wieland, V. and D. W. Wilcox, 2003. A Quantitative Exploration of the Opportunistic Approach to Disinflation. CEPR Discussion Paper No. 4073.

Baum, C.F. and M. Karasulu, 1998. Modelling Federal Reserve Discount Policy. *Computational Economics*, **11**, 53-70.

Chow, G., 1975. *Analysis and Control of Dynamic Economic Systems*. New York: John Wiley and Sons.

_____, 1981. *Econometric Analysis by Control Methods*. New York: John Wiley and Sons.

Fuhrer, J. and G. Moore, 1995. Inflation Persistence. *Quarterly Journal of Economics*, **110**:127-159.

Goodhart, C.A.E., 1995. Price Stability and Financial Fragility, in K. Sawamoto et al., eds., *Financial Stability in a Changing Environment*. London: St. Martin's Press.

King, M., 1996. How Should Central Banks Reduce Inflation? Conceptual Issues, in *Achieving Price Stability*. Kansas City: Federal Reserve Bank of Kansas City.

Kozicki, S. and P. Tinsley, 1998. Moving Endpoints and the Internal Consistency of Agents' Ex Ante Forecasts. *Computational Economics*, **11**, 21-40.

McCallum, B., 1995. Monetary Policy Rules and Financial Stability, in K. Sawamoto et al., eds., *Financial Stability in a Changing Environment*. London: St. Martin's Press.

Orphanides, A. and D. Wilcox, 2002. The Opportunistic Approach to Disinflation. *International Finance*, **5**, 47–71. Previously circulated as FEDS Working Paper 96–24, Federal Reserve Board of Governors.

Poole, W., 1994. Monetary Aggregates Targeting in a Low-Inflation Economy, in J. Fuhrer, ed., *Goals, Guidelines and Constraints Facing Monetary Policymakers*. Boston: Federal Reserve Bank of Boston.

Svensson, L., 1996. Commentary on "How should monetary policy respond to shocks while maintaining long run price stability–conceptual issues," in *Achieving Price Stability*. Kansas City: Federal Reserve Bank of Kansas City.

Taylor, J., 1993. *Macroeconomic Policy in a World Economy*. New York: W.W. Norton.

_____, 1994. The Inflation/Output Variability Trade-off Revisited, in J. Fuhrer, ed., *Goals, Guidelines and Constraints Facing Monetary Policymakers*. Boston: Federal Reserve Bank of Boston.

_____, 1995. Monetary Policy Implications of Greater Fiscal Discipline, in *Budget Deficits and Debt: Issues and Options*. Kansas City: Federal Reserve Bank of Kansas City.

INDEX

F

G

T

U